COLORED PENCIL
WORKBOOK

FABULOUS FLOWERS

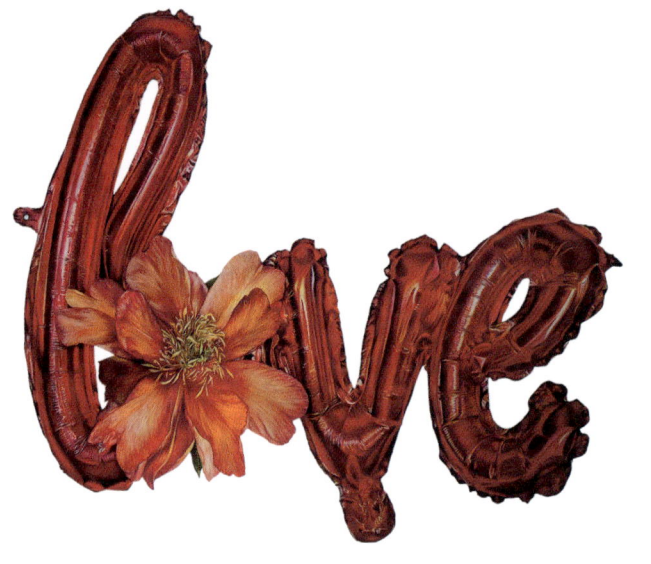

I would like to dedicate this book to my wonderful husband, John, and our beautiful children, Joshua and Isabel. Without their endless support, encouragement, and love this book would never have been possible.

Quarto.com

© 2025 Quarto Publishing Group USA Inc.
Text, Photos, Illustrations © 2024 Sun-Kyong An

First Published in 2025 by Quarry Books, an imprint of The Quarto Group,
100 Cummings Center, Suite 265-D, Beverly, MA 01915, USA.
T (978) 282-9590 F (978) 283-2742

Quarry Books titles are also available at discount for retail, wholesale, promotional, and bulk purchase. For details, contact the Special Sales Manager by email at specialsales@quarto.com or by mail at The Quarto Group, Attn: Special Sales Manager, 100 Cummings Center, Suite 265-D, Beverly, MA 01915, USA.

29 28 27 26 25   1 2 3 4 5

ISBN: 978-0-7603-9593-6

Digital edition published in 2025
eISBN: 978-0-7603-9594-3

Page design and layout: Samantha J. Bednarek, samanthabednarek.com

Printed in China

COLORED PENCIL
WORKBOOK

FABULOUS FLOWERS

Techniques, Templates, and Video Tutorials for Beginner-Friendly Projects

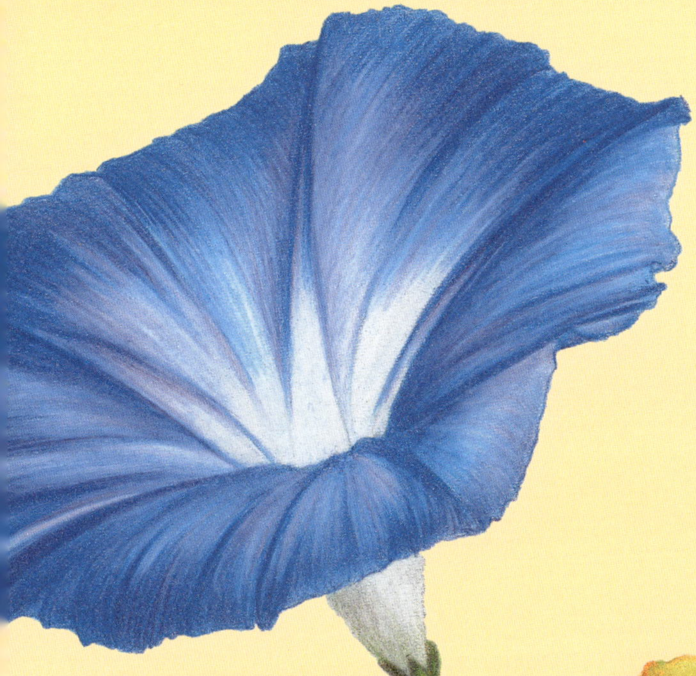

SUN-KYONG CLIFFORD
Fine Art by Sun

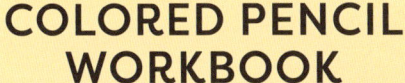
QUARRY

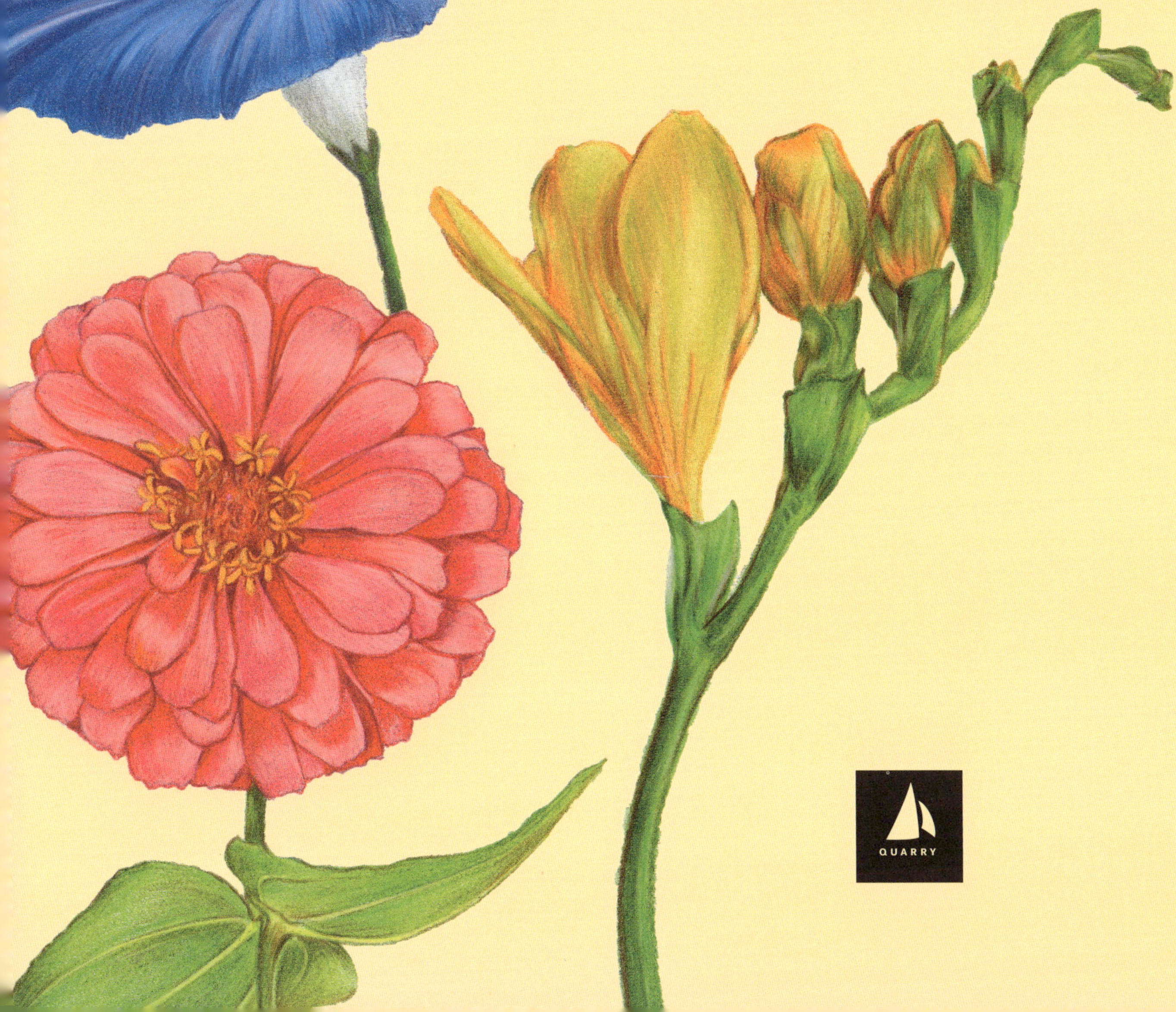

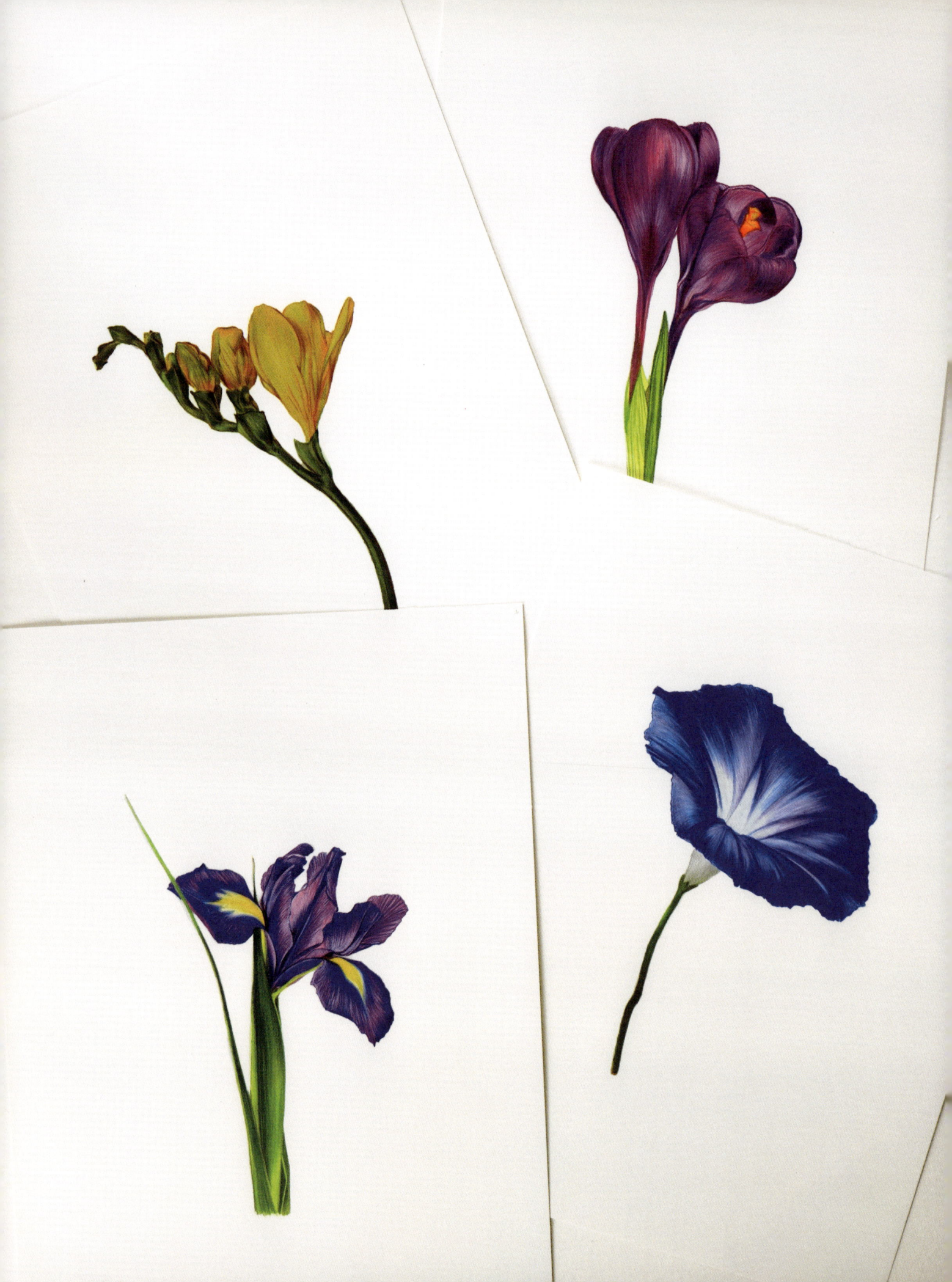

CONTENTS

PROJECT GALLERY 6

INTRODUCTION 10

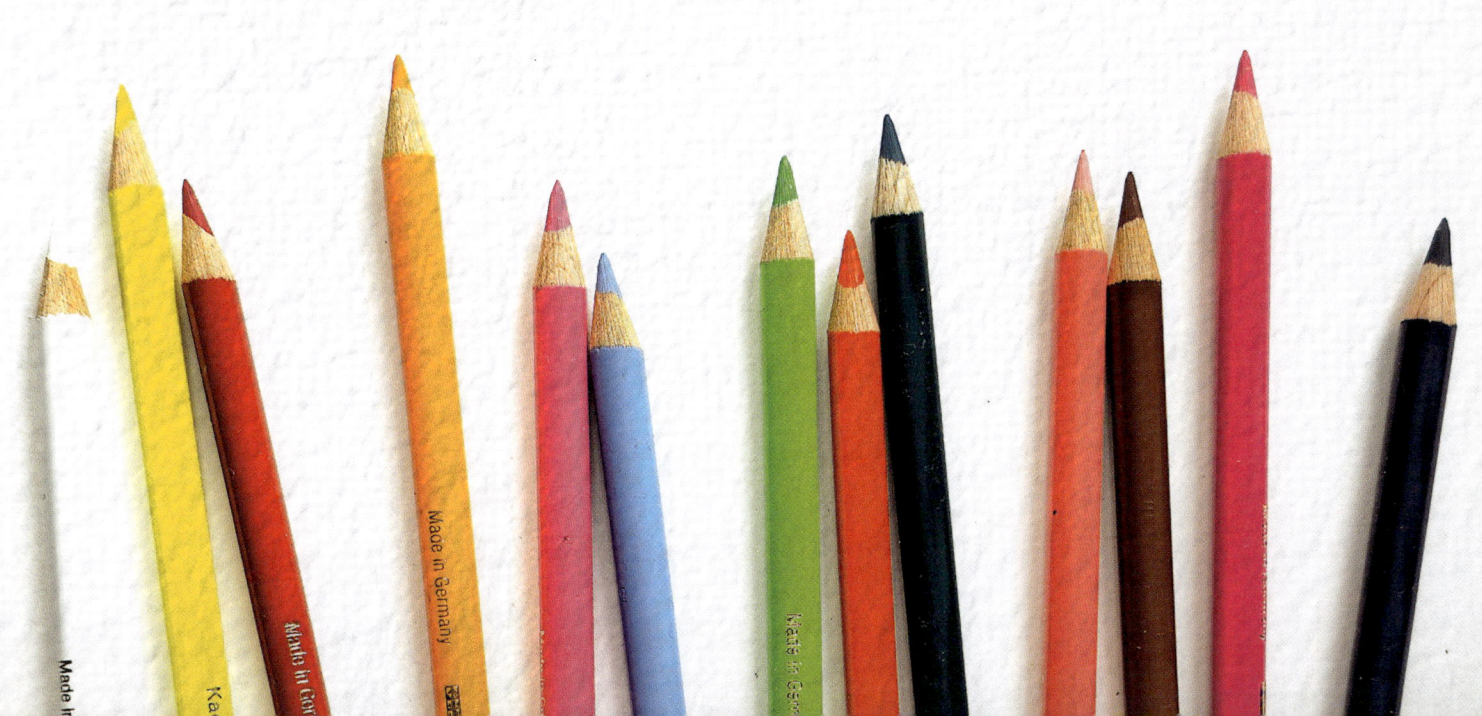

PROJECT GALLERY

IN THIS BOOK you will have the opportunity to create twenty different botanical drawings covering a range of flowers. This will allow you to try different techniques and color schemes as you start to learn the art of colored pencils. The first projects are designed to allow you to take your time and build up your confidence before you reach the final projects that will bring what you have learned together and expand upon those techniques further.

For easy reference, here are the flowers you will be drawing:

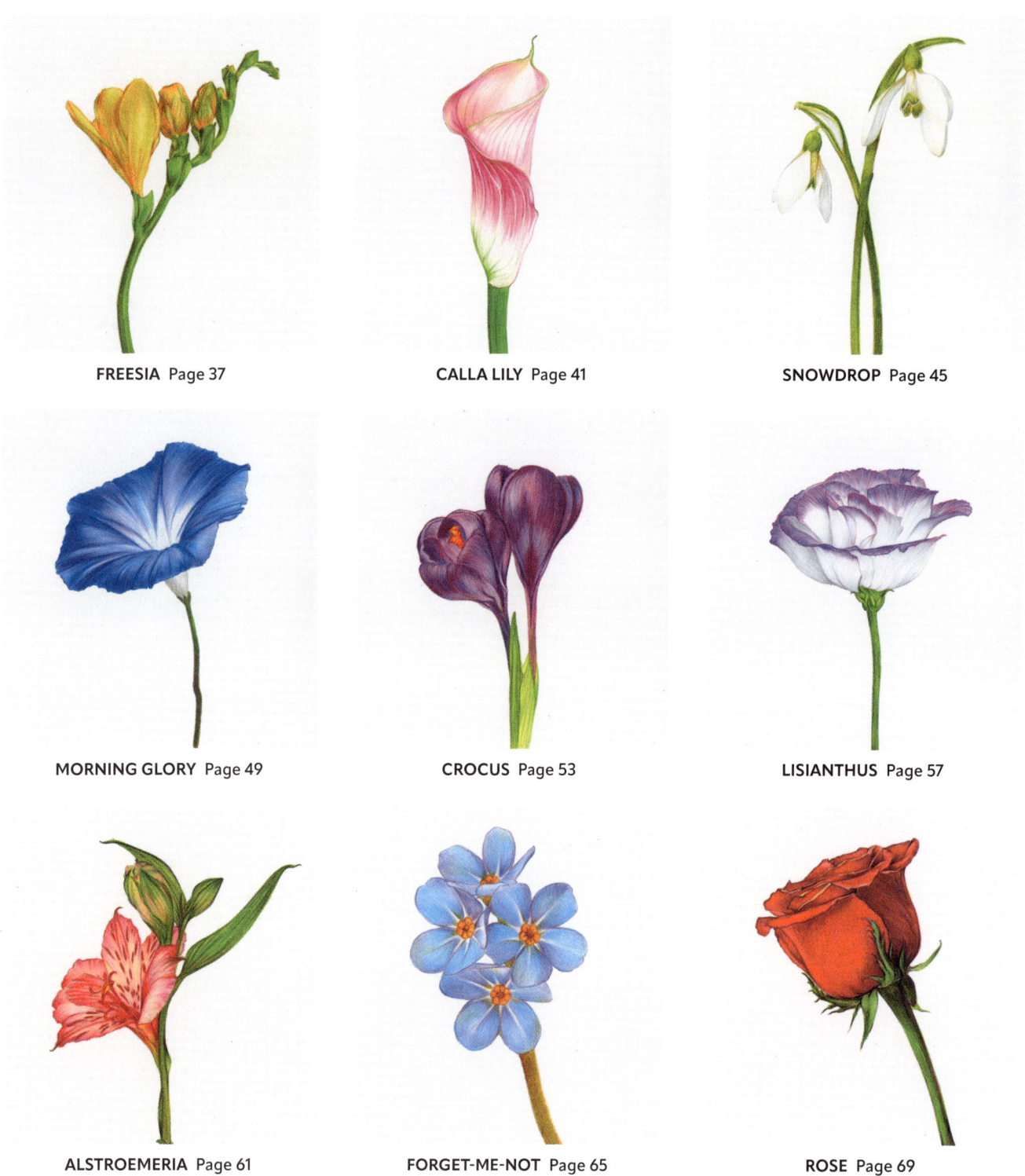

FREESIA Page 37

CALLA LILY Page 41

SNOWDROP Page 45

MORNING GLORY Page 49

CROCUS Page 53

LISIANTHUS Page 57

ALSTROEMERIA Page 61

FORGET-ME-NOT Page 65

ROSE Page 69

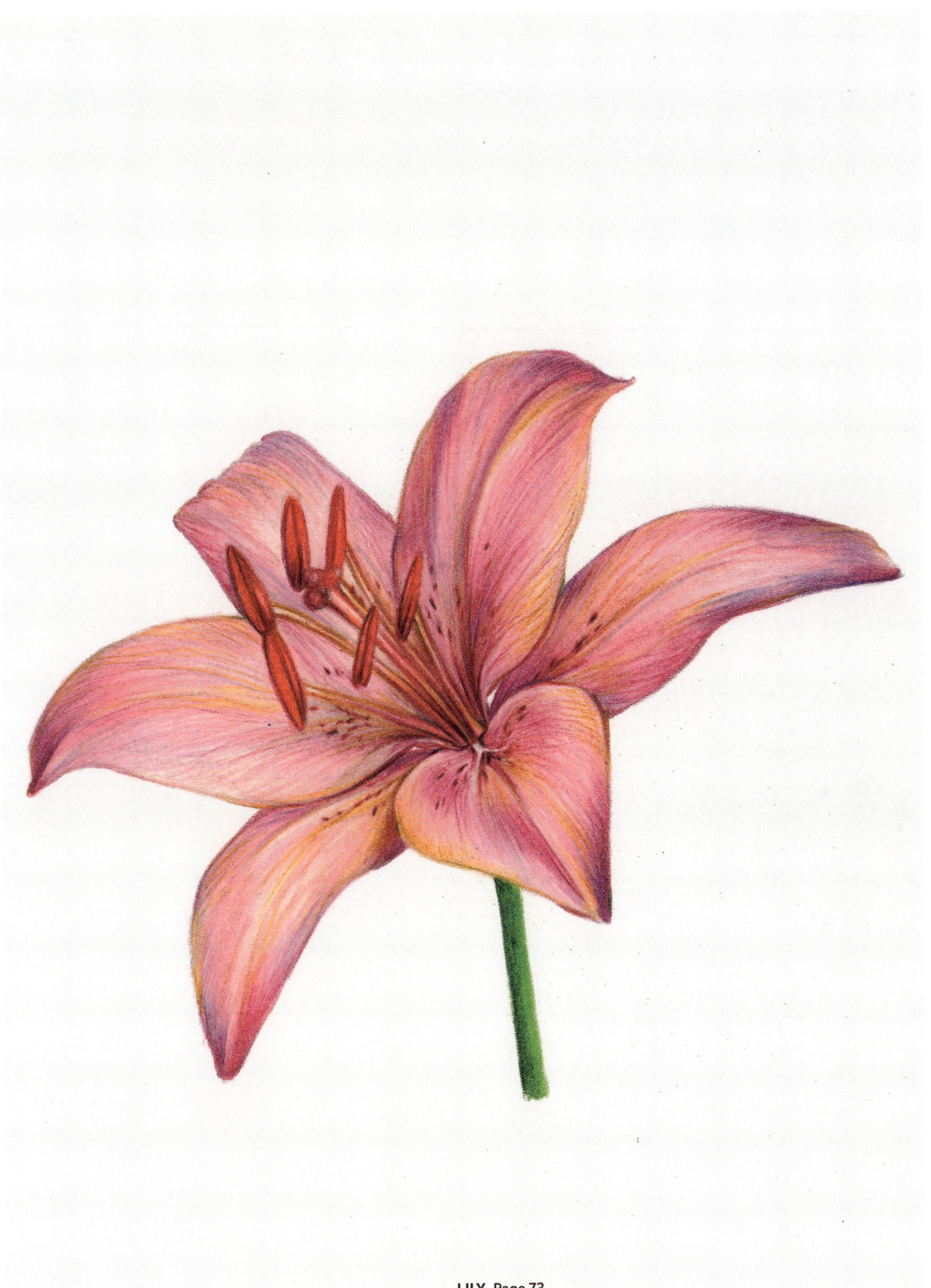

LILY Page 73

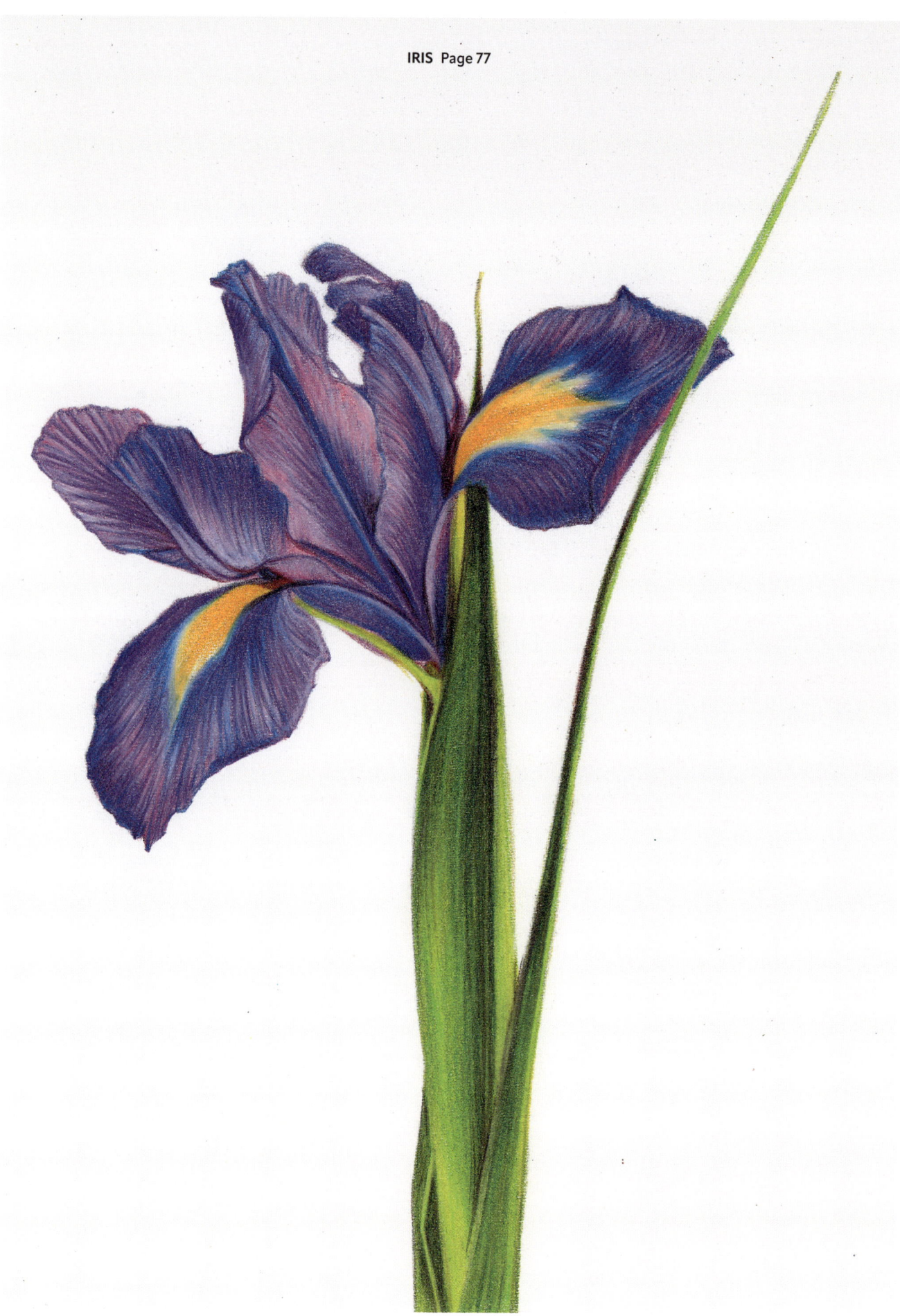

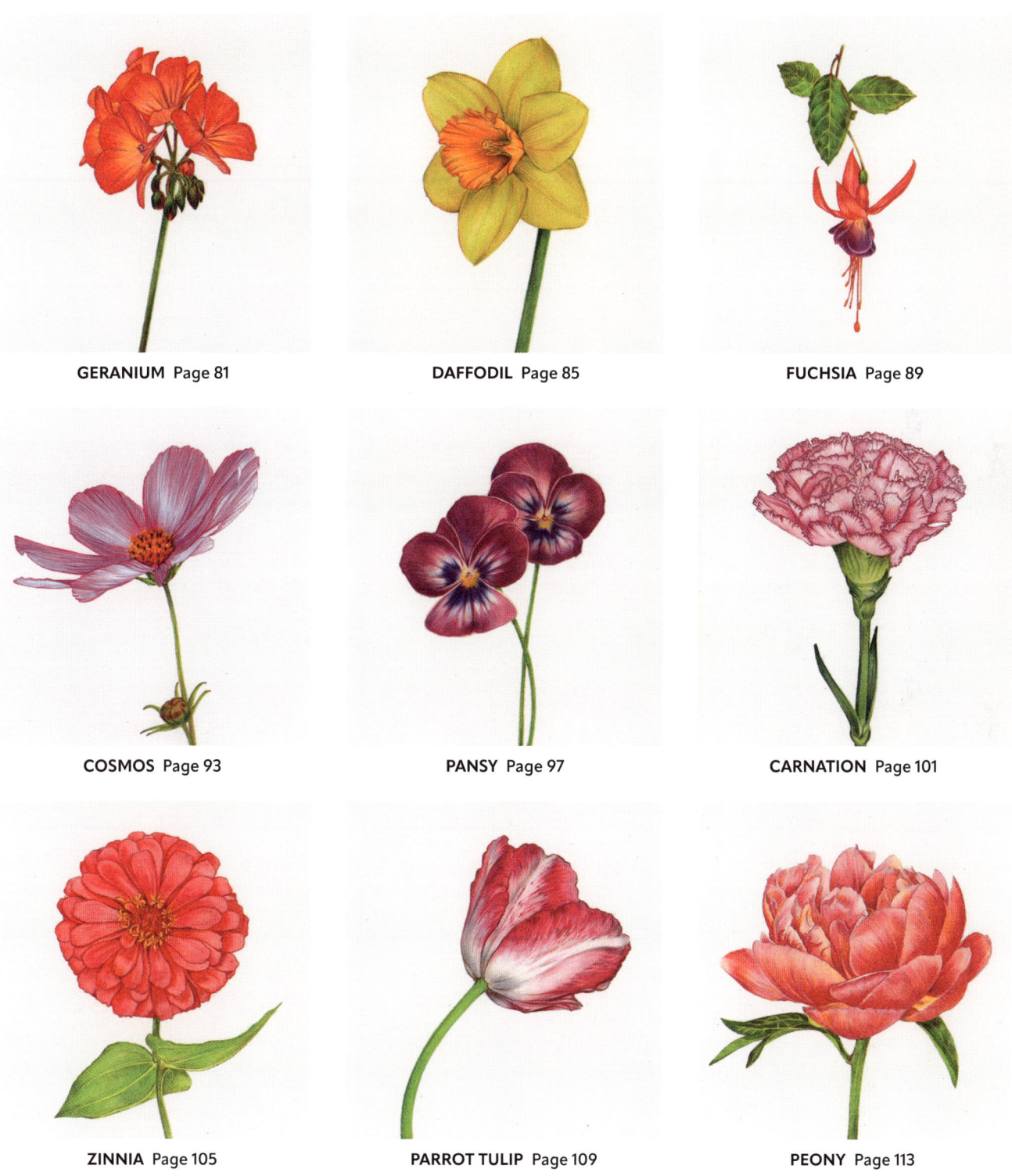

GERANIUM Page 81

DAFFODIL Page 85

FUCHSIA Page 89

COSMOS Page 93

PANSY Page 97

CARNATION Page 101

ZINNIA Page 105

PARROT TULIP Page 109

PEONY Page 113

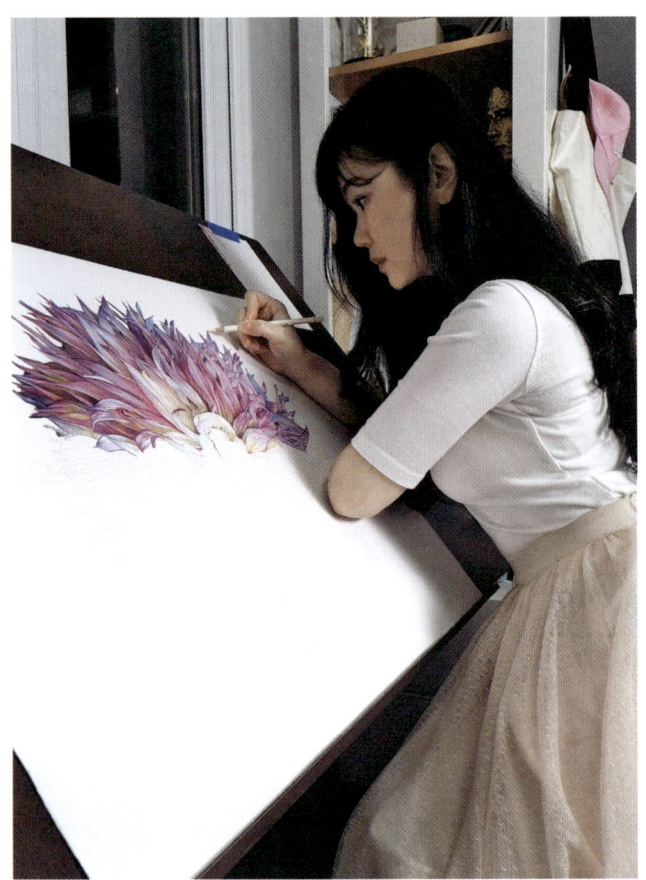
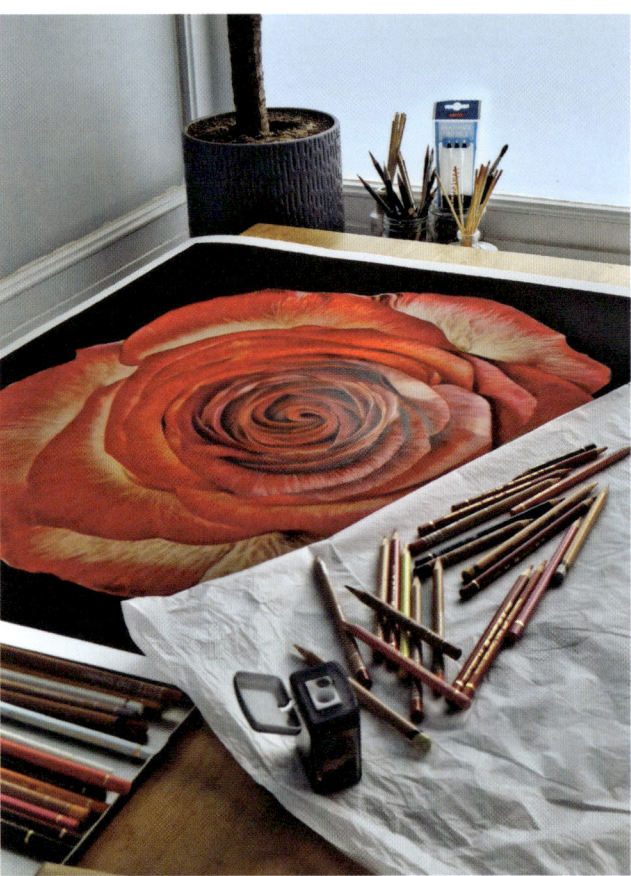

INTRODUCTION

WELCOME TO THE WONDERFUL world of colored pencil art. Things have advanced a lot since your childhood days using colored pencils in school and at home. Now you can create fantastic, realistic pieces of art using these familiar and highly accessible pencils.

Colored pencils are portable, easy to use, and a very familiar and forgiving medium. This gives us budding artists a fantastic place to start our artistic journey.

Colored pencils are good for both beginners and the more accomplished artist, bringing another way to capture and express the world around them through their art. With a selection of colored pencils, some paper, an eraser, and a sharpener, you are ready to start creating something beautiful.

In this book, I have selected twenty beautiful flowers to represent all the seasons, allowing you to capture them on paper to enjoy year-round. Through this book I hope to share the tools, techniques, tips, and ideas I have tried and tested over the years to help make your journey as rewarding as possible.

I recommend this book to anyone who loves flowers, wants to learn how to draw but doesn't know where to start, or those who simply want to spend time creating in a relaxed and peaceful way after a busy day.

I hope this book will introduce you to the beautiful and colorful world of colored pencil botanical art and help you create something special along the way. Colored pencils have become such an important part of my life, and I'm looking forward to sharing them with you.

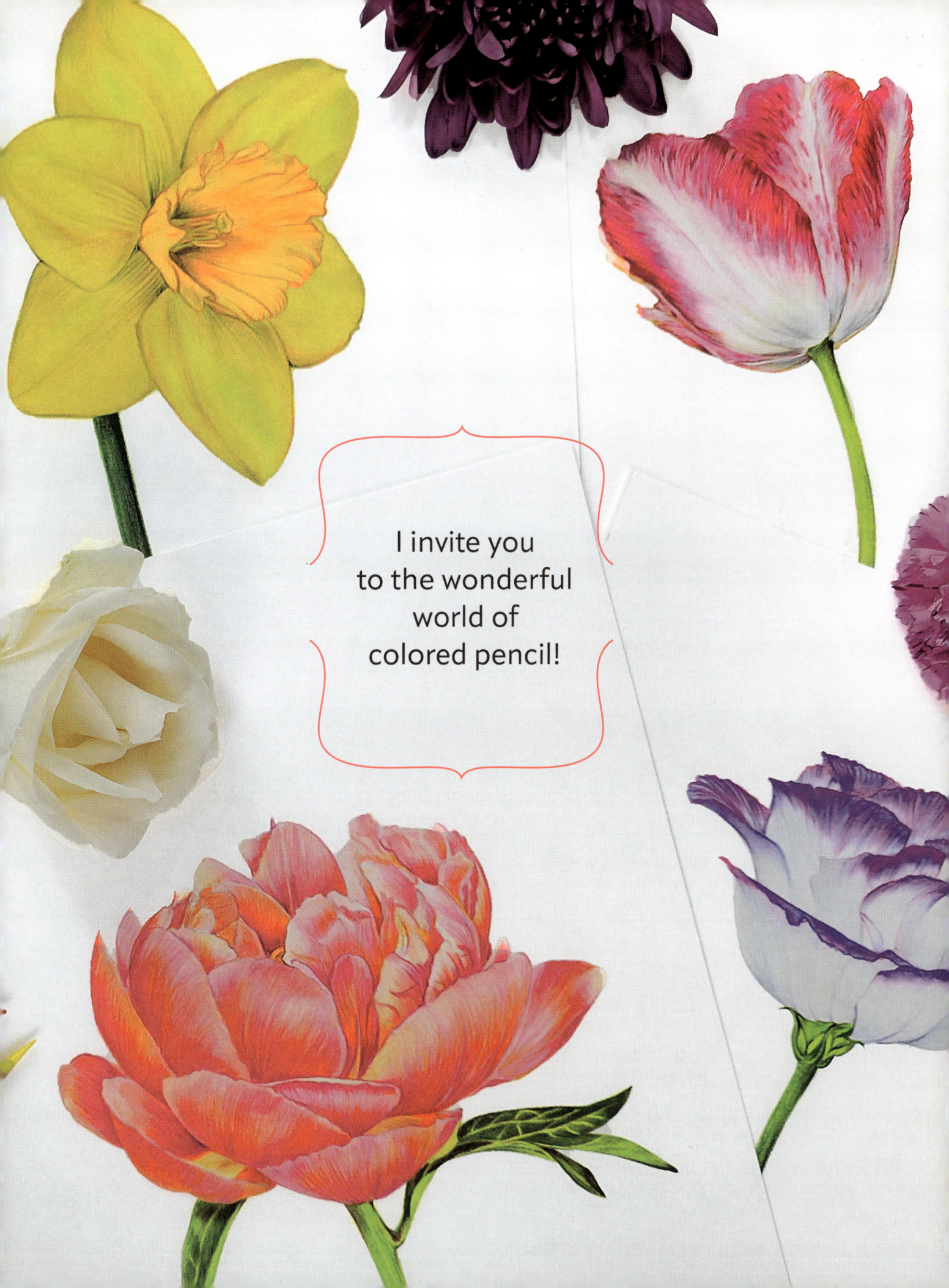

I invite you
to the wonderful
world of
colored pencil!

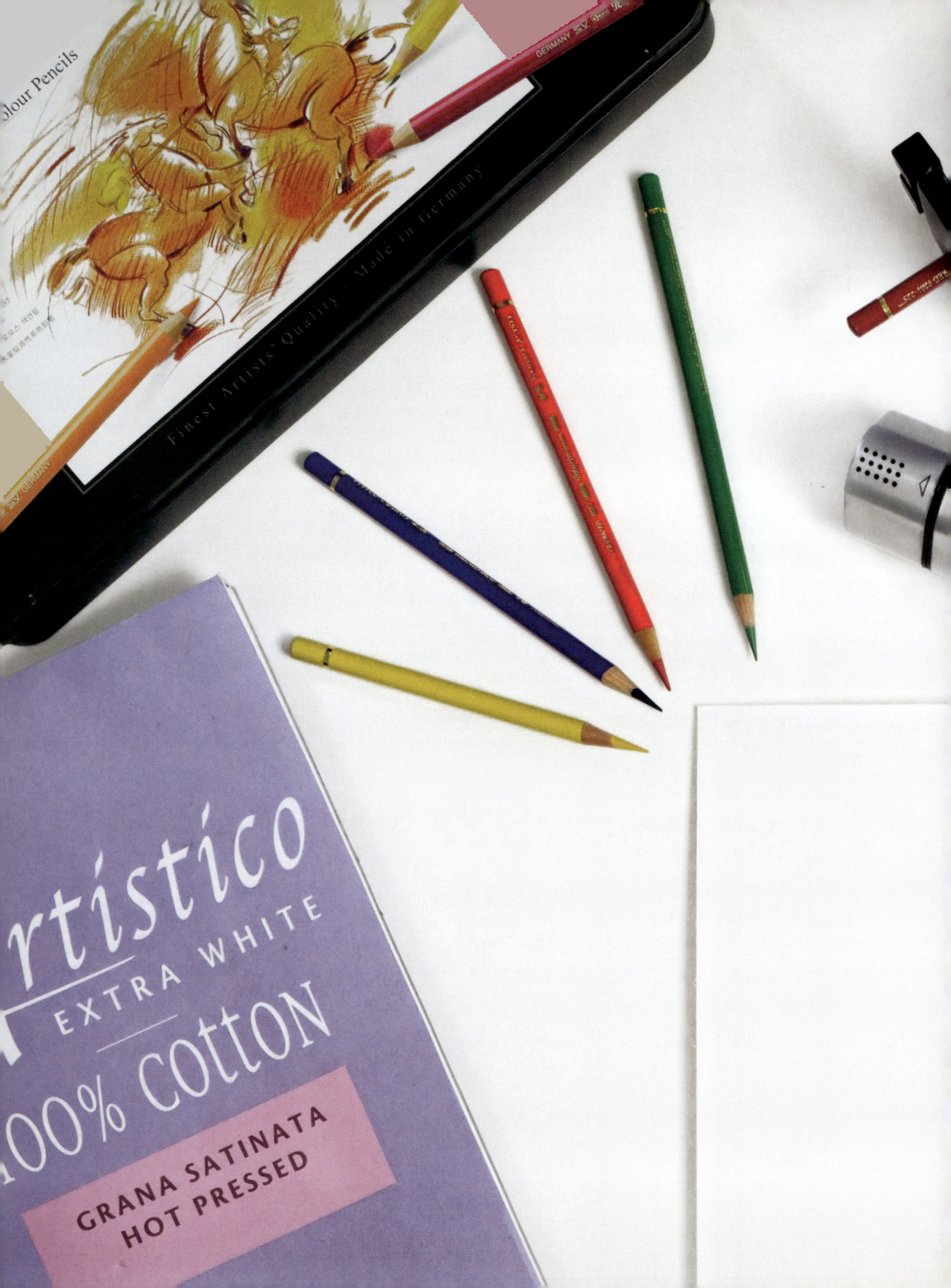

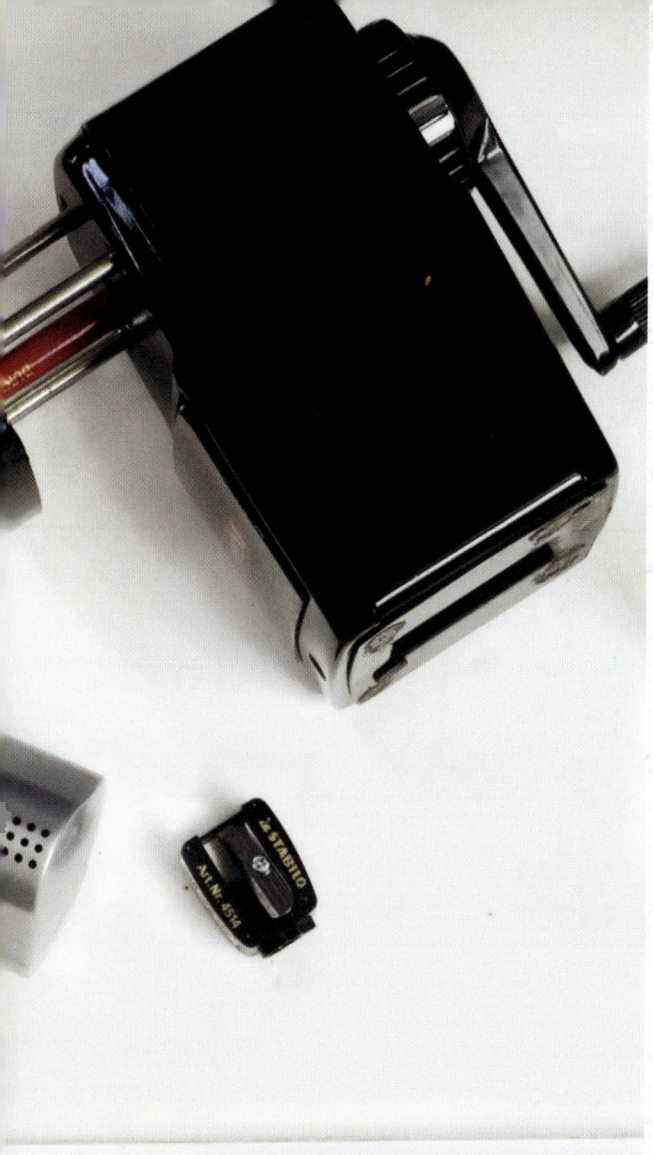

1

MATERIALS

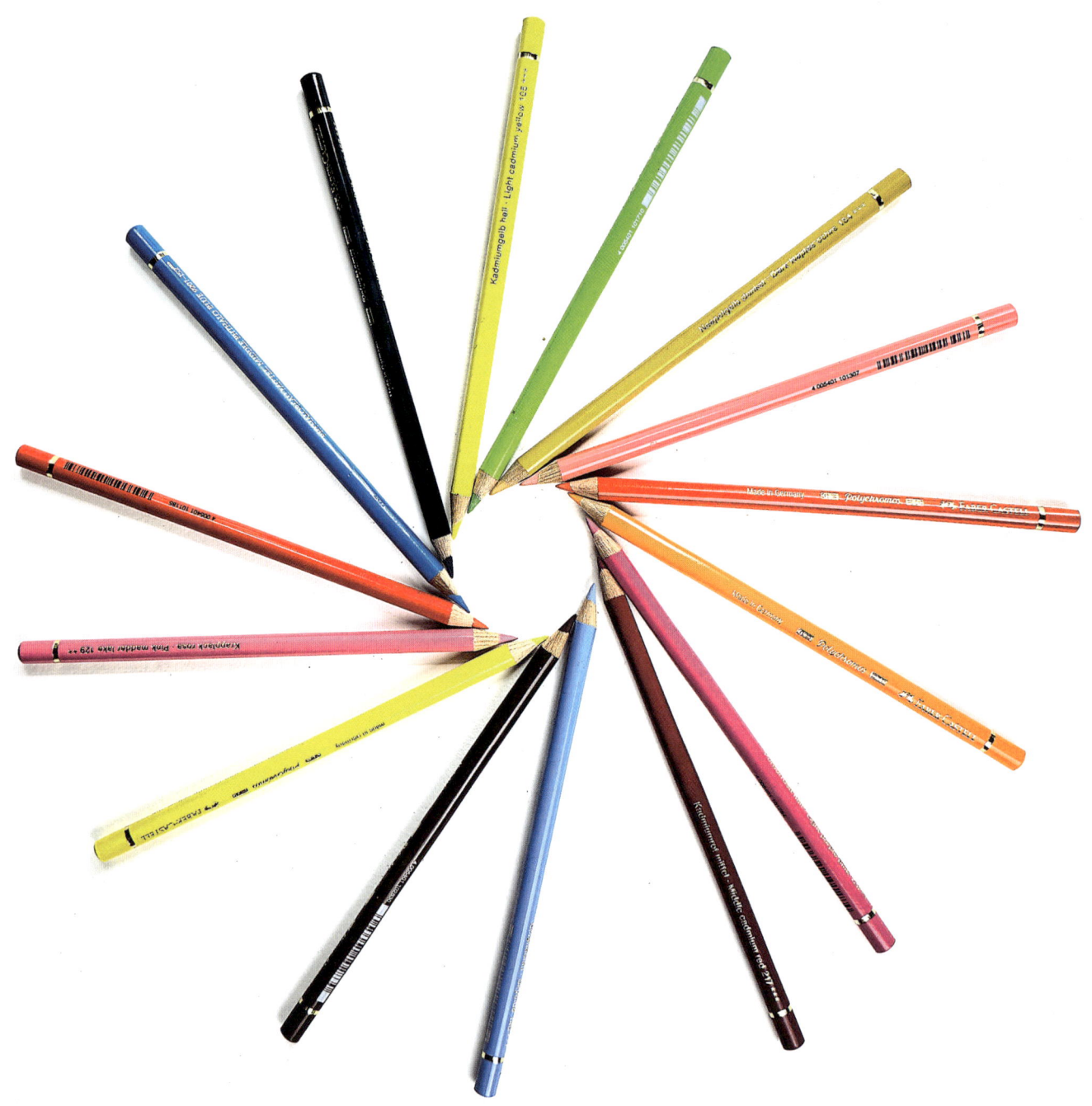

COLORED PENCILS

IN THIS BOOK I have used Faber-Castell Polychromos pencils. These professional artist-quality pencils have excellent pigmentation and sharpen to a very fine point, all of which is really important to get the best drawing onto the paper. These qualities also allow you to slowly build up many layers in order to bring your art to life.

I don't recommend rushing out to buy a full set of colored pencils if you're just starting out. You will find that many colors in these sets are not needed in botanical work

and will therefore not be used. It's better to buy single pencils and build up a collection of colors you know you will use. To help with this, I have minimized the color range for each project, allowing you to create each drawing with a minimum number of pencils as you grow your collection over time. Some of the flowers also use similar color palettes, so make sure to look at these as you expand your own pencil collection if you want to minimize the initial expense.

COLOR PALETTE FOR THIS BOOK

The selection of colors I have used for this book are shown below as a reference.
I have used Faber-Castell Polychromos pencils, but you can use similar colors from another brand or your own pencil collection if you already have some available.

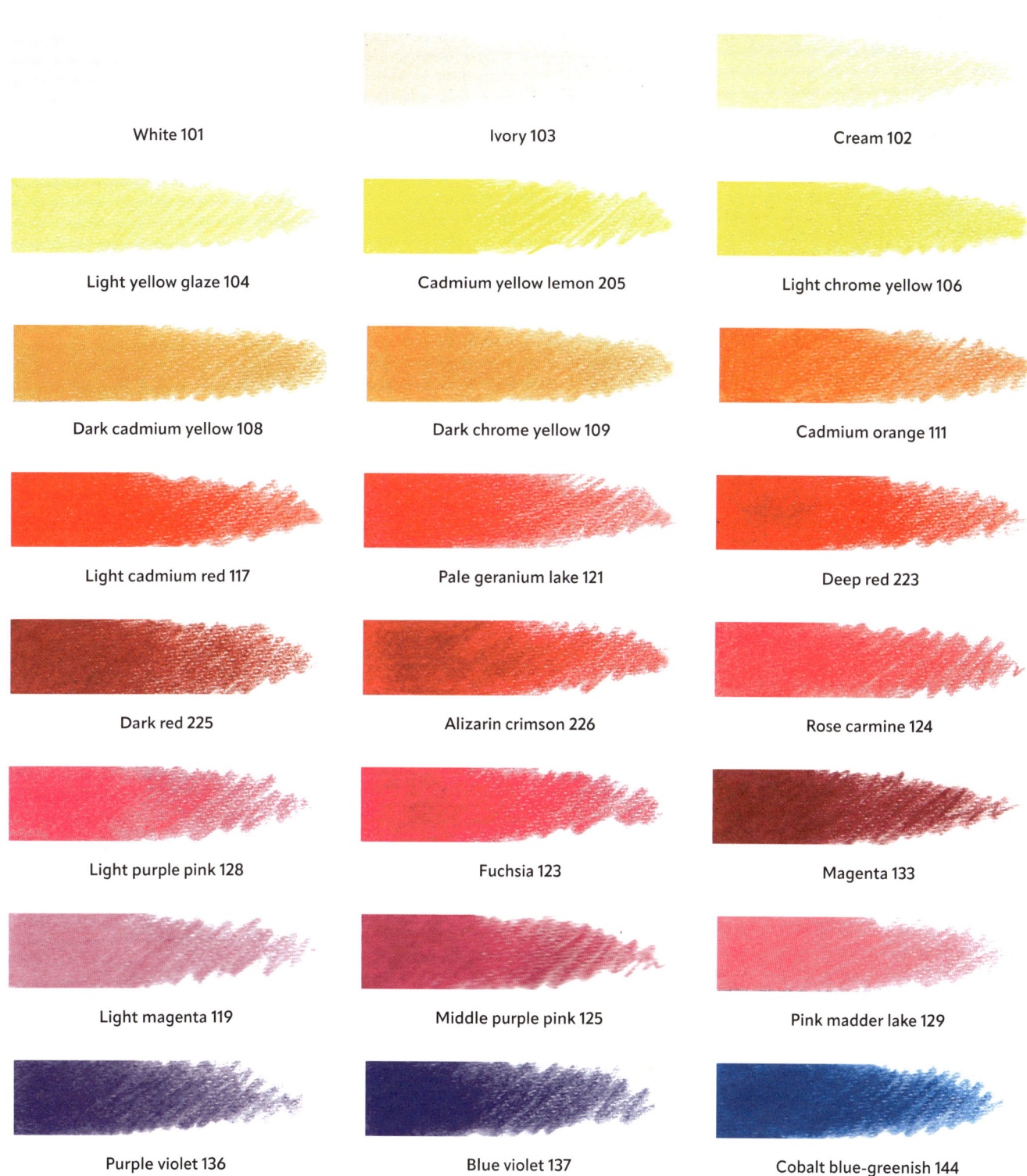

White 101

Ivory 103

Cream 102

Light yellow glaze 104

Cadmium yellow lemon 205

Light chrome yellow 106

Dark cadmium yellow 108

Dark chrome yellow 109

Cadmium orange 111

Light cadmium red 117

Pale geranium lake 121

Deep red 223

Dark red 225

Alizarin crimson 226

Rose carmine 124

Light purple pink 128

Fuchsia 123

Magenta 133

Light magenta 119

Middle purple pink 125

Pink madder lake 129

Purple violet 136

Blue violet 137

Cobalt blue-greenish 144

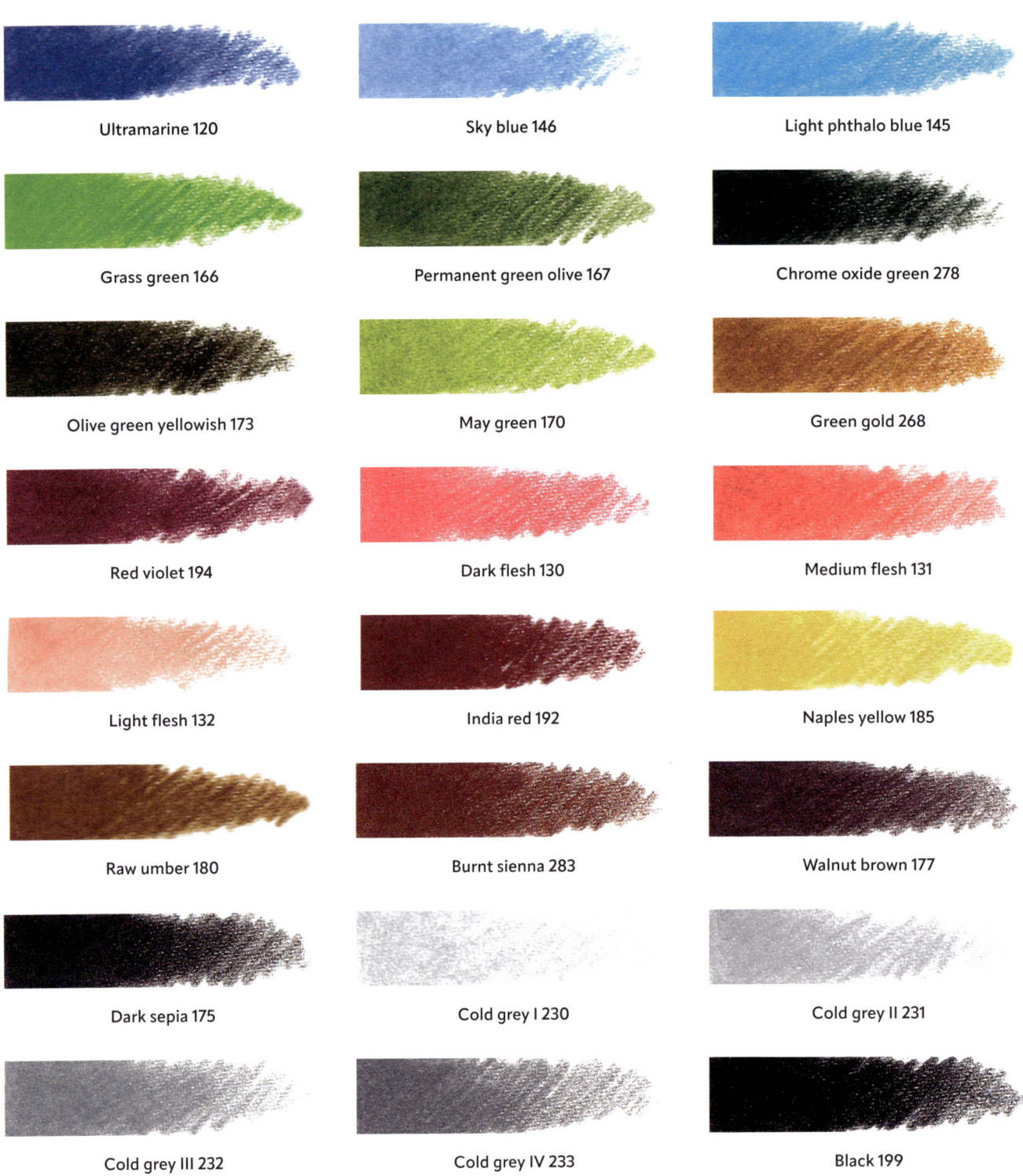

Ultramarine 120

Sky blue 146

Light phthalo blue 145

Grass green 166

Permanent green olive 167

Chrome oxide green 278

Olive green yellowish 173

May green 170

Green gold 268

Red violet 194

Dark flesh 130

Medium flesh 131

Light flesh 132

India red 192

Naples yellow 185

Raw umber 180

Burnt sienna 283

Walnut brown 177

Dark sepia 175

Cold grey I 230

Cold grey II 231

Cold grey III 232

Cold grey IV 233

Black 199

PAPER

FOR COLORED PENCIL DRAWING, it's very important to know what type of paper you prefer to work with. Some artists like to work on textured paper whereas others prefer a smoother surface. I recommend buying a sample of different types of paper to see what suits you and your style best. However, whatever type of surface you choose to work with, it is very important you have good-quality paper for your work.

To make learning to paint with colored pencils and recreate the projects in this book as easy as possible, we've included templates of the projects on premium coloring paper. As you continue your colored pencil journey, you'll want to buy paper to draw on. If you'll be coloring a large number of layers, and maybe using solvent, you need to use a heavier paper.

Your paper should have a good thickness of at least 300 gsm (140 lb) in order to handle the constant pressure of the

pencils on the surface, as you'll be using sharp points to create multiple layers. The use of erasers and solvents will quickly wear out a lightweight paper, leading to damage, tears, or holes in the paper, making repairs almost impossible.

There are many different types of paper on the market. I use hot-pressed watercolor paper. I use Fabriano Artistico hot press 100% cotton paper, either 640gsm (300 lb) or 300 gsm (140 lb). This is fairly smooth hot-pressed paper and is very resilient to corrections. It is available in bright white or traditional white. I prefer bright white, as this provides a clear background and makes my work stand out more.

Now that you understand some of the basics, don't be afraid to experiment and find the best paper for you and your art, and if it changes during your artistic journey that's fine. Each artist is different and there are no right or wrong answers when it comes to what suits you best. Have fun finding your personal preferences, as I did.

OTHER ESSENTIALS

COLORED PENCILS AND PAPER are the must-have materials for colored pencil art, but there are a few other supplies you'll want to have on hand.

PENCIL SHARPENERS

It's worth investing in a good-quality pencil sharpener for your colored pencils. Good pencil sharpeners are key to getting a sharp, fine point to your pencil, which allows you to draw sharp lines, as well as gives you better control while shading. A good-quality sharpener will make a huge difference in how your coloring turns out.

Colored pencils are made with oil and wax, and their leads are quite soft, which means they can break easily. Combining this soft material with a poor-quality pencil sharpener often results in breakages, which you really don't want. A quality sharpener reduces this risk and gives you a consistent sharp point, making the whole process more enjoyable.

DUSTING BRUSH

A large, soft brush is very useful for gently brushing away loose pencil dust from the paper surface. Keeping the paper clean and smudge-free is very important to ensure as clean a surface as possible to avoid any mistakes.

ERASERS

For light erasing, I use a kneaded eraser, and the Tombow MONO Zero is great for fine and precision erasing. When I have a large area to erase, I use a hard plastic art eraser. Just don't erase too hard, which could damage the surface of the paper. Take your time and use gentle movements and you can see the result, ensuring you don't take too much away and damage the paper underneath.

Just like paper, each artist has their own preference when it comes to erasers. I personally like hard plastic erasers for most of my erasing needs. I use the Tombow MONO Zero or an eraser pencil with a brush for those precision eraser tasks. However, many artists prefer kneaded erasers over hard plastic, as there is less risk of damaging the paper surface. I have never had an issue with hard plastic erasers.

Like everything in art, it is about personal preference. Try a few and see what best suits you. As most erasers are relatively inexpensive, this is one supply for which you can try many options before you settle on what works best for you and your paper.

FIXATIVE

Fixative is a solution that protects your drawings from smudging and damage. Applying fixative can be done once you have fully completed your work, or once you have completed various sections that are fully finished. Depending on the type of fixative you use you may not be able to work on your art again, whereas others allow you to continue. Please make sure you check the fixative before applying to ensure you select the correct one. My general rule is I do not apply any fixative until I have fully completed my artwork.

Fixative acts as a protective layer for your work. Some incorporate UV protection, ensuring the colors remain as you intended them to for a very long time.

Some artists do use fixative between layers or to add additional texture to the paper if it has been overworked. For example, if you have multiple layers or have used the eraser a lot, applying fixative can bring some of the texture back to the paper.

Use a good-quality fixative suitable for colored pencil work, and make sure you use it outside or in a well-ventilated room. Some artists use hairspray instead of fixative; however, I highly recommend not doing this. Hairspray is not designed for art and will eventually discolor your paper.

TIPS

Pencil sharpeners become clogged with waxy residue after frequent use, but regularly sharpening a graphite pencil in them helps keep them clean.

Brush your paper often and keep your brush close by at all times. It will become second nature to gently wipe away your pencil dust and keep your paper perfectly clean in no time.

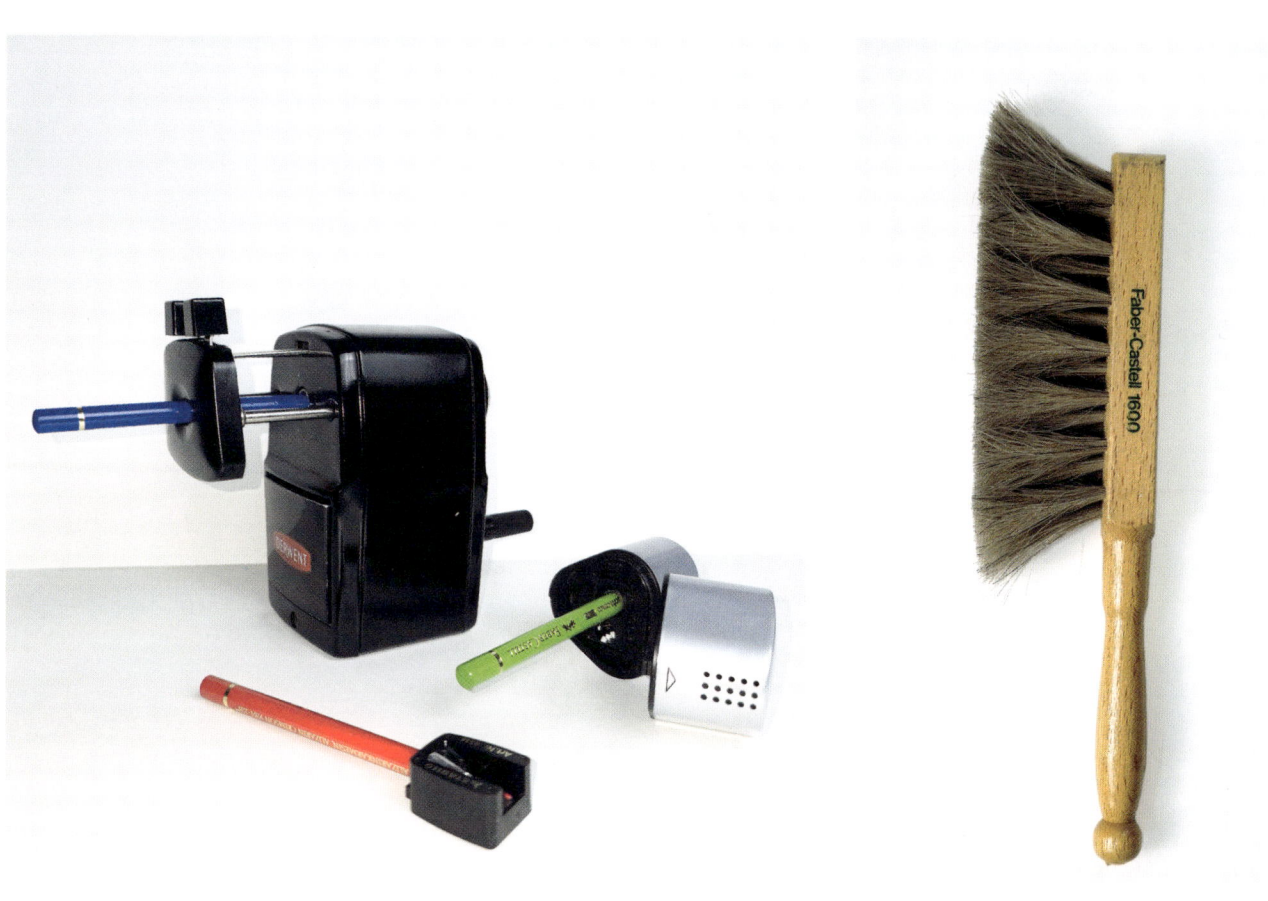

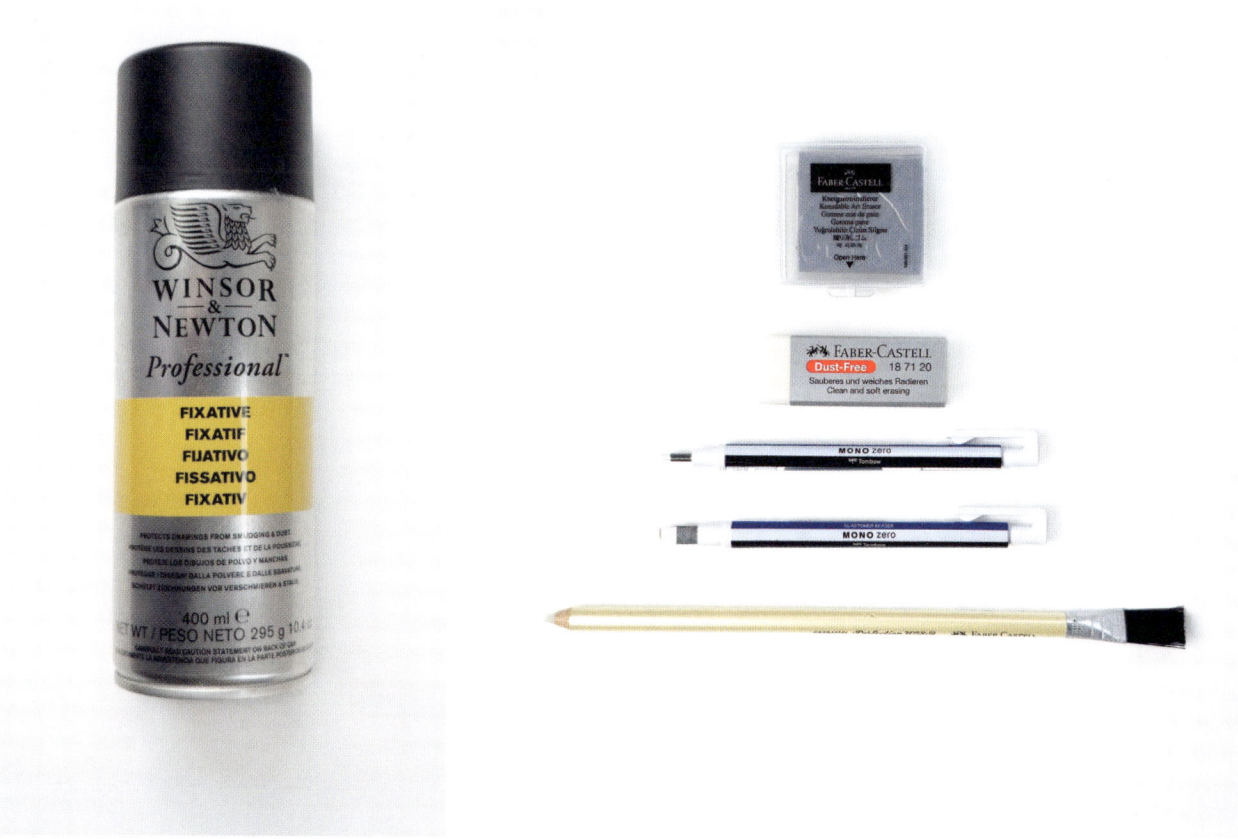

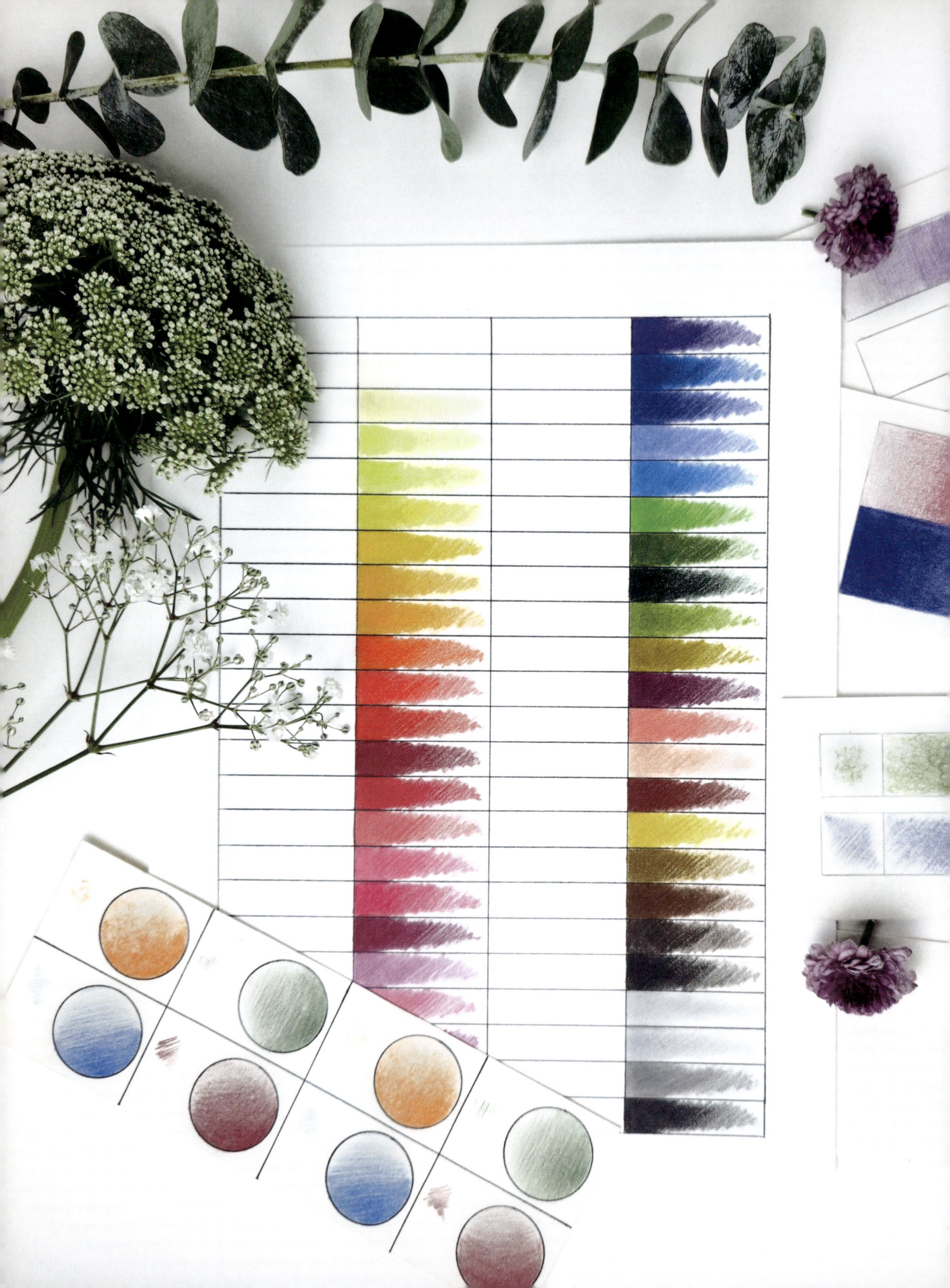

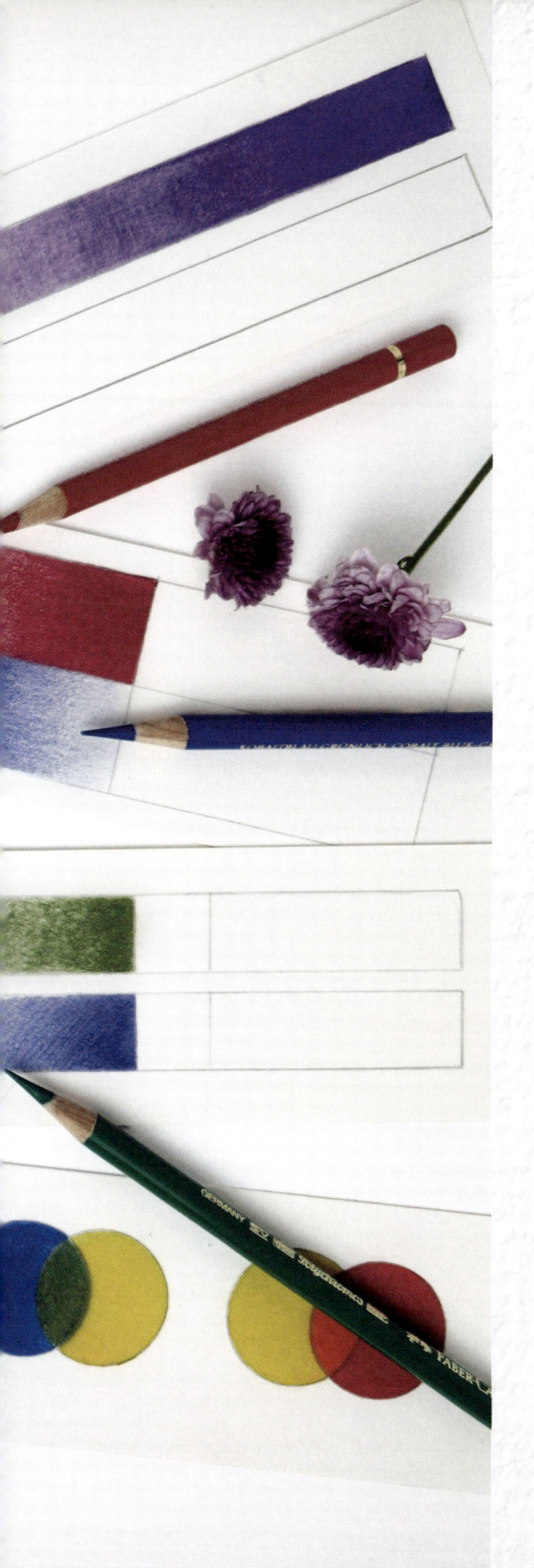

2

BASIC TECHNIQUES

COLORED PENCIL EXERCISES

IT'S IMPORTANT TO LEARN basic pencil techniques before attempting the projects. This will give you a good understanding of how the pencils will react under different circumstances as you start using them to create more detailed drawings.

I see this process as learning to dance with my pencils. I move around the paper and apply different pressure and techniques to create the outcome I am looking for.

This becomes much easier the more you do it, so don't be afraid to experiment and use the exercises in this book to see what your pencils will create for you.

As you start drawing with colored pencils you will naturally start to pick up some techniques and ways of drawing that come more naturally to you.

To help you get started, the following are some simple exercises. Use the QR code for a video showing you each exercise. It's important to maintain a sharp point on the pencil throughout every stage of the drawing process.

This is not an exhaustive list of techniques, as you don't need to worry about more advanced techniques at this stage. The following are examples of the techniques I use the most in my work, which will allow you to create your own drawings.

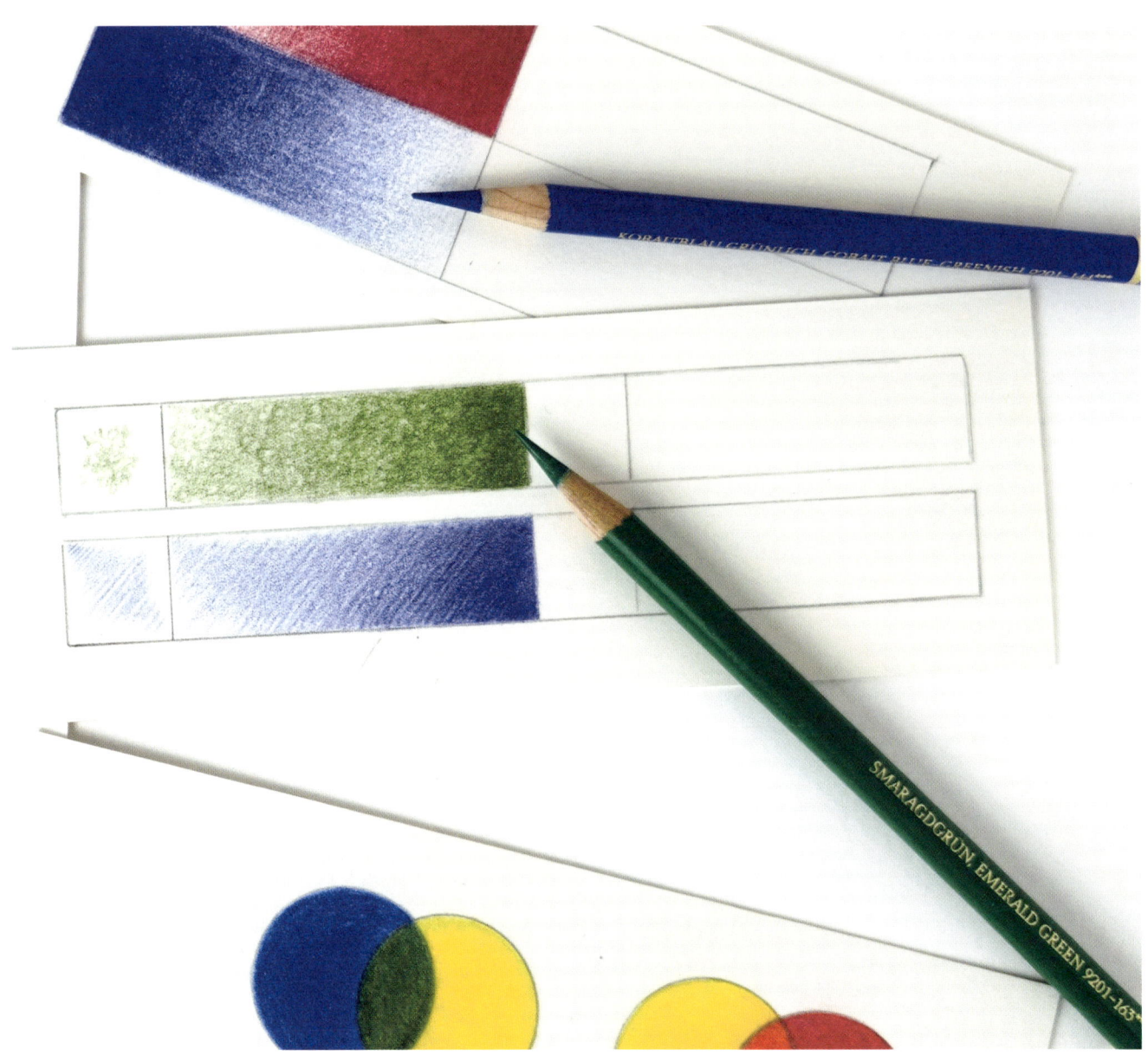

LINE PRACTICE

THESE LINE EXERCISES MIGHT SEEM SIMPLE, and you might be tempted to skip them. But I encourage you to take the time to try them and practice making your lines. It will help you get used to working with the colored pencil and increase the confidence of your strokes.

EXERCISE 1: HORIZONTAL LINES

Draw a line using constant pencil pressure. Make the pencil strokes uniform and neat.

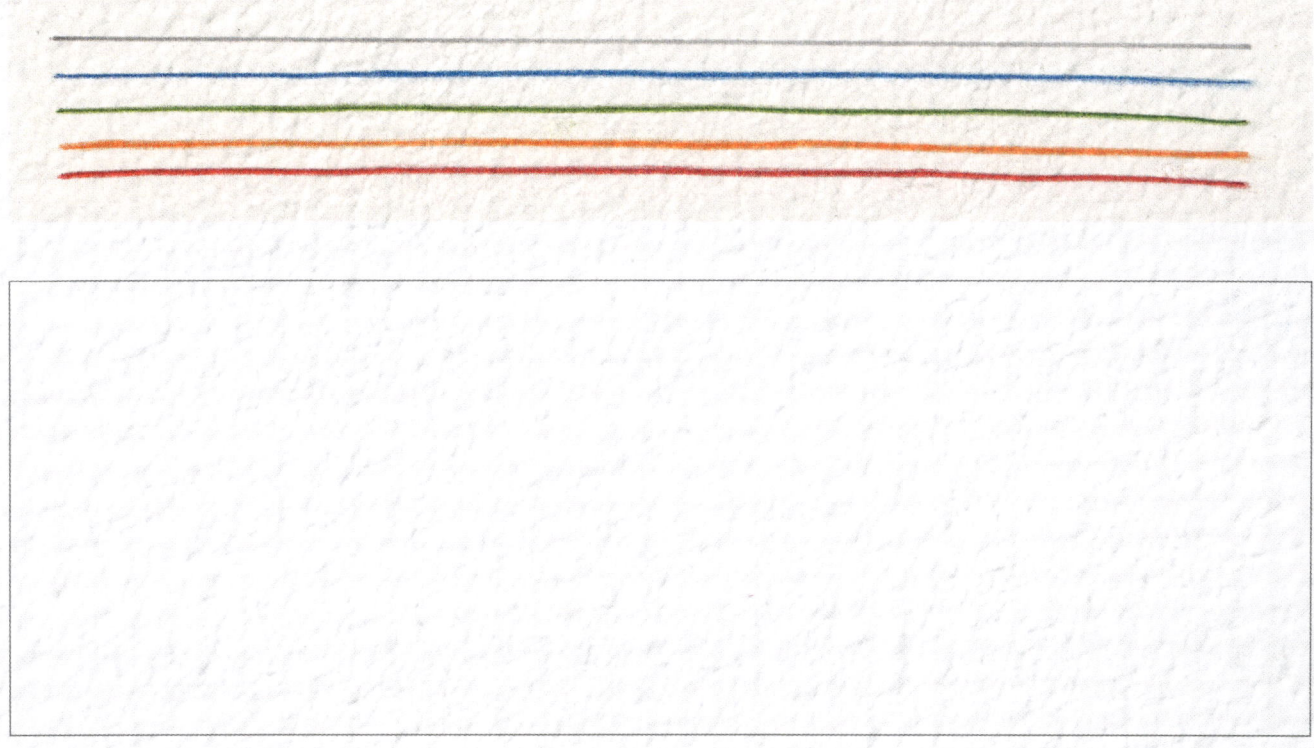

Your turn!

SCAN TO WATCH
A TUTORIAL.

EXERCISE 2: VERTICAL LINES

Draw a line vertically using hard-to-light pencil pressure. Start with a thick line, applying more pressure and slowly release it to create a thinner and weaker line as you move down. The line should look like it is fading from top to bottom.

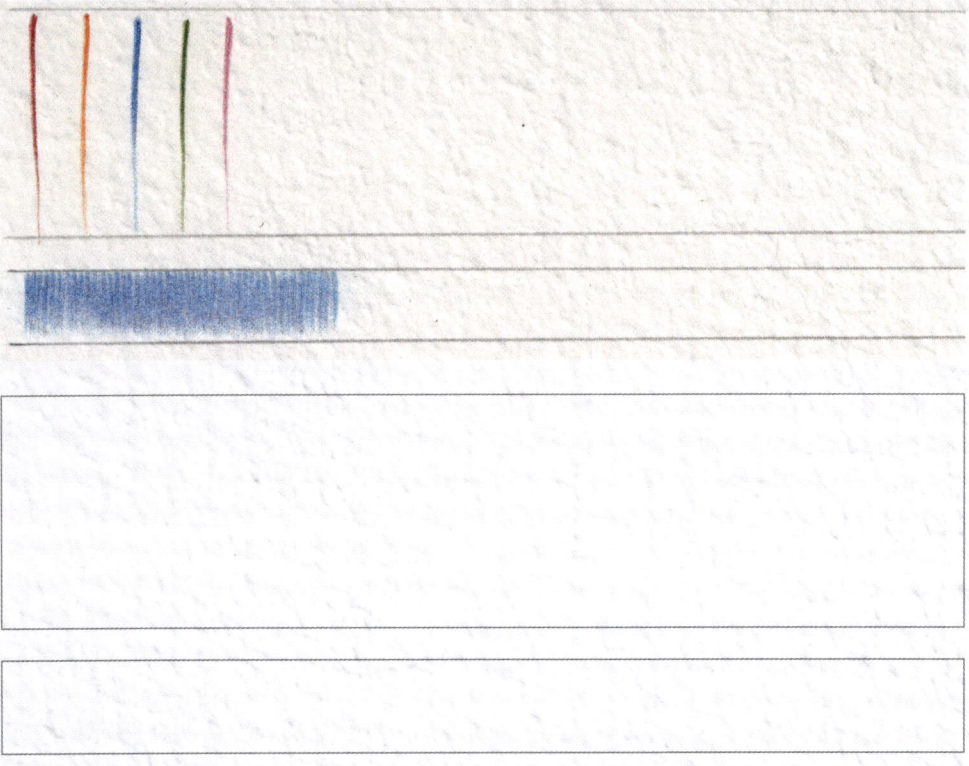

SCAN TO WATCH
A TUTORIAL.

Your turn!

EXERCISE 3: CURVES

When you draw a curve, hold your pencil at a 45-degree angle to the paper. While applying more pressure at the beginning of the stroke, move the pencil and gently reduce the pressure, as if you are carefully removing the pencil from the paper toward the end of each stroke.

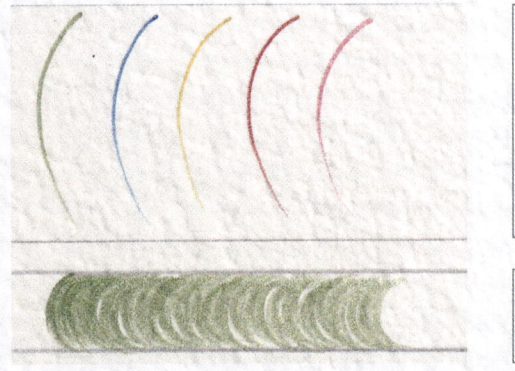

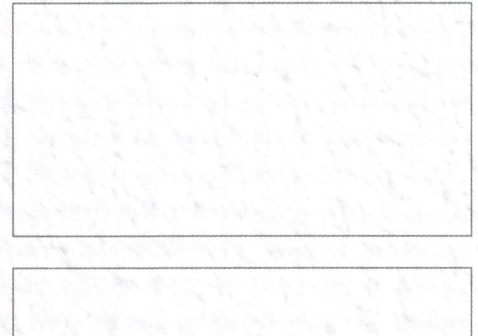

SCAN TO WATCH
A TUTORIAL.

Your turn!

EXERCISE 4: S- AND C-TYPE LINES

An S- or C-type line is often used to create the flowing details on a petal in botanical artwork. When you do this make sure you are consistent. Each S shape should look uniform and build upon the one before it. Keep layering the S line and you will start to see the effect shown here. This gets easier the more you do it.

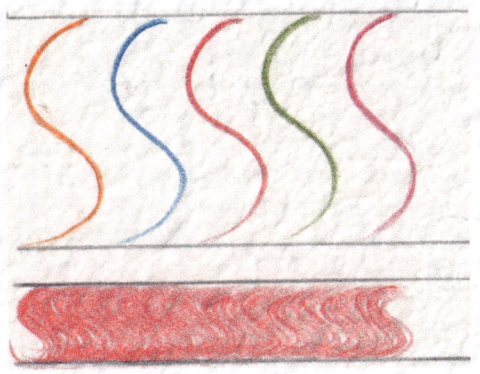

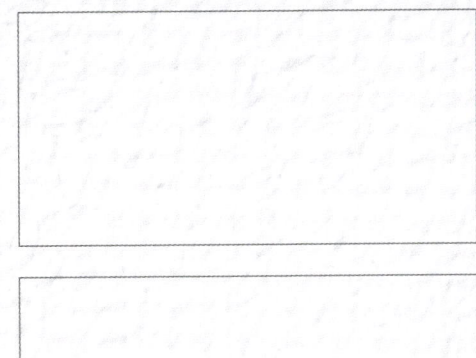

Your turn!

SCAN TO WATCH
A TUTORIAL.

EXERCISE 5: LITTLE HOOKS

This technique is useful for creating the edge of a petal or leaf. It is similar to drawing a little hook.
Practice drawing the curves in both directions, applying light pressure.

SCAN TO WATCH
A TUTORIAL.

Your turn!

LAYERING PRACTICE

I URGE YOU TO TRY these layering exercises here and even on additional paper.
It takes a little practice to get smooth, even coverage, but it's worth the effort.

EXERCISE 1: GRADATED SHADING

Starting from the left, lightly apply pressure and color in the entire box. Now go back to the left-hand side and leave space at the beginning before adding another layer. You will see the color start to deepen toward the right-hand side the more layers you add, as can be seen here.

**SCAN TO WATCH
A TUTORIAL.**

Your turn!

EXERCISE 2: BACK AND FORTH

Similar to exercise 1, fill the box starting with light pressure before pressing heavier towards the end, as can be seen in the red example shown. Now do the same in reverse, as shown in the blue example. Practice shading in both directions to become more comfortable. This exercise is great for getting used to pencil pressure and the changes it can make.

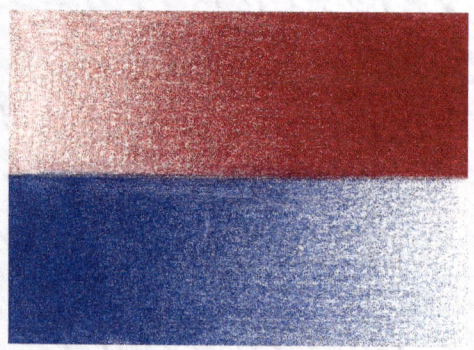

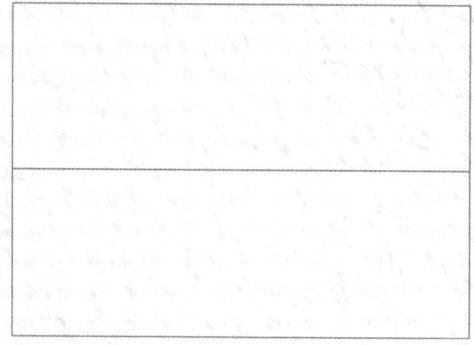

**SCAN TO WATCH
A TUTORIAL.**

Your turn!

EXERCISE 3: TINY CIRCLES

Draw a tiny circle without lifting the point of the pencil.
Move across the paper so that the whole box is colored in, as shown in the green example.

SCAN TO WATCH
A TUTORIAL OF
EXERCISES 3 AND 4.

Your turn!

EXERCISE 4: HATCHING

Using a very light touch, begin to shade in the box using parallel hatch lines.
Lift the pencil tip at the end of each stroke, as seen in the blue example.

Your turn!

EXERCISE 5: STRAIGHT LINES

Apply light pressure to fill in the box using vertical straight lines.
Lift the pencil tip at the end of each stroke before making the next, as shown in the orange example.

SCAN TO WATCH
A TUTORIAL OF
EXERCISES 5 AND 6.

Your turn!

EXERCISE 6: ZIGZAG

Use the lightest pressure with a zigzagging motion to fill the box. This technique is useful to fill in large areas, creating depth. Make sure to keep light pressure on the paper so the color builds evenly without leaving unnecessary pencil lines, as shown in the blue example.

Your turn!

COLOR MIXING PRACTICE

IN SCHOOL YOU PROBABLY LEARNED how to create new colors by mixing other colors. In the same way, you can create new colors by combining your pencils. Blending two pencils together allows you to create additional colors, as shown here. This is a useful way to add a color you may not have, instead of purchasing new pencils straightaway. If you find yourself using that color frequently, you might want to add it to your pencil collection.

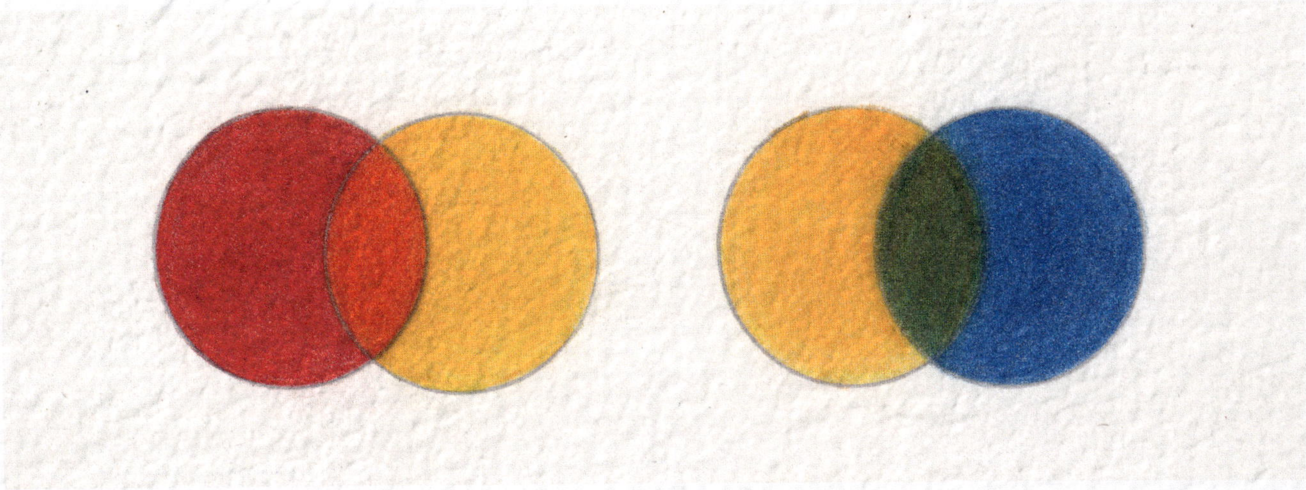

Your turn!

SCAN TO WATCH
A TUTORIAL.

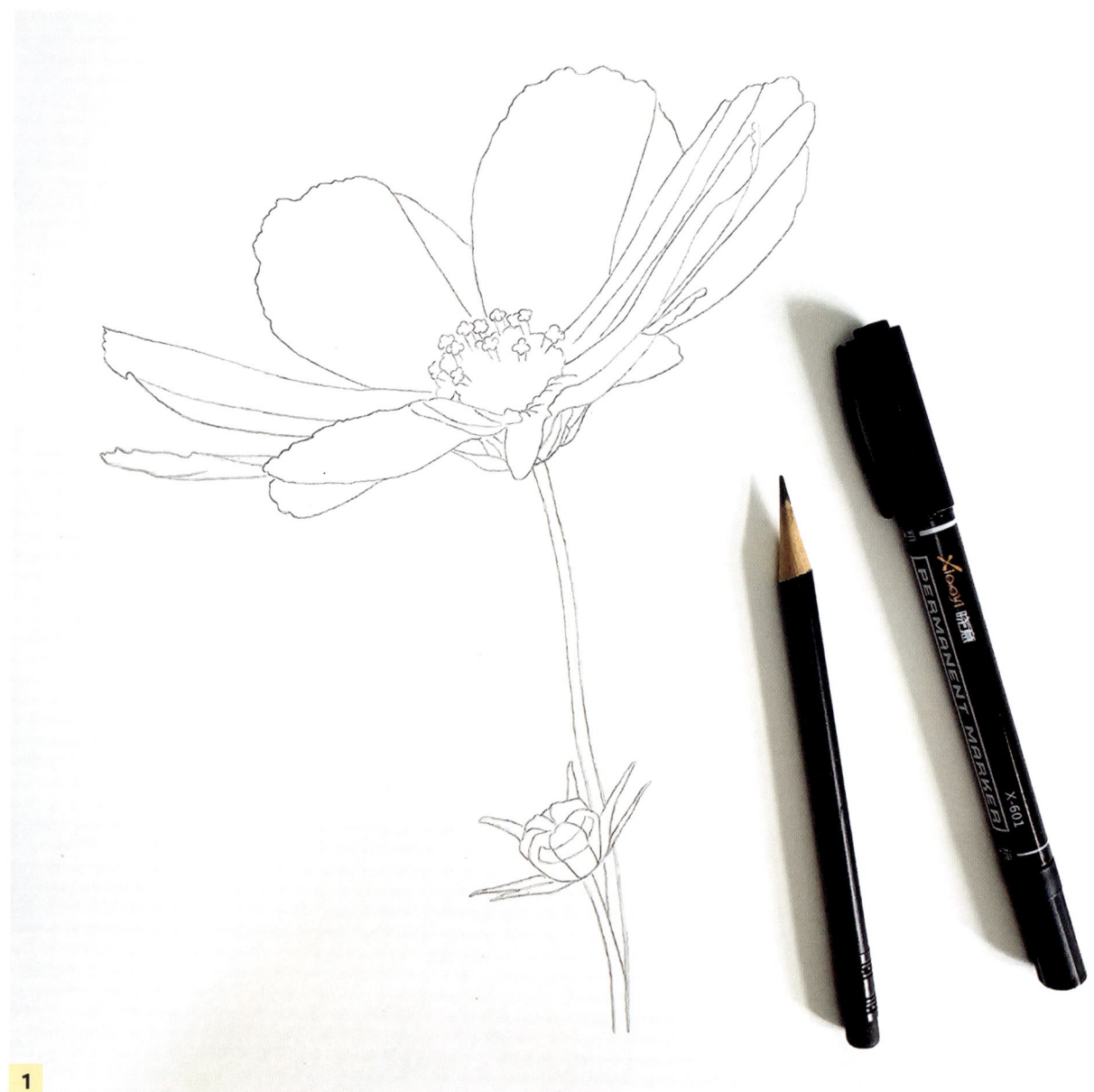

1

TRANSFERRING IMAGES

EACH PROJECT IN THIS BOOK includes an outline of the flower so you can start coloring right in the book. You can also download the templates to transfer onto your own paper. You also might want to transfer other images to your colored pencil paper, such as when you're creating other artworks beyond this book.

You can draw your image right on the paper, but the paper surface can be easily damaged by overuse of an eraser, as mentioned before. A heavily applied pencil point may indent the surface, leaving a permanent mark. If you don't feel confident enough with your drawing skills, or feel the use of an eraser is inevitable, it might be worth considering doing your preliminary outline on a piece of tracing paper first and transferring it to your better-quality paper. I will walk you through the steps to easily transfer your drawing. You can also purchase specialized transfer paper.

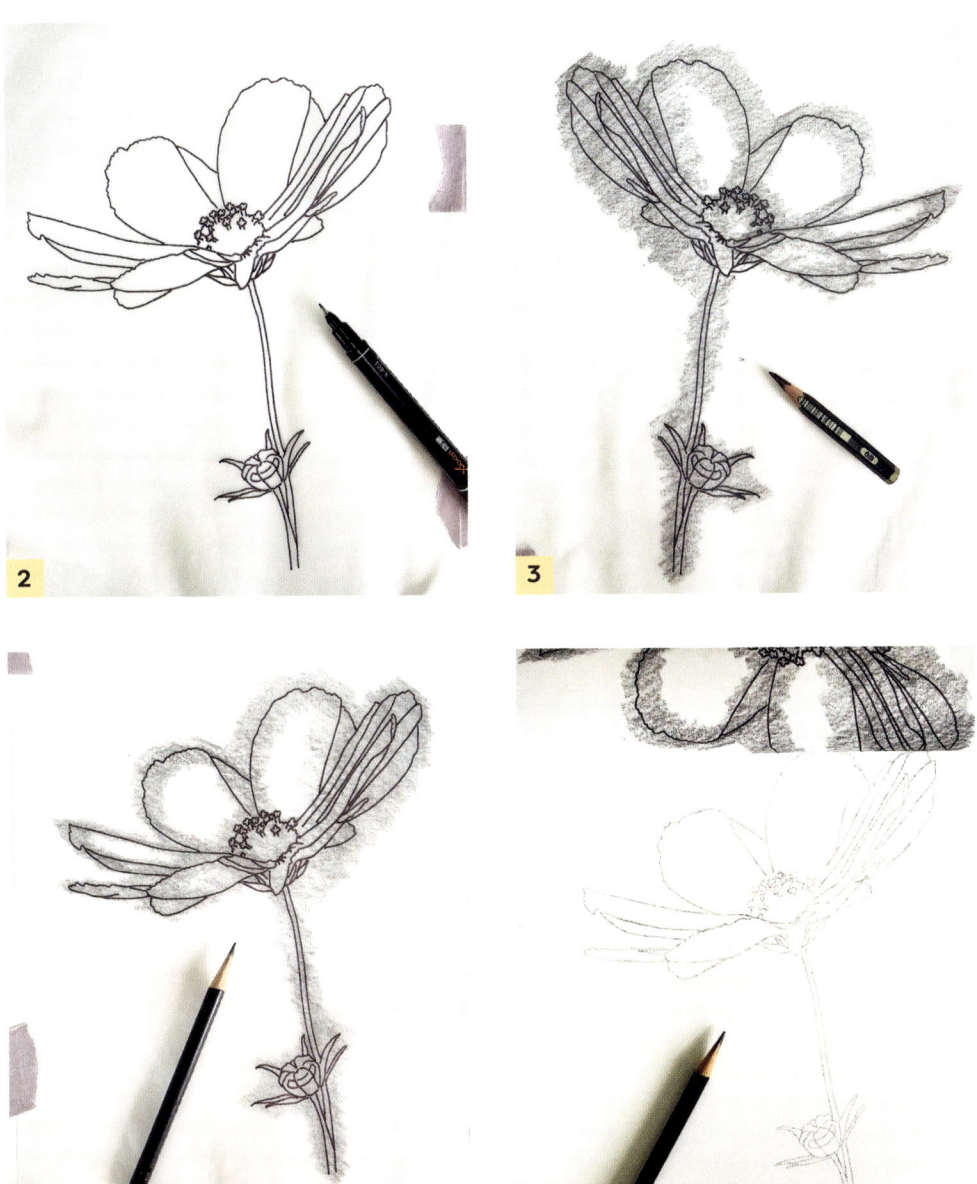

1 First, draw a sketch on the tracing paper with an HB pencil.

2 Now go back over your pencil lines with a fineliner pen or colored pencil/pen. The colored pencil/pen will make it easier to see after you have completed the next stage.

3 Turn the tracing paper over and blacken the area behind the sketch using a dark pencil, such as a 6B.

4 Place tracing paper on top of the paper you want to transfer your sketch onto. Secure it with masking tape to make sure it doesn't move around. Now go back over the traced sketch lines to transfer the image onto the drawing paper.

5 Remove the masking tape and then gently lift the tracing paper leaving the outline of your sketch on your drawing paper. You are now ready to draw. Well done!

You might have done something similar to this transfer technique in school. This is an easy and effective way to copy any sketch onto your drawing paper. It might be simple, but it's really useful.

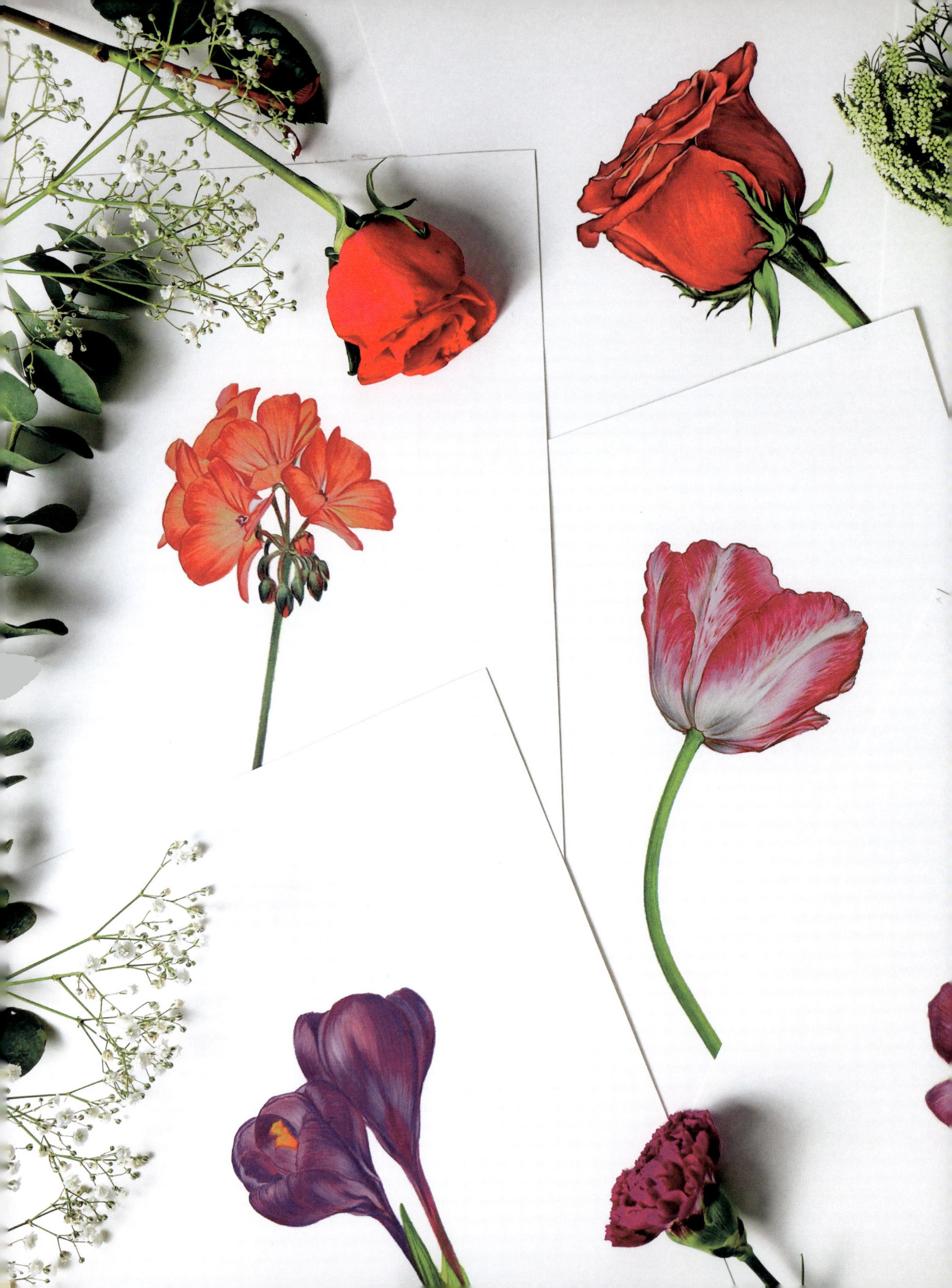

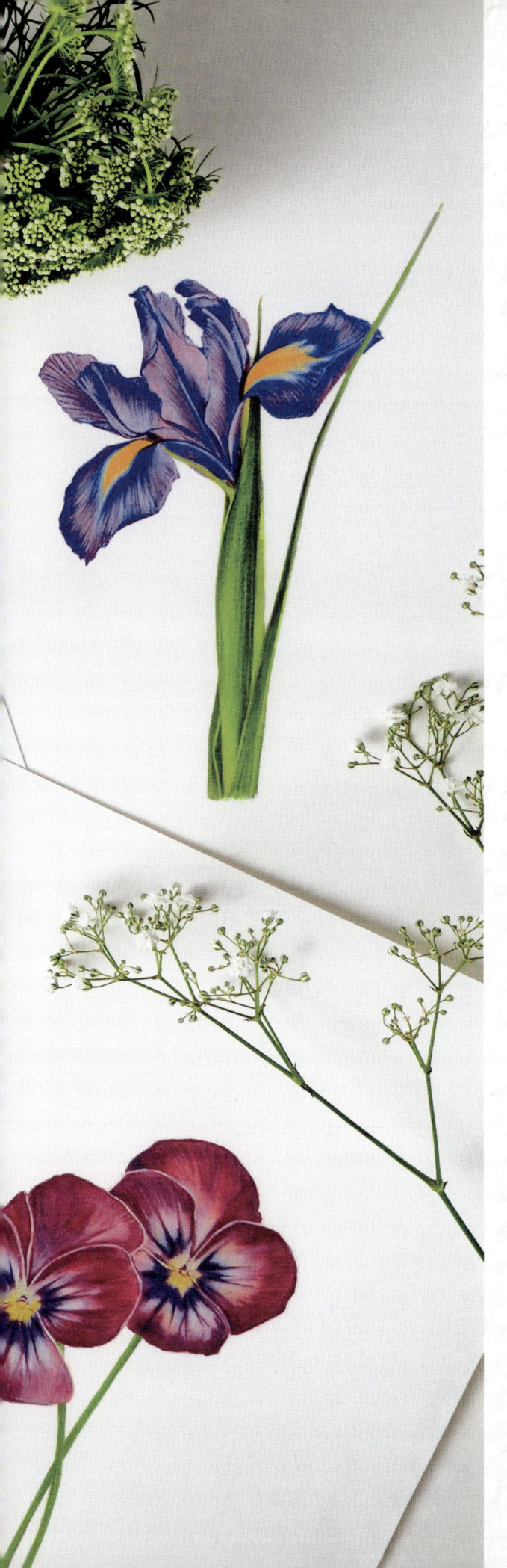

3

THE
PROJECTS

HOW TO USE THIS BOOK

EACH PROJECT IN THIS BOOK is laid out in the same way to allow you to move from one to another easily. In order to set yourself up in the best possible way, I recommend you take the following steps before beginning.

Finished project

Scan the QR code to watch a sped-up video of the steps

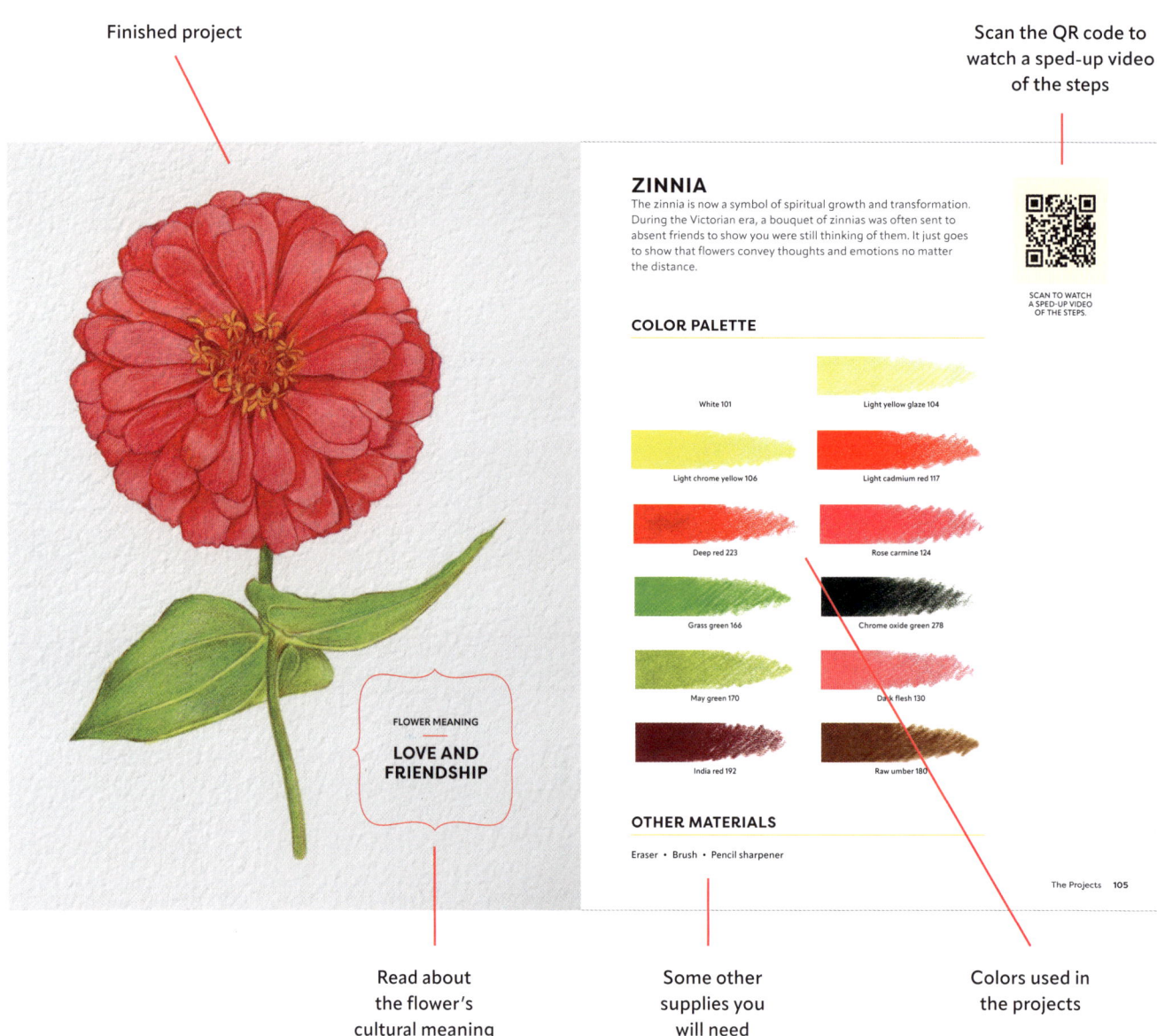

ZINNIA

The zinnia is now a symbol of spiritual growth and transformation. During the Victorian era, a bouquet of zinnias was often sent to absent friends to show you were still thinking of them. It just goes to show that flowers convey thoughts and emotions no matter the distance.

SCAN TO WATCH A SPED-UP VIDEO OF THE STEPS.

COLOR PALETTE

White 101

Light yellow glaze 104

Light chrome yellow 106

Light cadmium red 117

Deep red 223

Rose carmine 124

Grass green 166

Chrome oxide green 278

May green 170

Dark flesh 130

India red 192

Raw umber 180

OTHER MATERIALS

Eraser • Brush • Pencil sharpener

The Projects   105

FLOWER MEANING

LOVE AND FRIENDSHIP

Read about the flower's cultural meaning

Some other supplies you will need

Colors used in the projects

SCAN TO DOWNLOAD
ADDITIONAL TEMPLATES
OF THE PROJECTS.

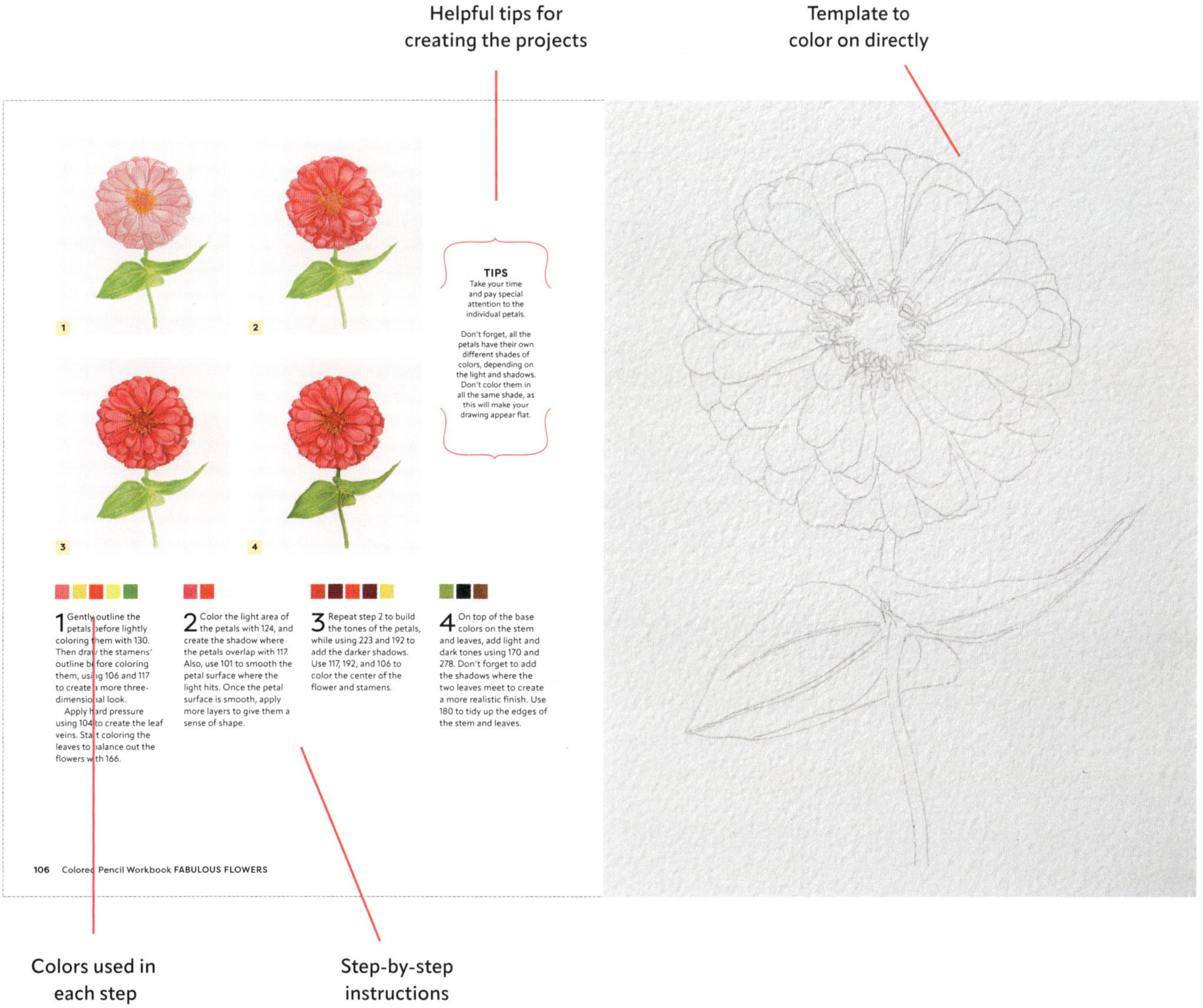

Helpful tips for
creating the projects

Template to
color on directly

TIPS

Take your time
and pay special
attention to the
individual petals.

Don't forget, all the
petals have their own
different shades of
colors, depending on
the light and shadows.
Don't color them in
all the same shade, as
this will make your
drawing appear flat.

1 Gently outline the petals before lightly coloring them with 130. Then draw the stamens' outline before coloring them, using 106 and 117 to create a more three-dimensional look.
Apply hard pressure using 104 to create the leaf veins. Start coloring the leaves to balance out the flowers with 166.

2 Color the light area of the petals with 124, and create the shadow where the petals overlap with 117. Also, use 101 to smooth the petal surface where the light hits. Once the petal surface is smooth, apply more layers to give them a sense of shape.

3 Repeat step 2 to build the tones of the petals, while using 223 and 192 to add the darker shadows. Use 117, 192, and 106 to color the center of the flower and stamens.

4 On top of the base colors on the stem and leaves, add light and dark tones using 170 and 278. Don't forget to add the shadows where the two leaves meet to create a more realistic finish. Use 180 to tidy up the edges of the stem and leaves.

106 Colored Pencil Workbook **FABULOUS FLOWERS**

Colors used in
each step

Step-by-step
instructions

- Study the finished drawing so you have a clear idea of what you want to achieve.

- A template for each project is included. You can use your own paper to trace the template if you would like to reuse it in the future. More information on how to use the templates can be found on page 30.

- Review the color palette information and select your pencils.

- Make sure you have your eraser, brush, and sharpener ready.

- Review the steps before you begin so you know what the end result of each step should look like.

- Use the QR code to watch a sped-up version of me coloring each flower.

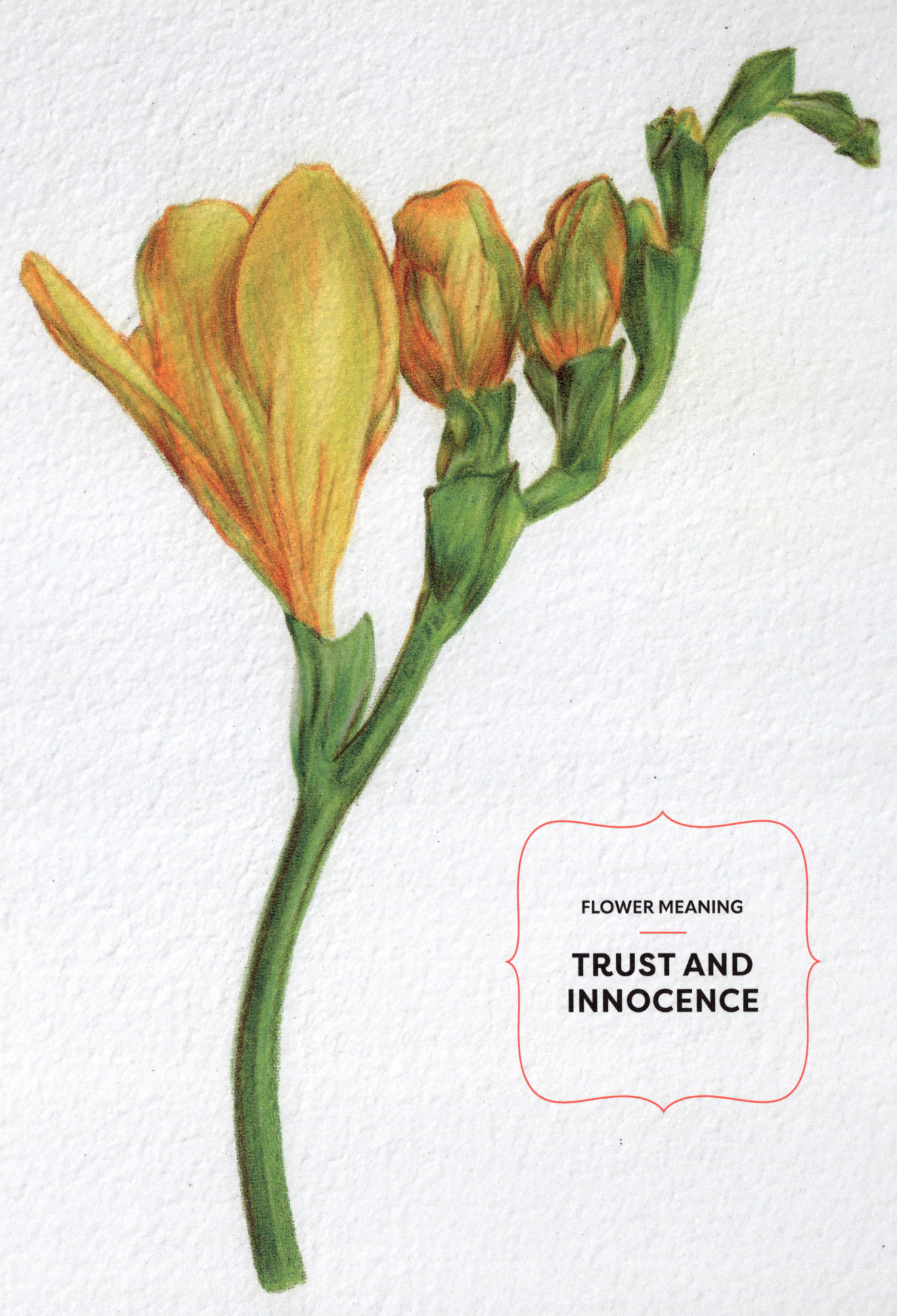

FLOWER MEANING

TRUST AND INNOCENCE

FREESIA

The freesia is a symbol of friendship, trust, and innocence. In South Korea, however, it is often given as a graduation day flower. It is the most popular flower during this very happy time.

SCAN TO WATCH A SPED-UP VIDEO OF THE STEPS.

COLOR PALETTE

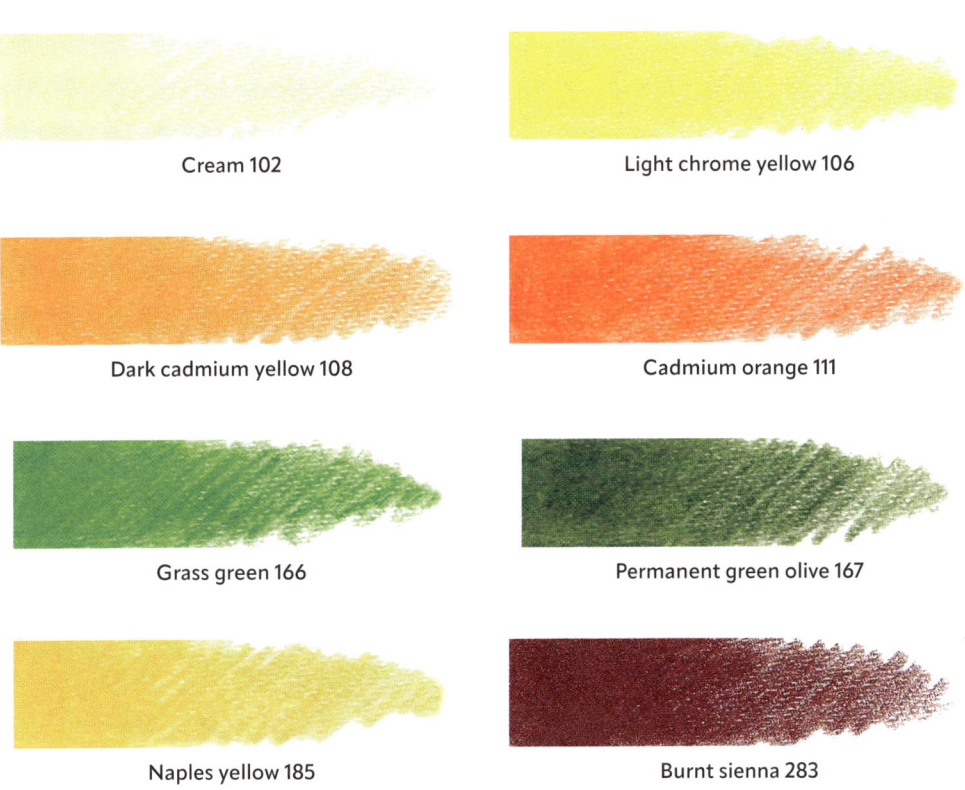

Cream 102

Light chrome yellow 106

Dark cadmium yellow 108

Cadmium orange 111

Grass green 166

Permanent green olive 167

Naples yellow 185

Burnt sienna 283

OTHER MATERIALS

Eraser • Brush • Pencil sharpener

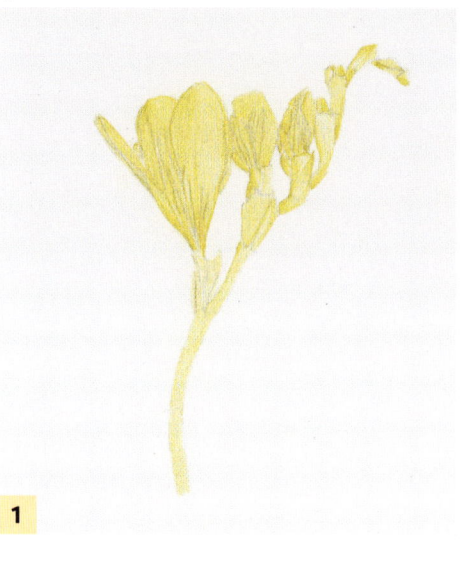

1

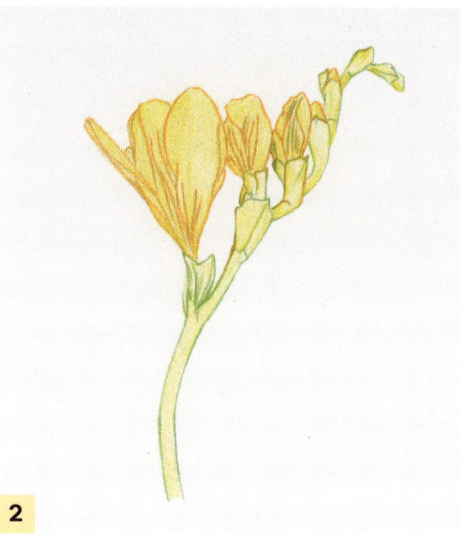

2

TIP
Where the petals haven't opened fully yet, they are greener. Make sure to represent this with your color application.

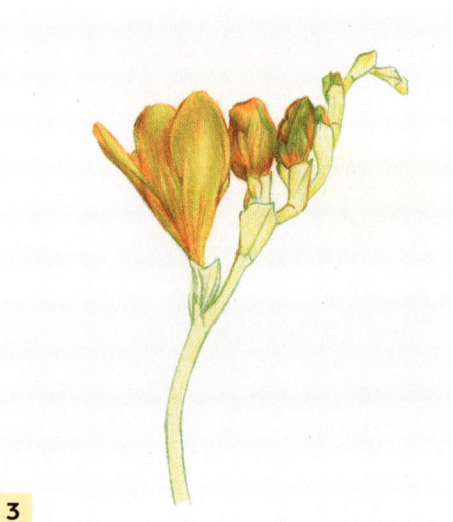

3

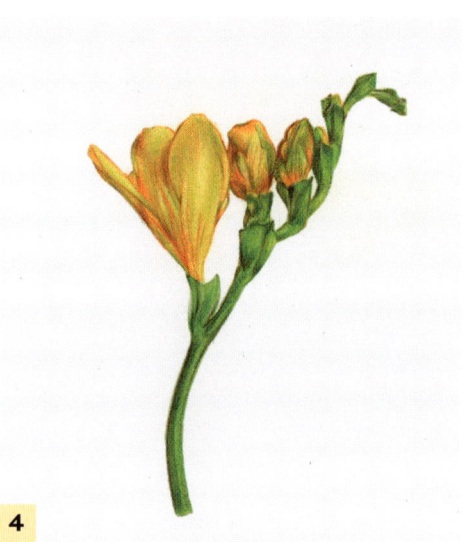

4

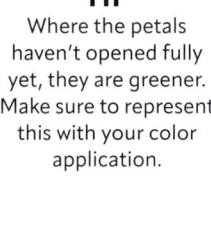

1 Use 106 to apply a base layer to the entire flower, including petals, buds, and stem.

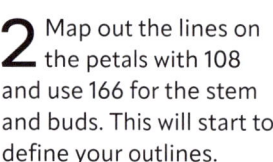

2 Map out the lines on the petals with 108 and use 166 for the stem and buds. This will start to define your outlines.

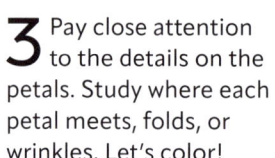

3 Pay close attention to the details on the petals. Study where each petal meets, folds, or wrinkles. Let's color!

Apply a light layer to the petals using 106 and 108. Color the dark shadows where the petals overlap using 185 and 111. Once you have layered the colors, blend them with 102. Use 166 to give a hint of light green shine to the petals. Using 283, create the detailed outline around the petals, and create the darker shadows.

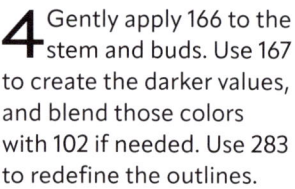

4 Gently apply 166 to the stem and buds. Use 167 to create the darker values, and blend those colors with 102 if needed. Use 283 to redefine the outlines.

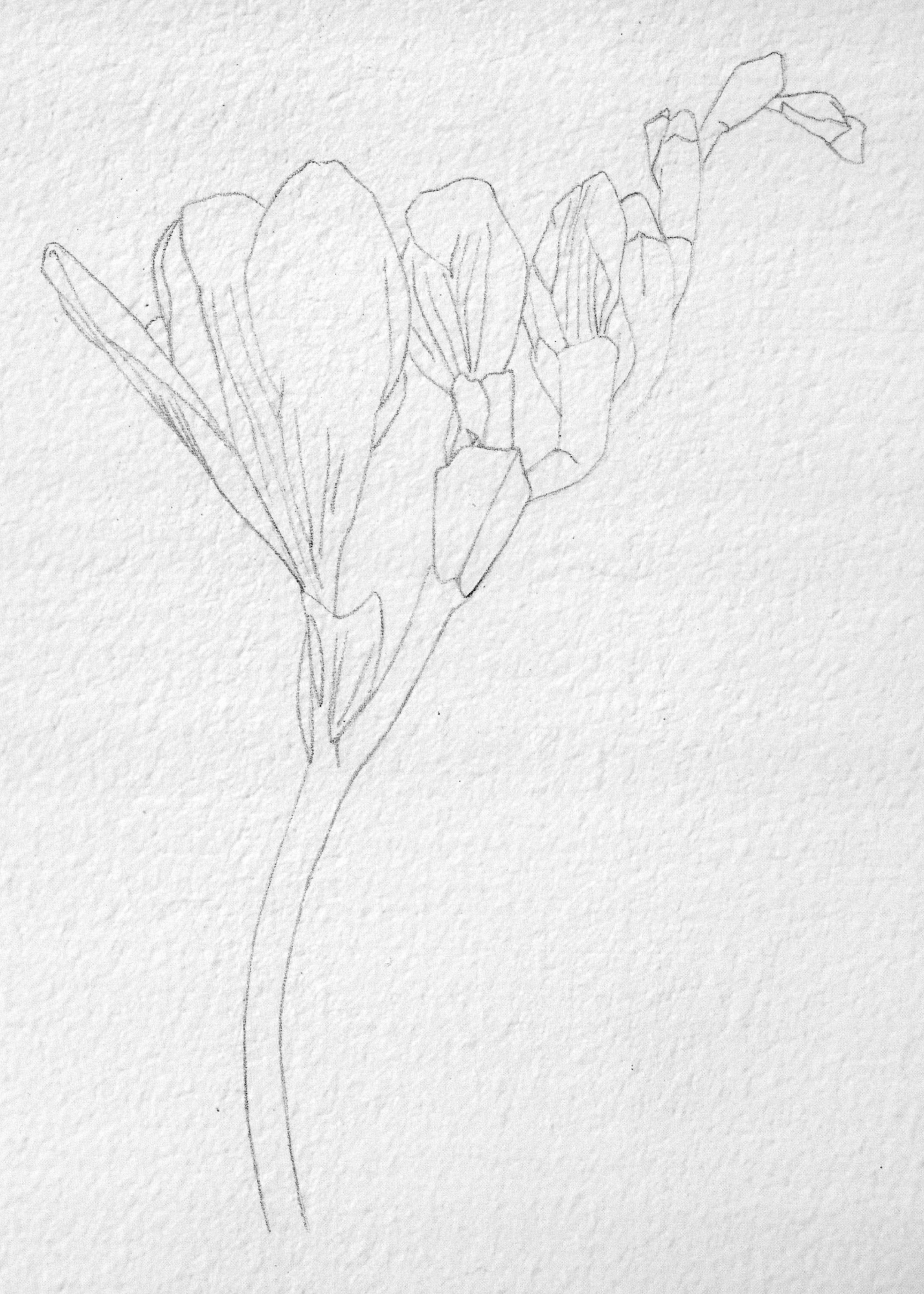

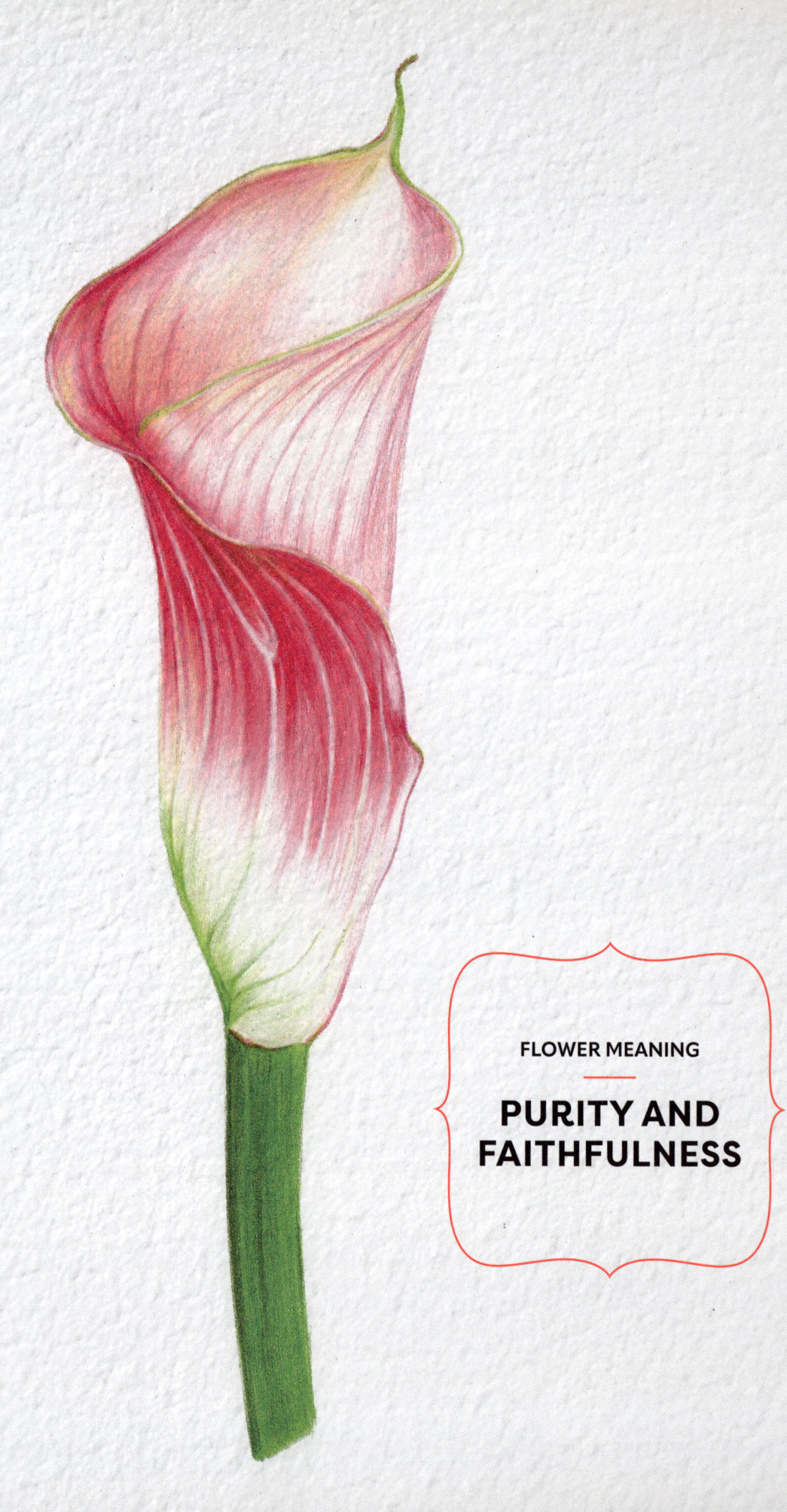

FLOWER MEANING

PURITY AND FAITHFULNESS

CALLA LILY

The calla lily comes in many colors, with several meanings ranging from admiration to rebirth. It has been seen as a chalice for the ancient Greeks and Romans, but to me, it is simply my favorite flower.

SCAN TO WATCH A SPED-UP VIDEO OF THE STEPS.

COLOR PALETTE

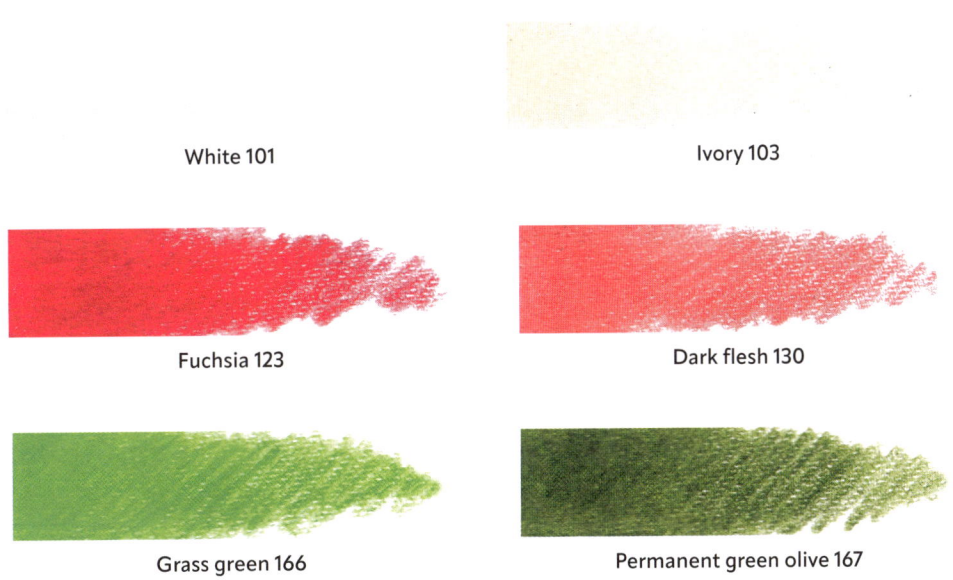

White 101

Ivory 103

Fuchsia 123

Dark flesh 130

Grass green 166

Permanent green olive 167

OTHER MATERIALS

Eraser • Brush • Pencil sharpener

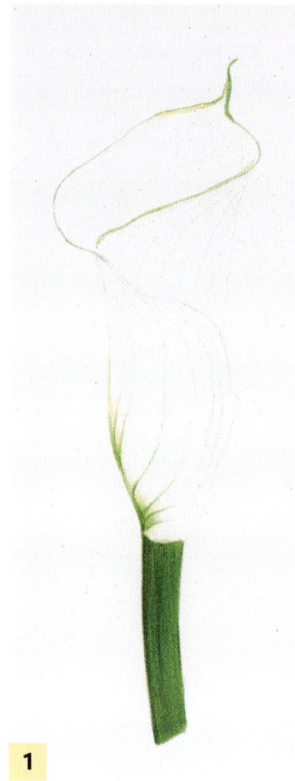

1

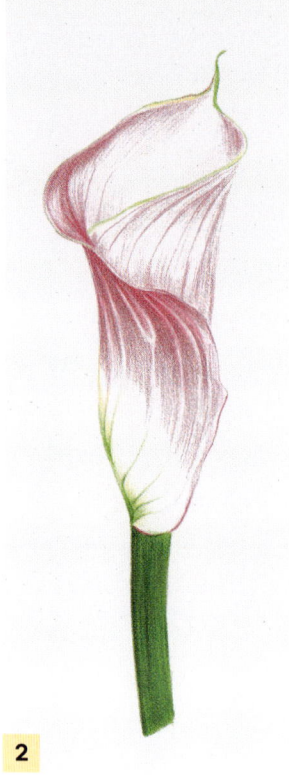

2

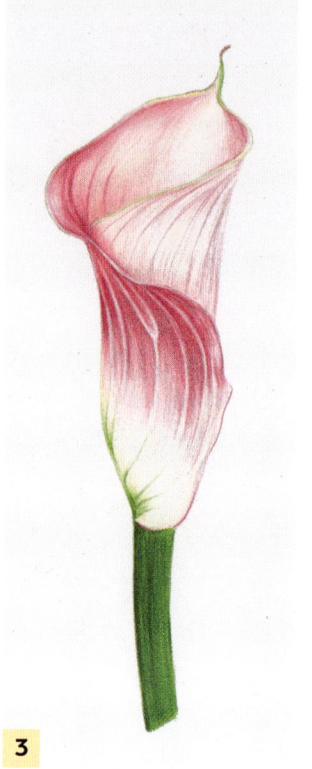

3

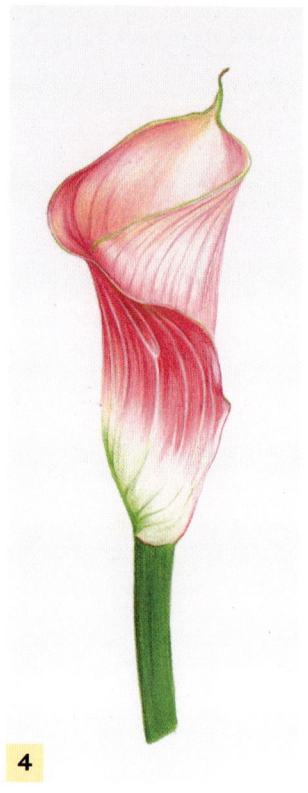

4

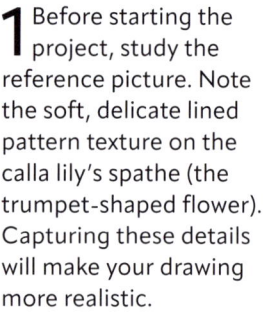

1 Before starting the project, study the reference picture. Note the soft, delicate lined pattern texture on the calla lily's spathe (the trumpet-shaped flower). Capturing these details will make your drawing more realistic.

Use 101 to mark the lines on the spathe. Use 166 to lightly outline the edges of the spathe, naturally meeting the lines you just added. With 166 and 167 use short strokes to follow the vertical lines of the stem, gently adding layers (Line Practice, Exercise 2).

2 Use 123 to color the flower, using light pressure strokes. Starting from the top, follow the flower's lines, adding more layers to increase the tone on the darker areas. Avoid the masked lines you added earlier in step 1 to create the desired pattern.

3 This is the blending step. Use 103 to gently apply a light layer to the entire spathe, blending with the 123 applied in step 2. Take your time, and don't rush this step. Slowly build up the layers to fill in the spathe as you go.

Once you have achieved a smoother look by blending the two colors, apply 130 to the inner part of the spathe to create some contrast. Repeat this step until you achieve the desired details and colors.

4 Step 4 is all about the details. Use 101 to gently blend the entire spathe, smoothing out the surface. Once all the colors are nicely blended, use 123 and 130 to greatly enhance the main color of the flower, while focusing on the details. Use 166 and 167 to define the edge of the spathe.

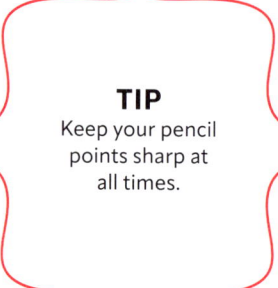

TIP
Keep your pencil points sharp at all times.

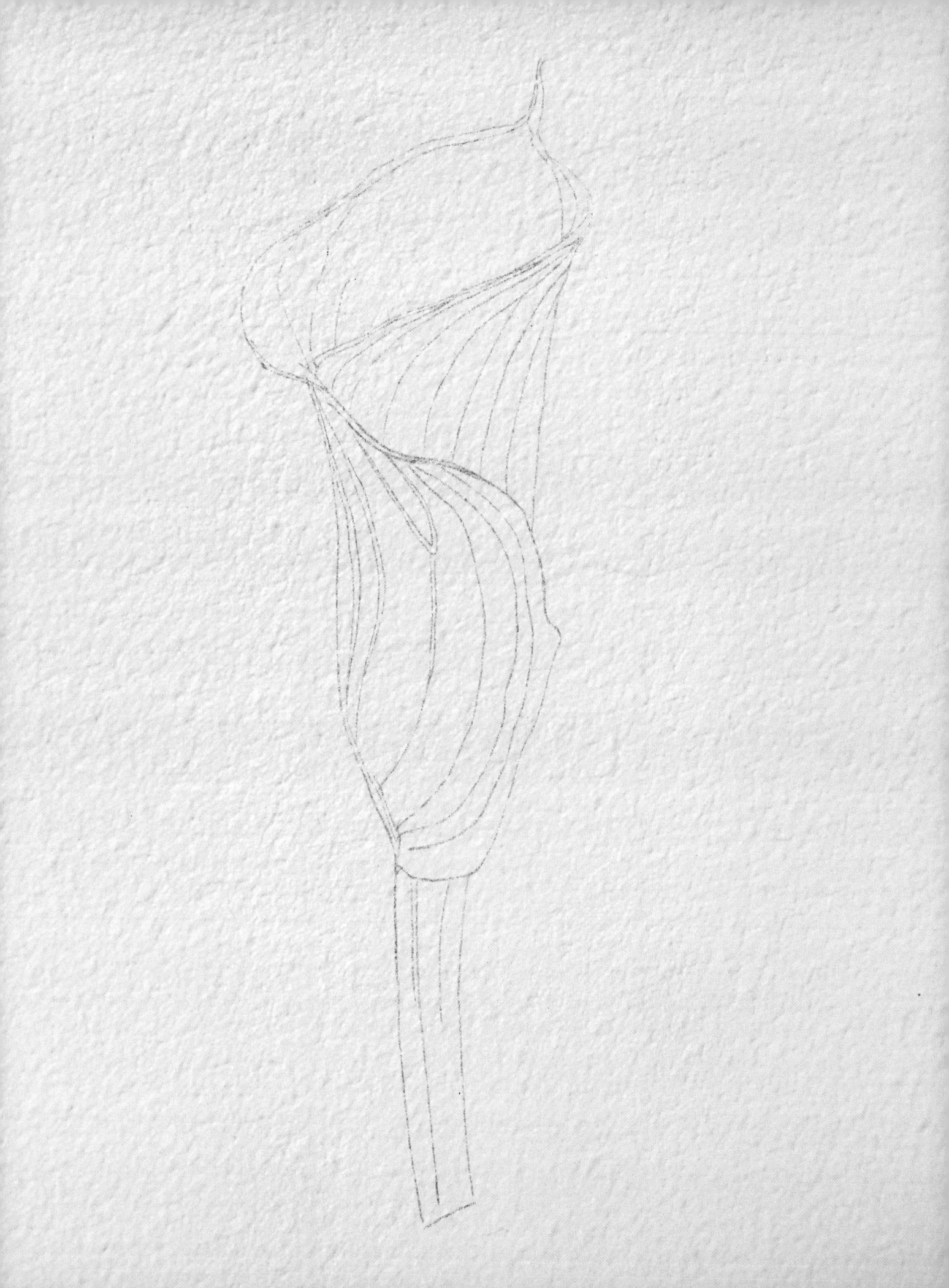

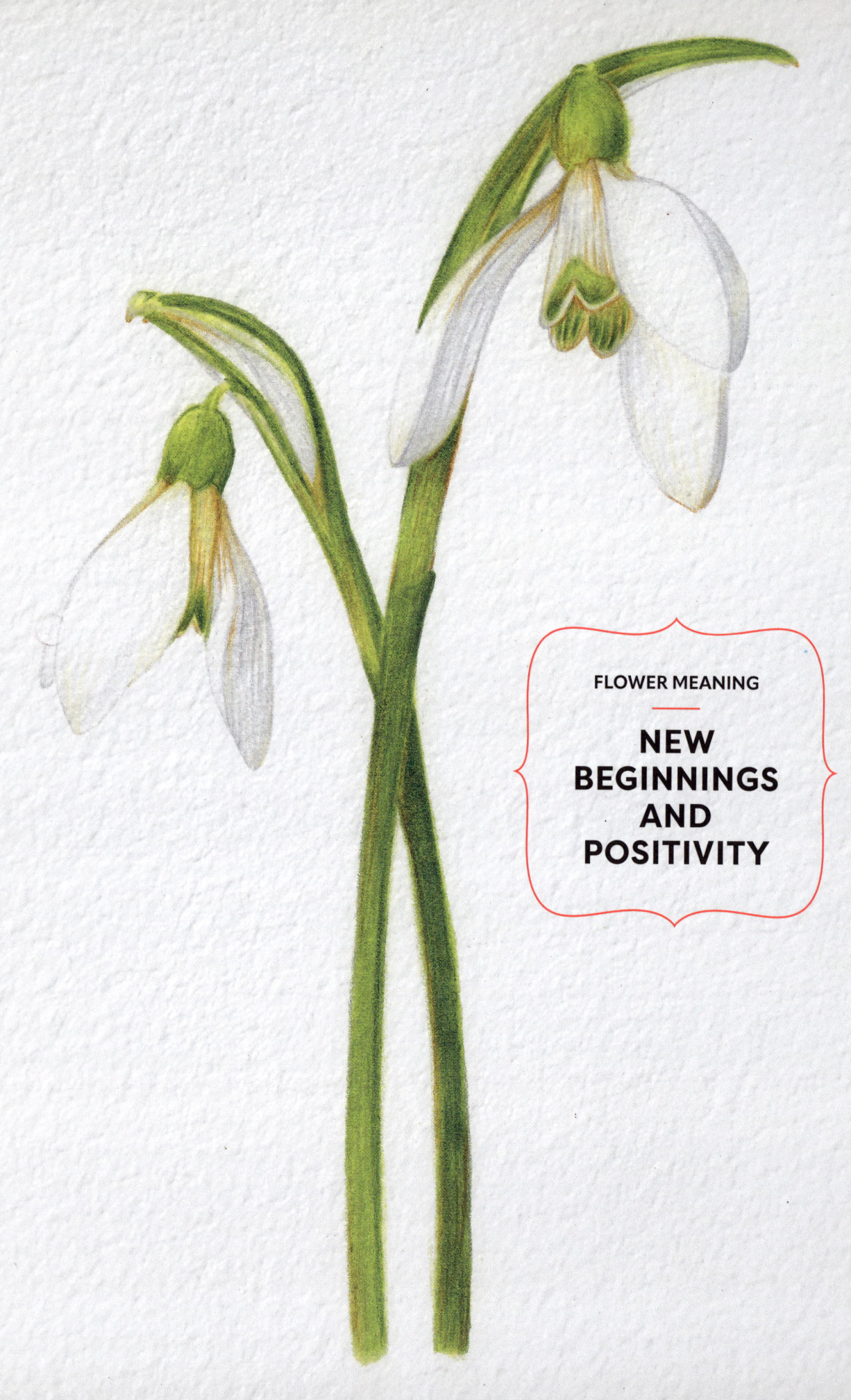

FLOWER MEANING

NEW BEGINNINGS AND POSITIVITY

SNOWDROP

The snowdrop is one of the first flowers you will see introducing spring, even when winter hasn't left the forest yet. It reminds me of a white butterfly gently warming itself on a green stem.

SCAN TO WATCH A SPED-UP VIDEO OF THE STEPS.

COLOR PALETTE

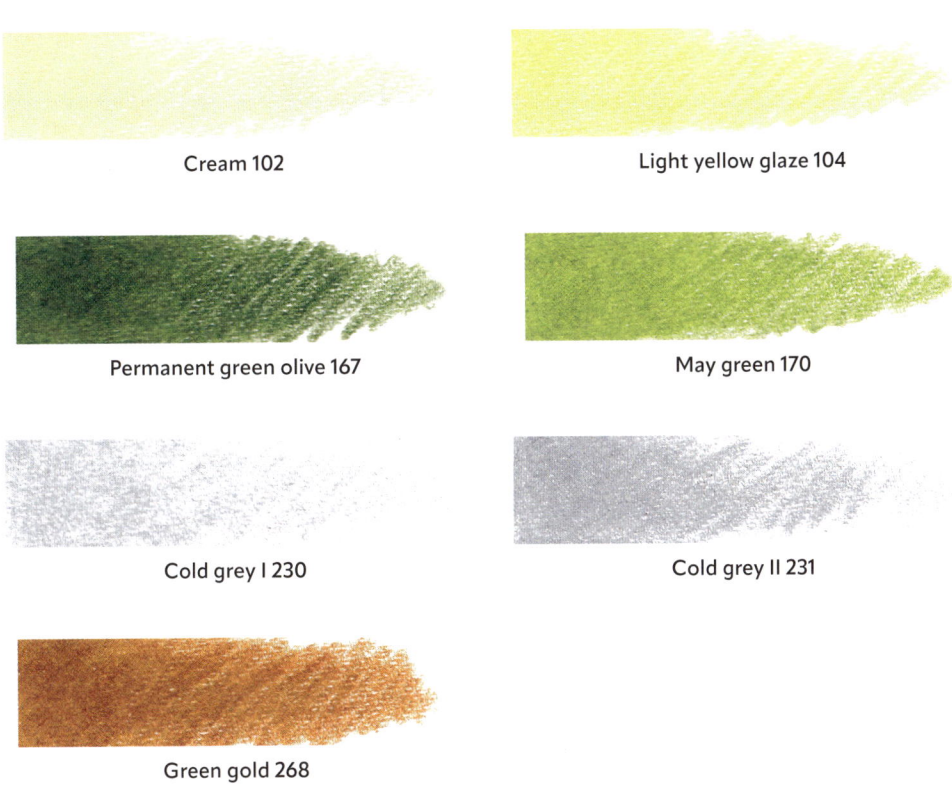

Cream 102

Light yellow glaze 104

Permanent green olive 167

May green 170

Cold grey I 230

Cold grey II 231

Green gold 268

OTHER MATERIALS

Eraser • Brush • Pencil sharpener

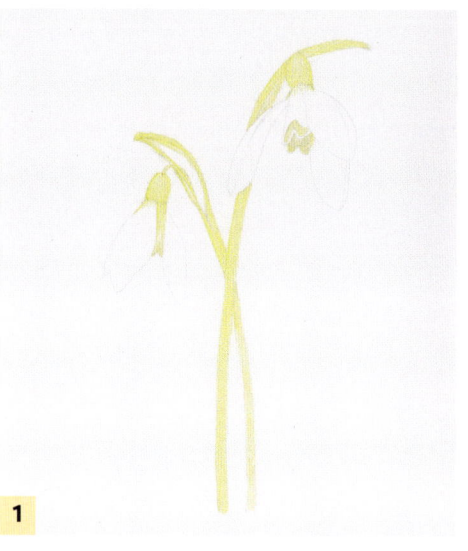

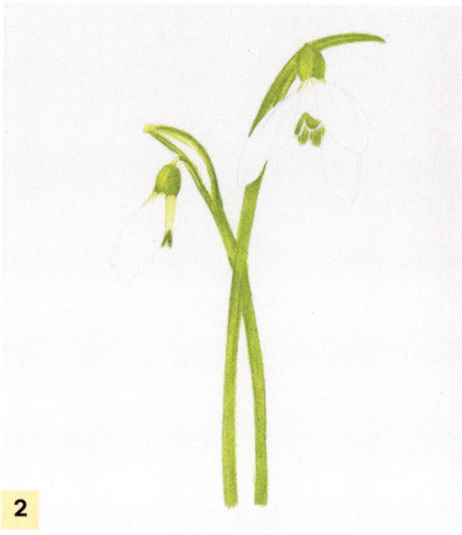

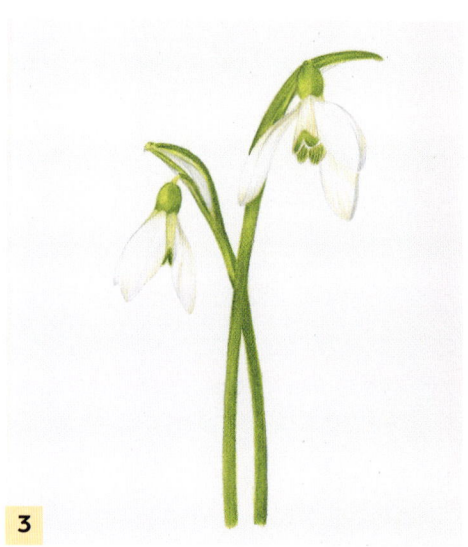

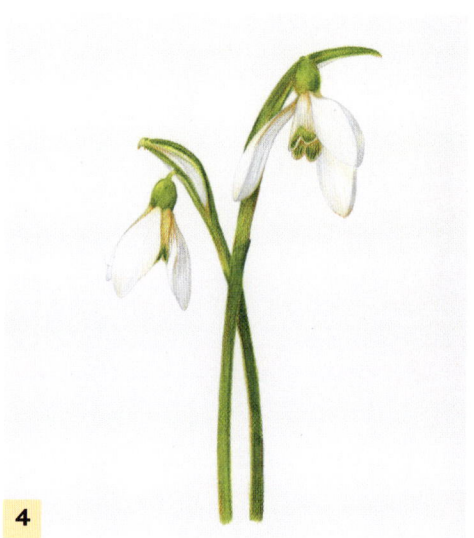

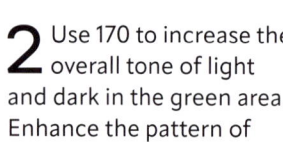

1 Use 104 and start applying the base layer for the areas of the flower that will eventually be colored green, such as the stem.

2 Use 170 to increase the overall tone of light and dark in the green area. Enhance the pattern of the petals too.

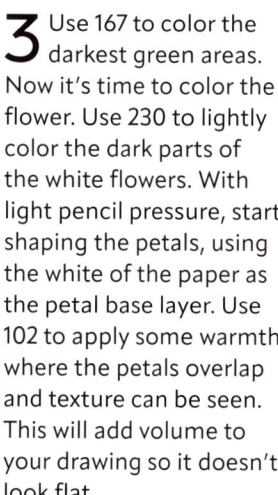

3 Use 167 to color the darkest green areas. Now it's time to color the flower. Use 230 to lightly color the dark parts of the white flowers. With light pencil pressure, start shaping the petals, using the white of the paper as the petal base layer. Use 102 to apply some warmth where the petals overlap and texture can be seen. This will add volume to your drawing so it doesn't look flat.

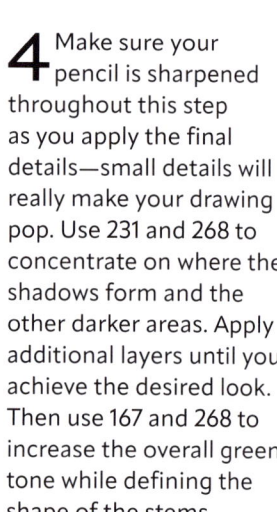

4 Make sure your pencil is sharpened throughout this step as you apply the final details—small details will really make your drawing pop. Use 231 and 268 to concentrate on where the shadows form and the other darker areas. Apply additional layers until you achieve the desired look. Then use 167 and 268 to increase the overall green tone while defining the shape of the stems.

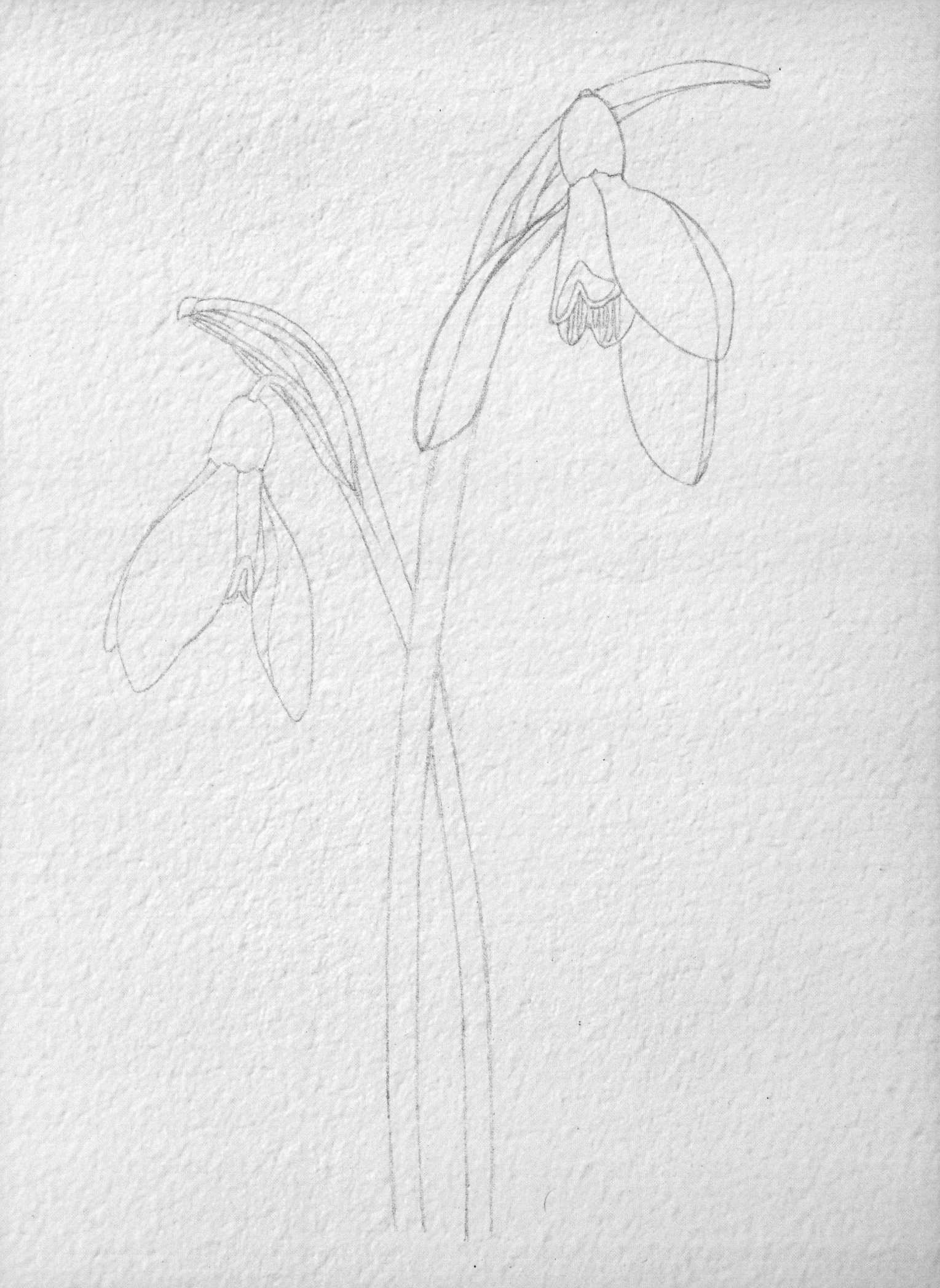

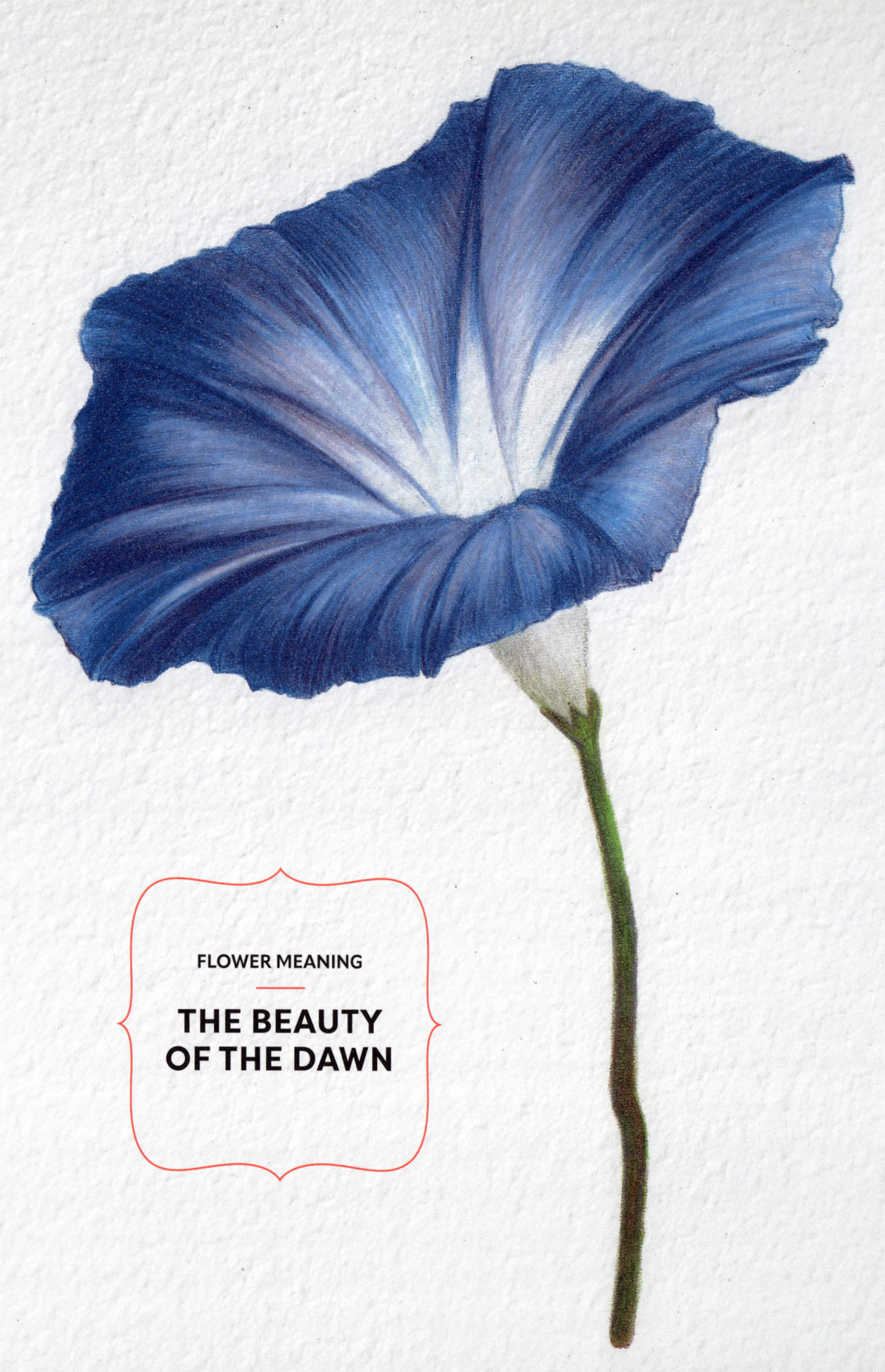

FLOWER MEANING

THE BEAUTY OF THE DAWN

MORNING GLORY

The morning glory is able to bloom, open, and close before sunset every day, which is probably why it is associated with fresh starts. The morning glory is also a close relative of the sweet potato—how interesting!

SCAN TO WATCH
A SPED-UP VIDEO
OF THE STEPS.

COLOR PALETTE

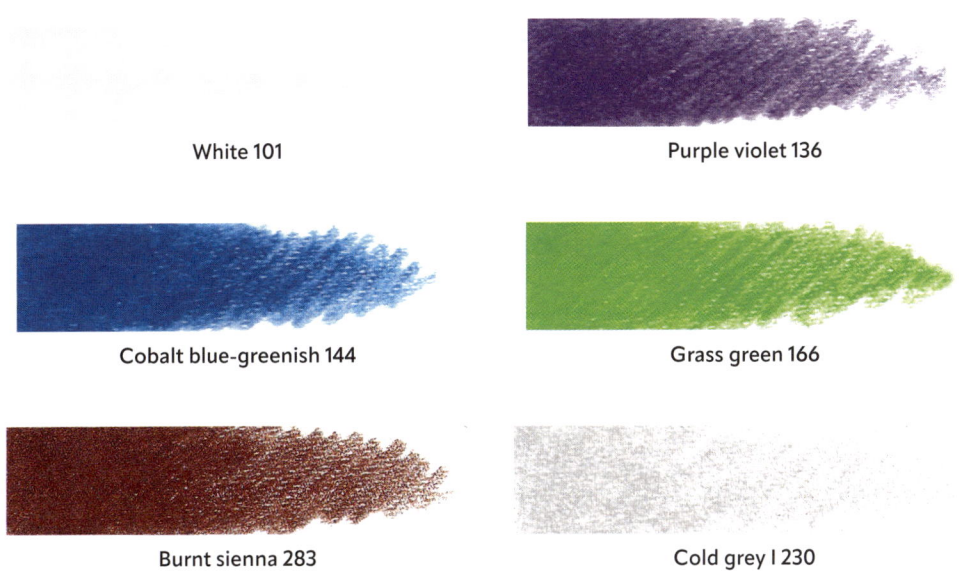

White 101

Purple violet 136

Cobalt blue-greenish 144

Grass green 166

Burnt sienna 283

Cold grey I 230

OTHER MATERIALS

Eraser • Brush • Pencil sharpener

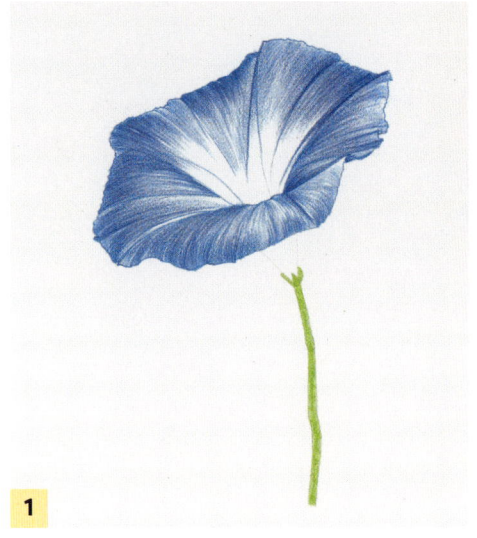

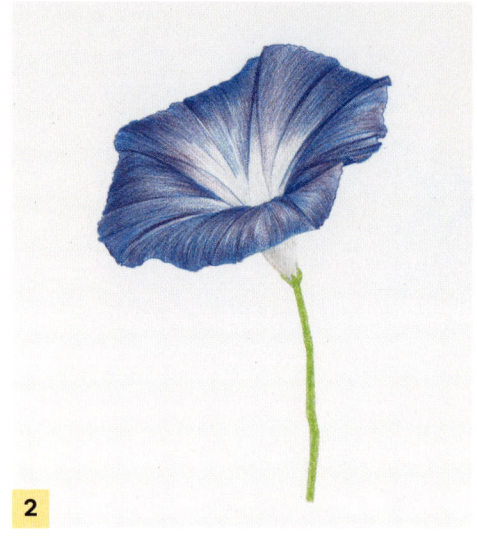

TIP
The key here is blending and layering! Blend blue and purple with white to achieve the smooth texture. Add additional layers to achieve a more realistic look.

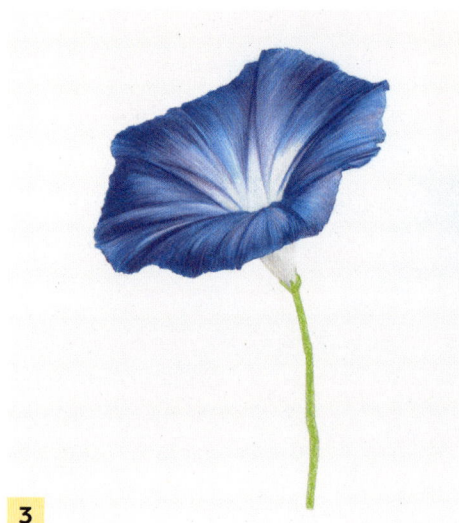

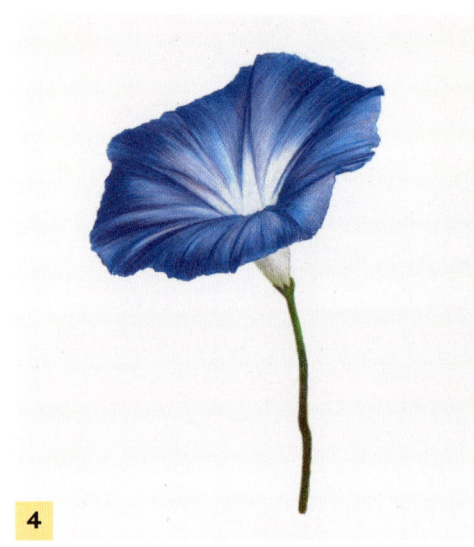

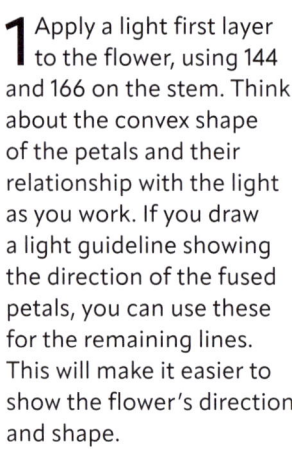

1 Apply a light first layer to the flower, using 144 and 166 on the stem. Think about the convex shape of the petals and their relationship with the light as you work. If you draw a light guideline showing the direction of the fused petals, you can use these for the remaining lines. This will make it easier to show the flower's direction and shape.

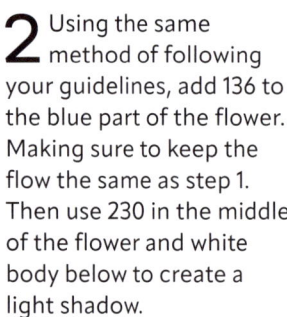

2 Using the same method of following your guidelines, add 136 to the blue part of the flower. Making sure to keep the flow the same as step 1. Then use 230 in the middle of the flower and white body below to create a light shadow.

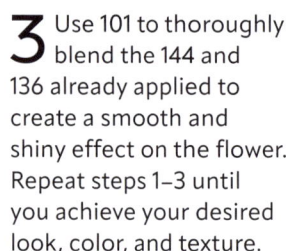

3 Use 101 to thoroughly blend the 144 and 136 already applied to create a smooth and shiny effect on the flower. Repeat steps 1–3 until you achieve your desired look, color, and texture.

4 First color and shape the stem using 166, and increase the darker tones with 283.Make sure you keep your pencil tip sharp as you color the long, skinny stem. Finish off the bottom of the tube with 230, creating a shadow.

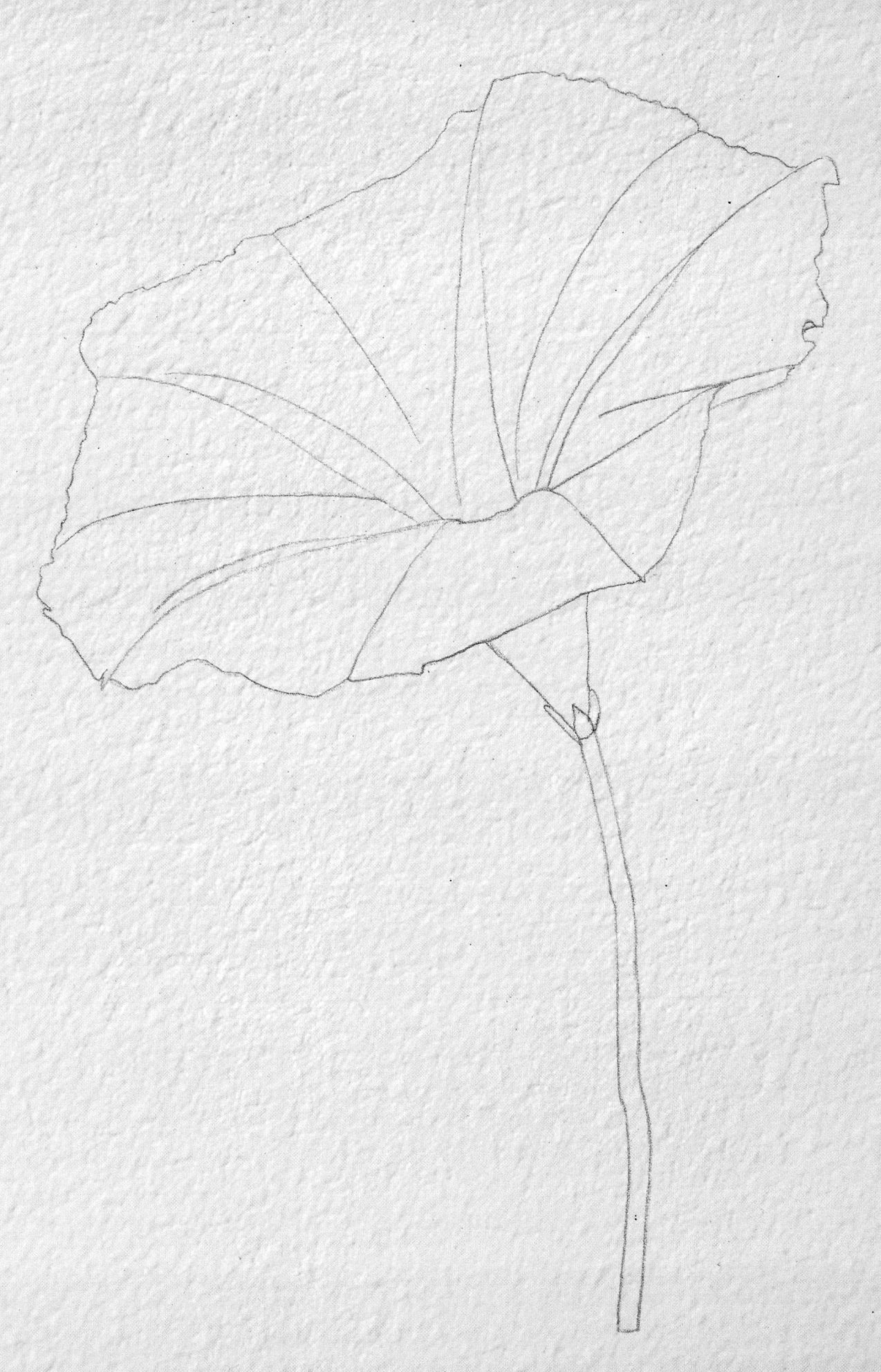

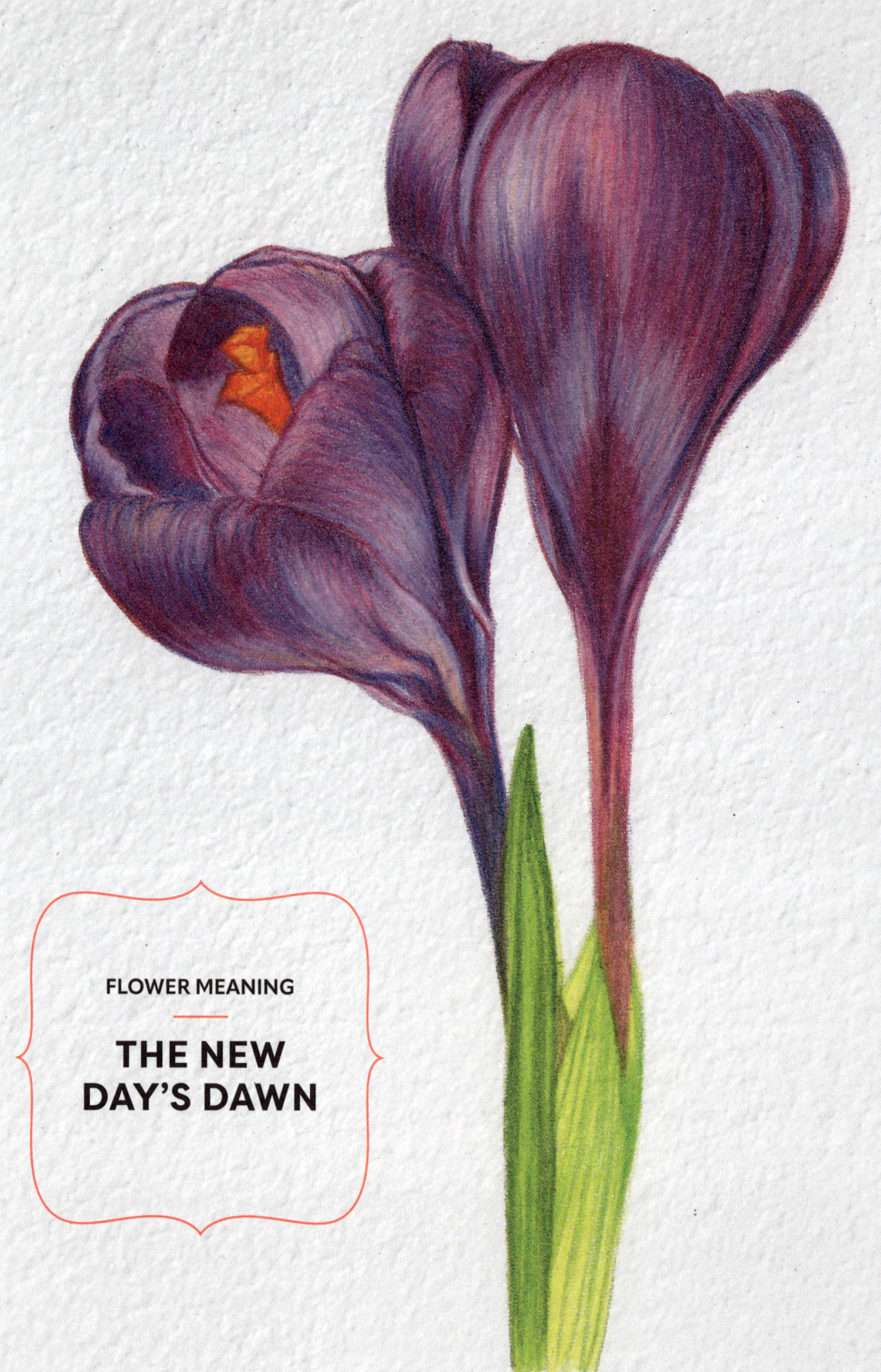

CROCUS

The crocus can symbolize hope and new beginnings, such as the transition from dark to light, night to day, and the coming of a new dawn. Maybe the crocus in this book is a symbol of the artist emerging from inside you.

SCAN TO WATCH
A SPED-UP VIDEO
OF THE STEPS.

COLOR PALETTE

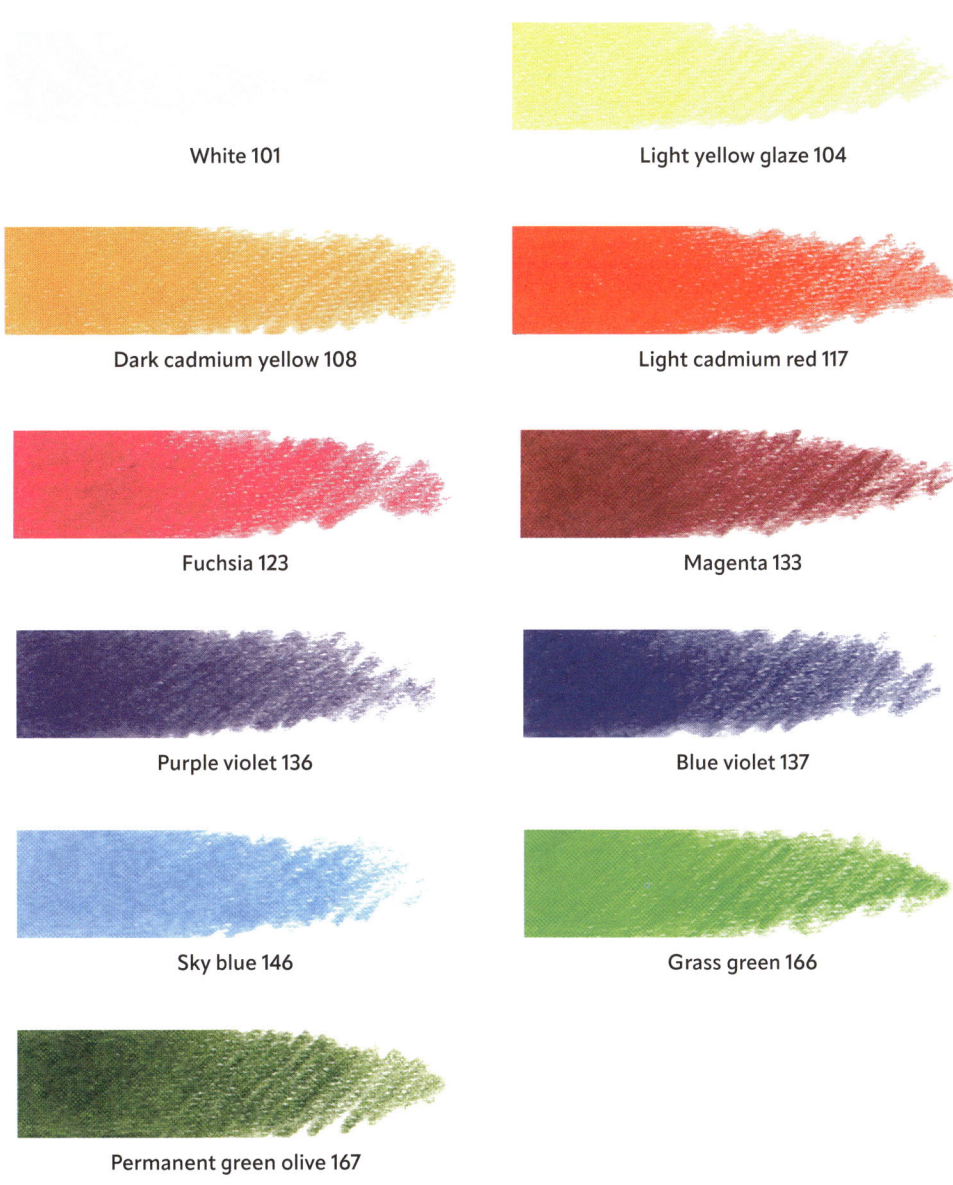

White 101

Light yellow glaze 104

Dark cadmium yellow 108

Light cadmium red 117

Fuchsia 123

Magenta 133

Purple violet 136

Blue violet 137

Sky blue 146

Grass green 166

Permanent green olive 167

OTHER MATERIALS

Eraser • Brush • Pencil sharpener

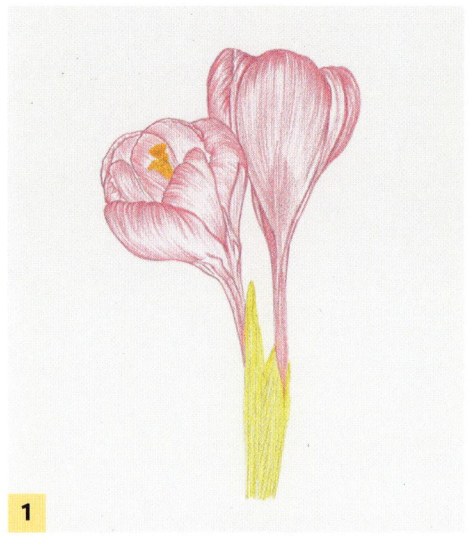

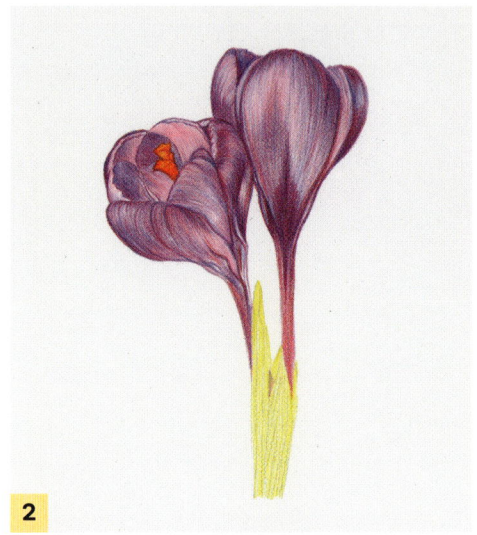

TIP

The crocus petal has a shiny surface. Use your white wisely to blend the colors to achieve the smooth, shiny surface.

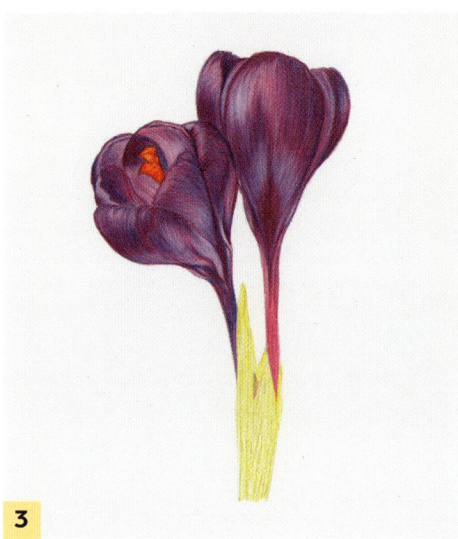

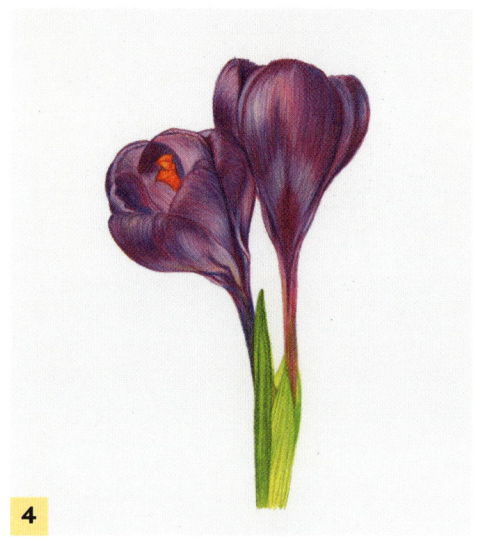

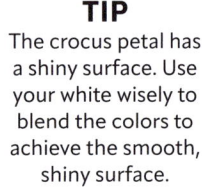

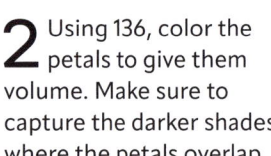

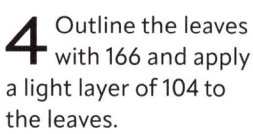

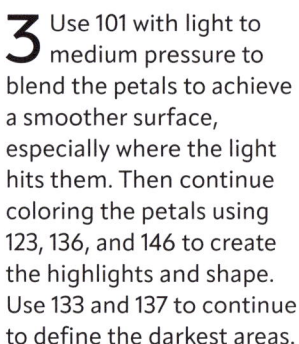

1 Map out the outline of the petals, using 123 and 104 for the base layer on the leaves. Use 108 to color the stamens. The edge of the crocus petal has a smooth curve. Pay special attention to the shape of the flower and follow its lines to start creating the shape.

2 Using 136, color the petals to give them volume. Make sure to capture the darker shades where the petals overlap.

Apply even strokes to achieve the underlayer colors and patterns, following the flow of the petals, using 123 and 136. Apply 117 to darken the stamens. Carefully blend 133 to emphasize the deepest shadow at the bottom of the flower and where the petals overlap.

3 Use 101 with light to medium pressure to blend the petals to achieve a smoother surface, especially where the light hits them. Then continue coloring the petals using 123, 136, and 146 to create the highlights and shape. Use 133 and 137 to continue to define the darkest areas.

4 Outline the leaves with 166 and apply a light layer of 104 to the leaves.

Lastly, use 167 to define the darkest lines on the leaves, creating a more realistic effect.

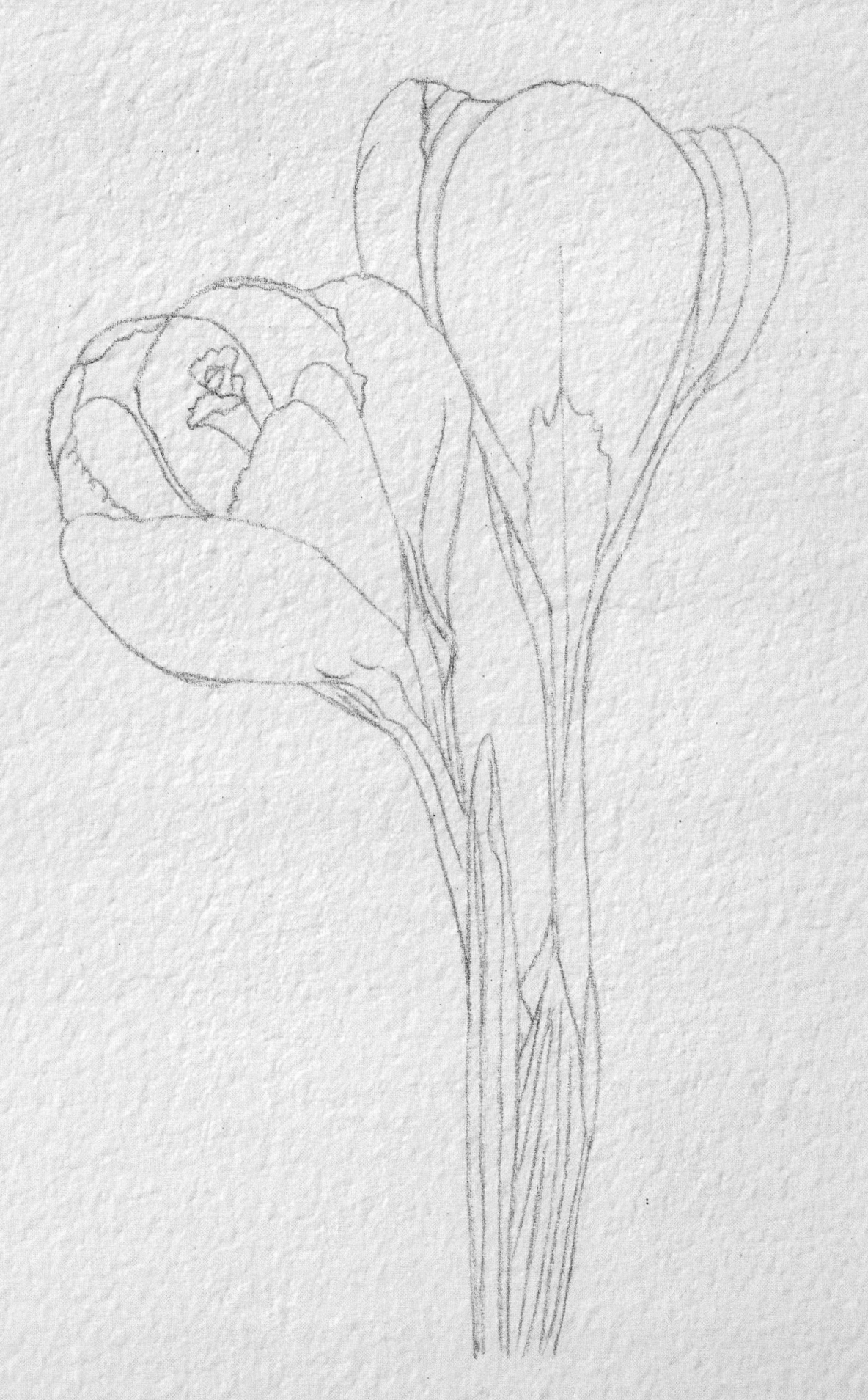

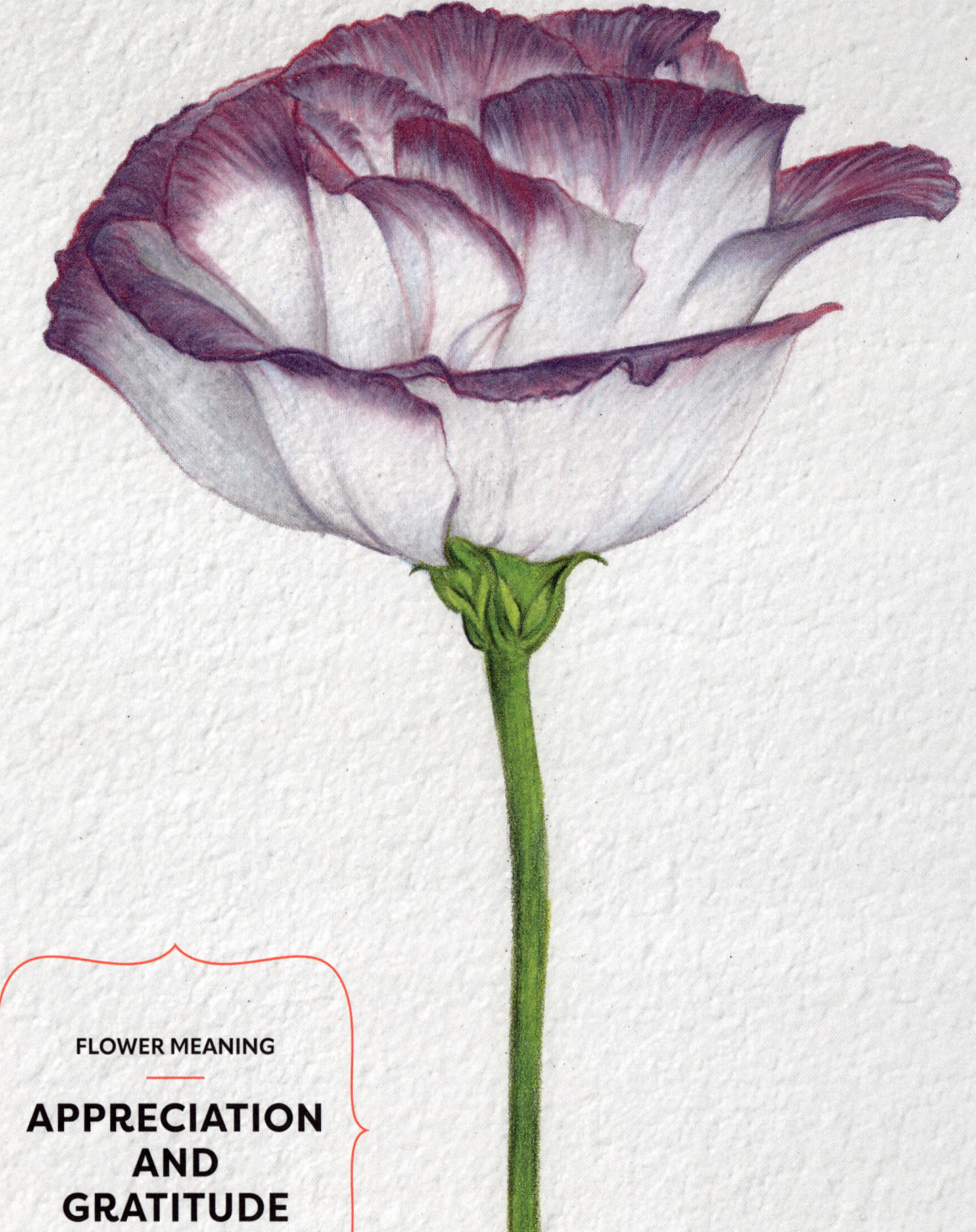

FLOWER MEANING
—

APPRECIATION AND GRATITUDE

LISIANTHUS

The lisianthus is often found in a wedding or thank-you bouquet. This flower is a symbol of real admiration and appreciation, so if you receive them the sender truly thinks the world of you. Keep that person close.

SCAN TO WATCH A SPED-UP VIDEO OF THE STEPS.

COLOR PALETTE

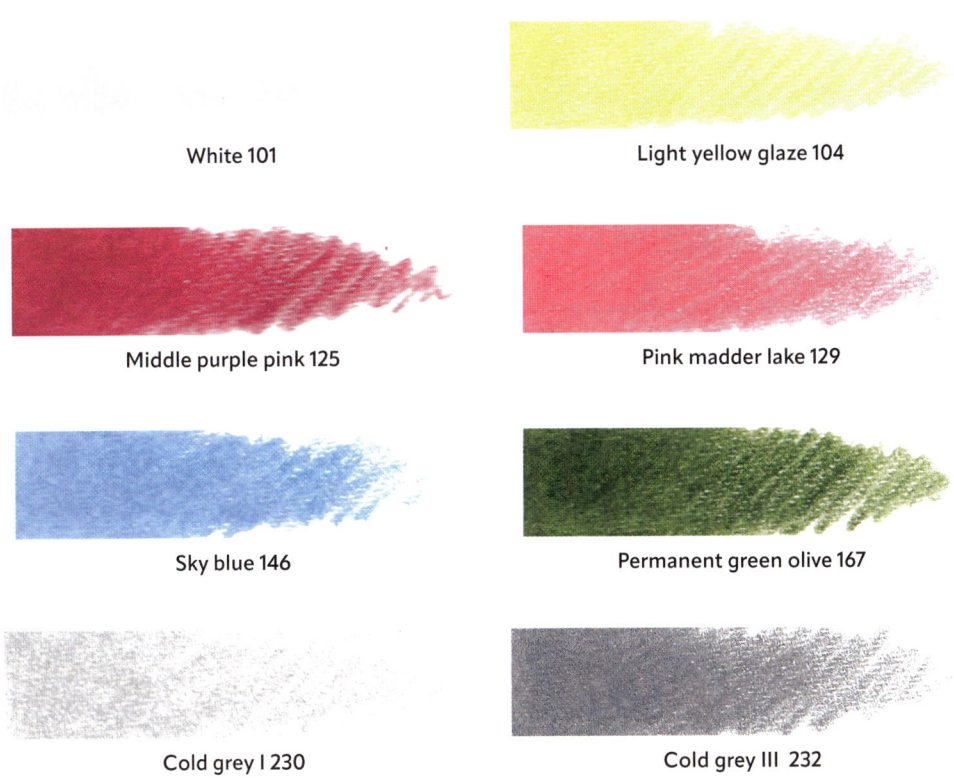

White 101

Light yellow glaze 104

Middle purple pink 125

Pink madder lake 129

Sky blue 146

Permanent green olive 167

Cold grey I 230

Cold grey III 232

OTHER MATERIALS

Eraser • Brush • Pencil sharpener

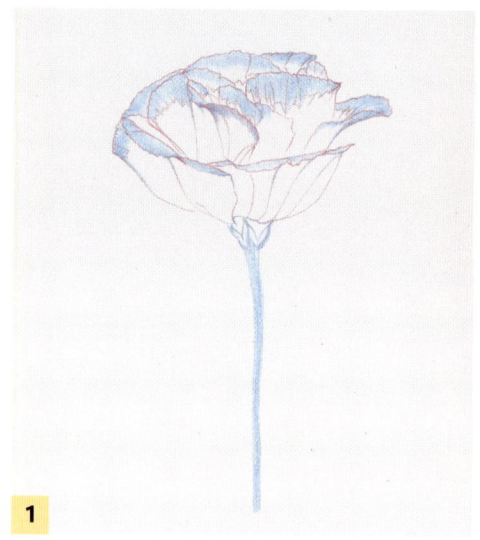

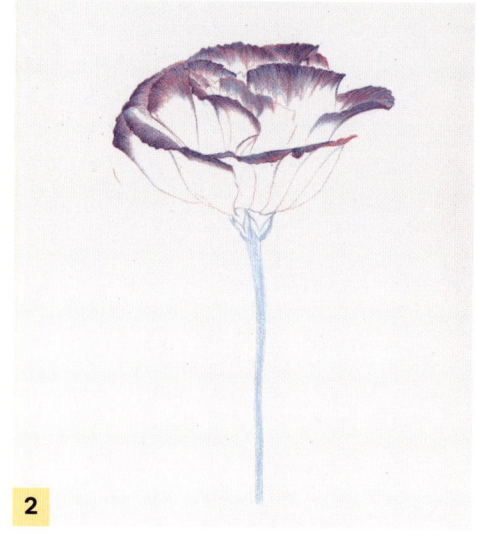

TIP
Take your time to blend in the edges of the petals so they do not appear too sharp. This will help you achieve a more flowing, natural look.

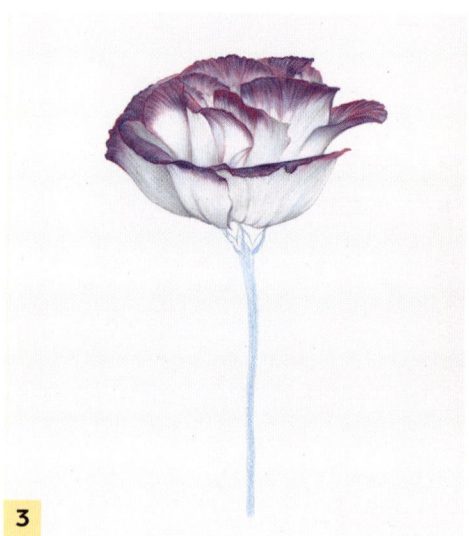

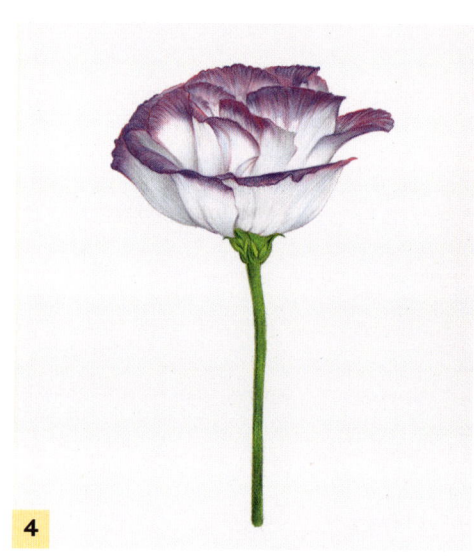

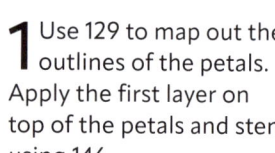

1 Use 129 to map out the outlines of the petals. Apply the first layer on top of the petals and stem using 146.

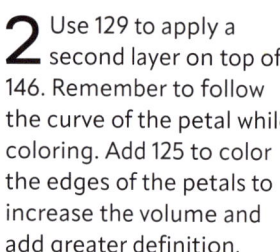

2 Use 129 to apply a second layer on top of 146. Remember to follow the curve of the petal while coloring. Add 125 to color the edges of the petals to increase the volume and add greater definition.

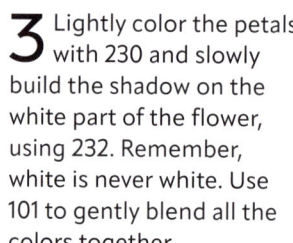

3 Lightly color the petals with 230 and slowly build the shadow on the white part of the flower, using 232. Remember, white is never white. Use 101 to gently blend all the colors together.

Add 125 on the ends of the petals and light touch of 146 on the white areas where the petals overlap to show more depth and texture. This process will make your flowers look livelier.

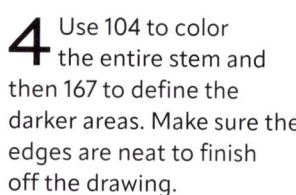

4 Use 104 to color the entire stem and then 167 to define the darker areas. Make sure the edges are neat to finish off the drawing.

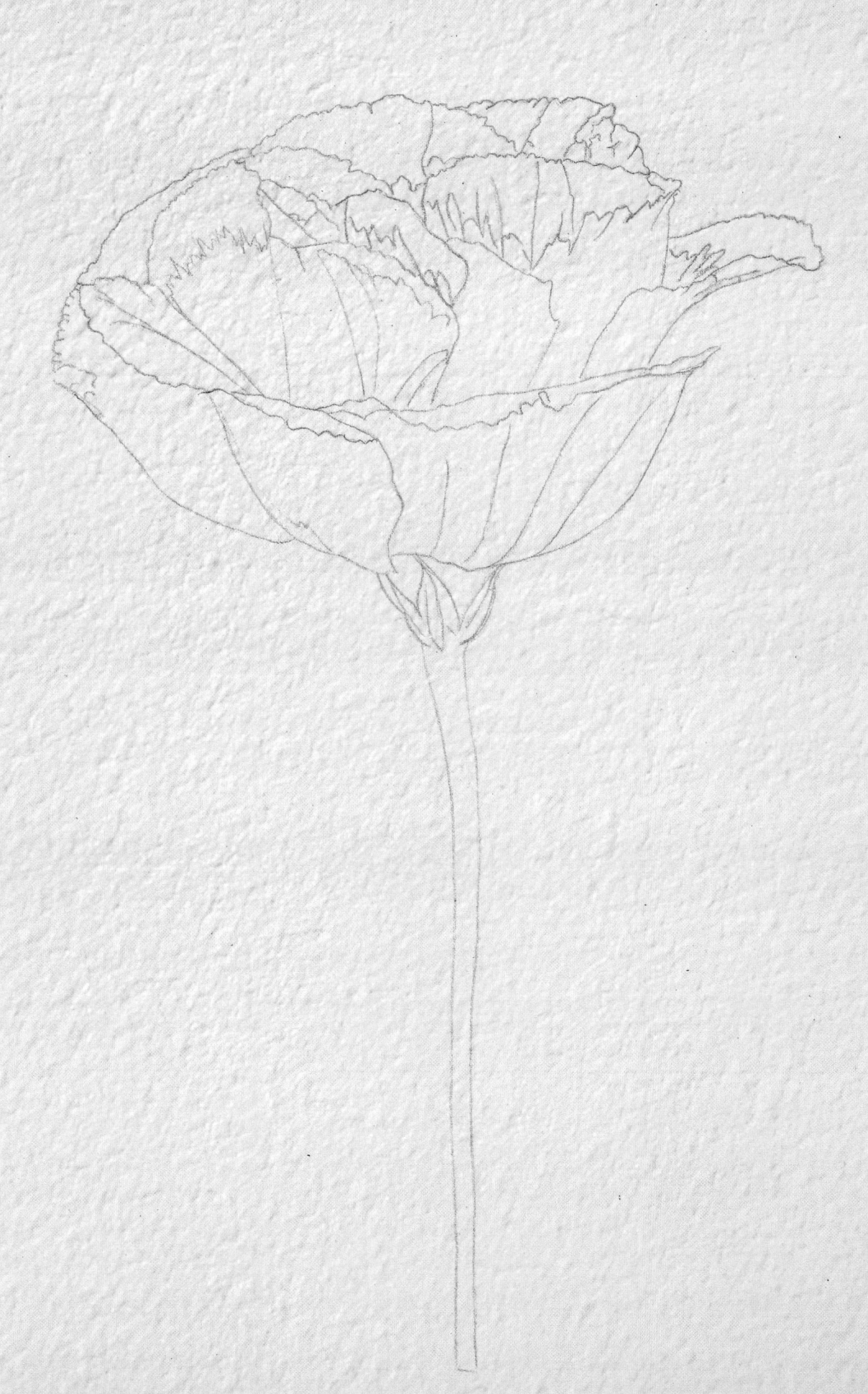

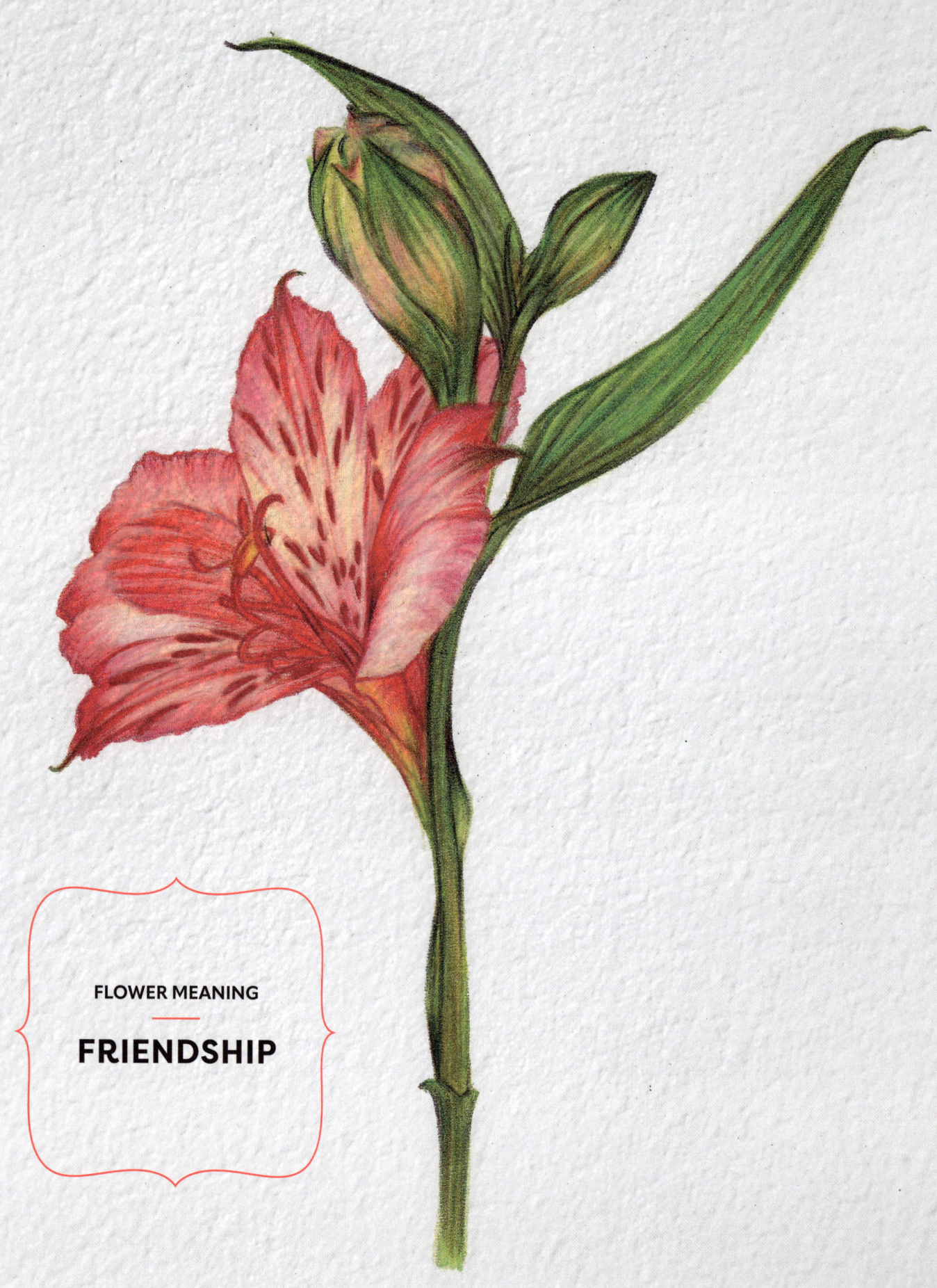

FLOWER MEANING

—

FRIENDSHIP

ALSTROEMERIA

The alstroemeria flower has many meanings, but most represent supporting each other and helping people through life's struggles. I love the fact that the twisted leaves symbolize overcoming adversities. A true flower of friendship and resilience.

SCAN TO WATCH
A SPED-UP VIDEO
OF THE STEPS.

COLOR PALETTE

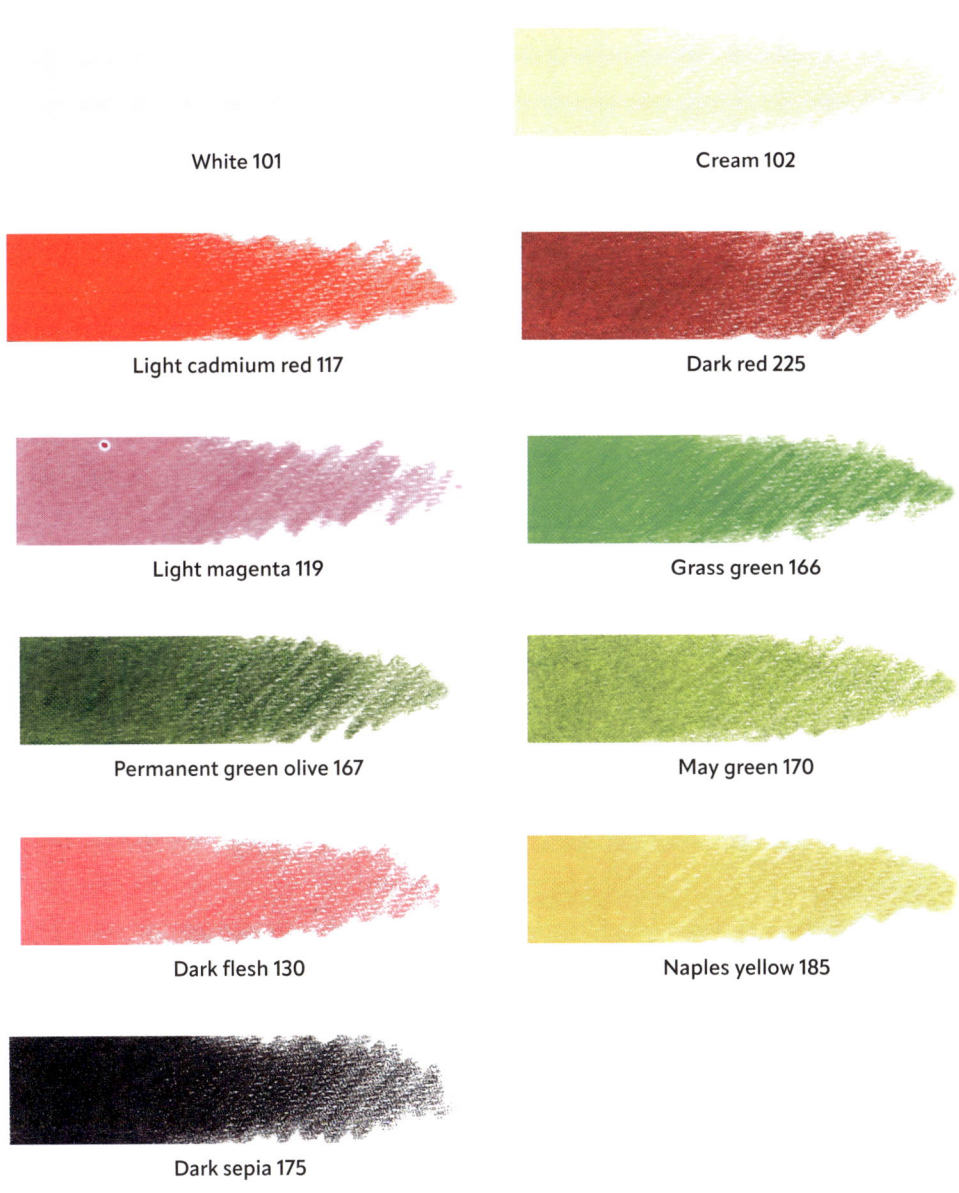

White 101

Cream 102

Light cadmium red 117

Dark red 225

Light magenta 119

Grass green 166

Permanent green olive 167

May green 170

Dark flesh 130

Naples yellow 185

Dark sepia 175

OTHER MATERIALS

Eraser • Brush • Pencil sharpener

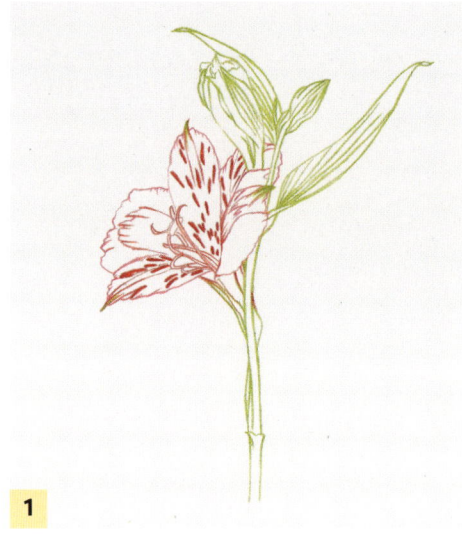

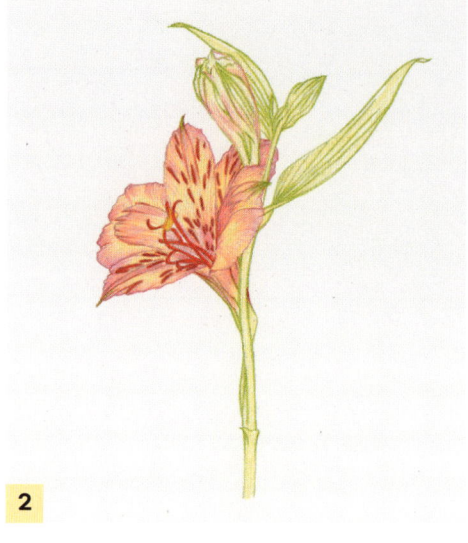

TIP

Blend each color on the petals thouroughly to create a natural and realistic texture.

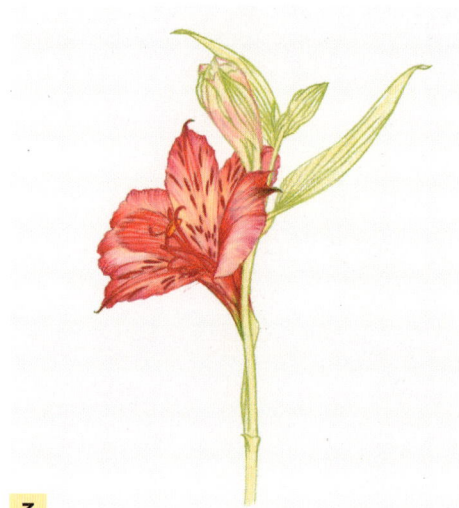

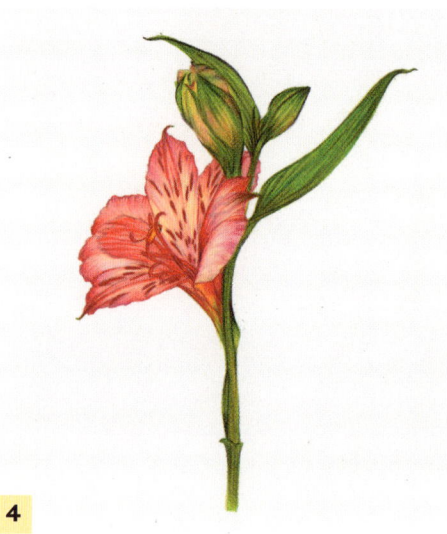

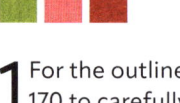

1 For the outline, use 170 to carefully mark out the stem and leaves. Then use 130 to outline the petals and 225 for the patterns on the petals and stamens.

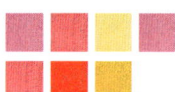

2 Use 119 to color the petal, working from the edge inward. Then use 130 to add the dark shaded area. Apply a gentle layer of 102 on the petals in order to blend the 119 and 130 colors to create a natural base. Sharpen your pencils and use 117 and 185 to color the stamens.

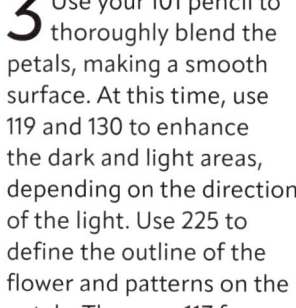

3 Use your 101 pencil to thoroughly blend the petals, making a smooth surface. At this time, use 119 and 130 to enhance the dark and light areas, depending on the direction of the light. Use 225 to define the outline of the flower and patterns on the petals. Then use 117 for the shadows.

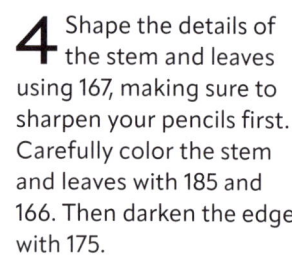

4 Shape the details of the stem and leaves using 167, making sure to sharpen your pencils first. Carefully color the stem and leaves with 185 and 166. Then darken the edge with 175.

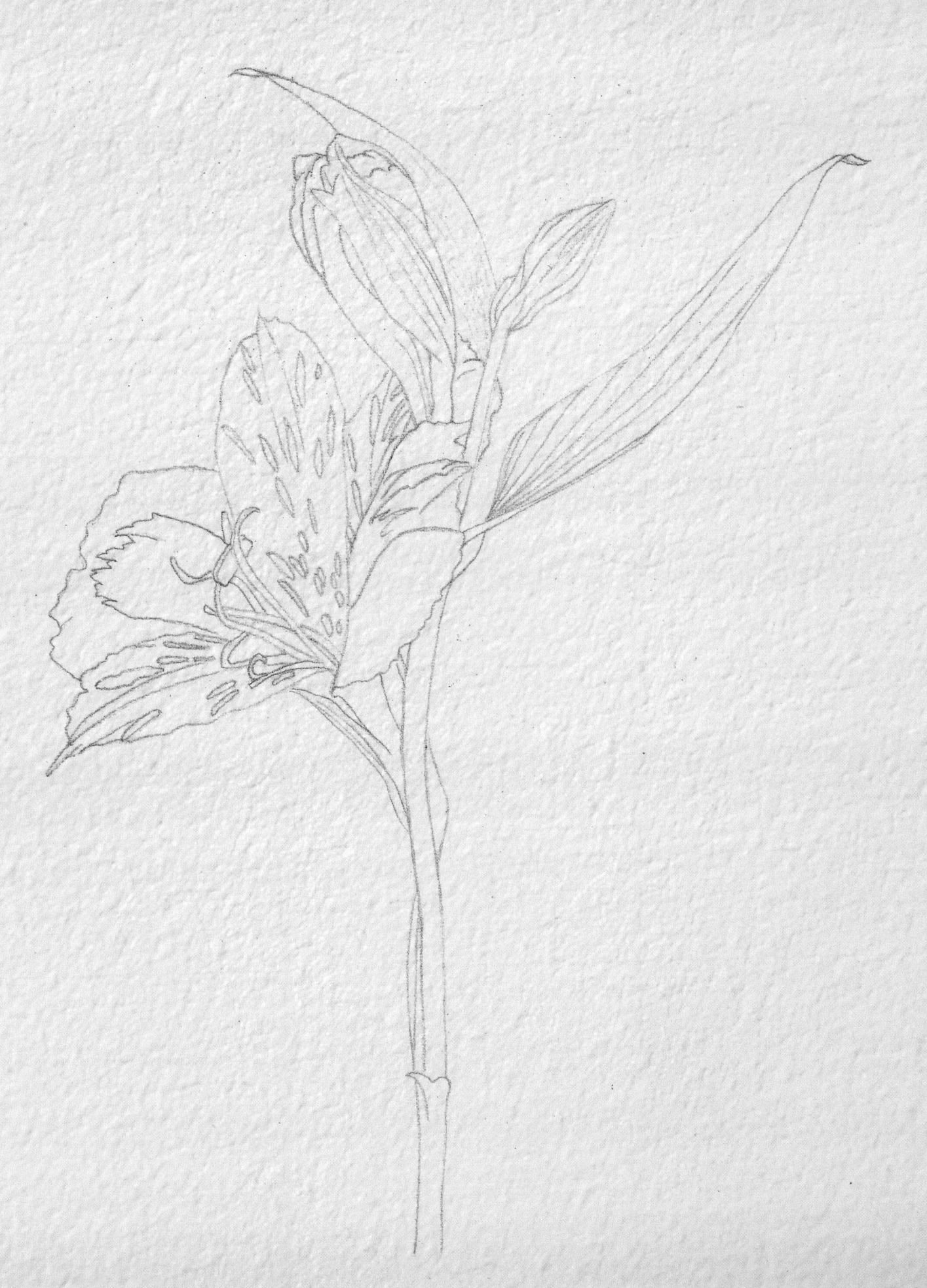

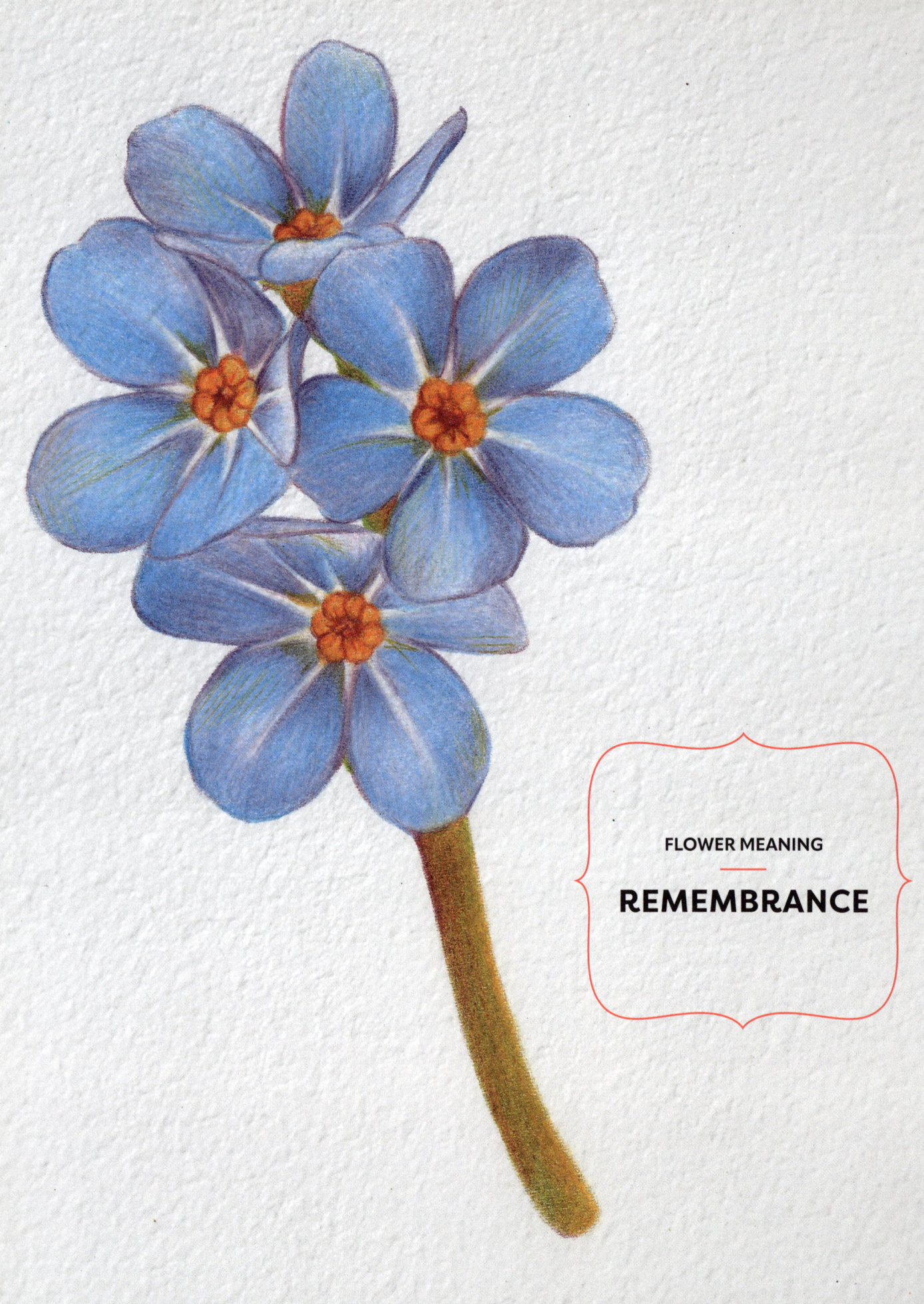

FLOWER MEANING

—

REMEMBRANCE

FORGET-ME-NOT

The forget-me-not flower is associated with an everlasting memory, unbreakable bonds, and eternal love. The forget-me-not was officially adopted as a symbol for Alzheimer's disease awareness, given its links to remembrance.

SCAN TO WATCH
A SPED-UP VIDEO
OF THE STEPS.

COLOR PALETTE

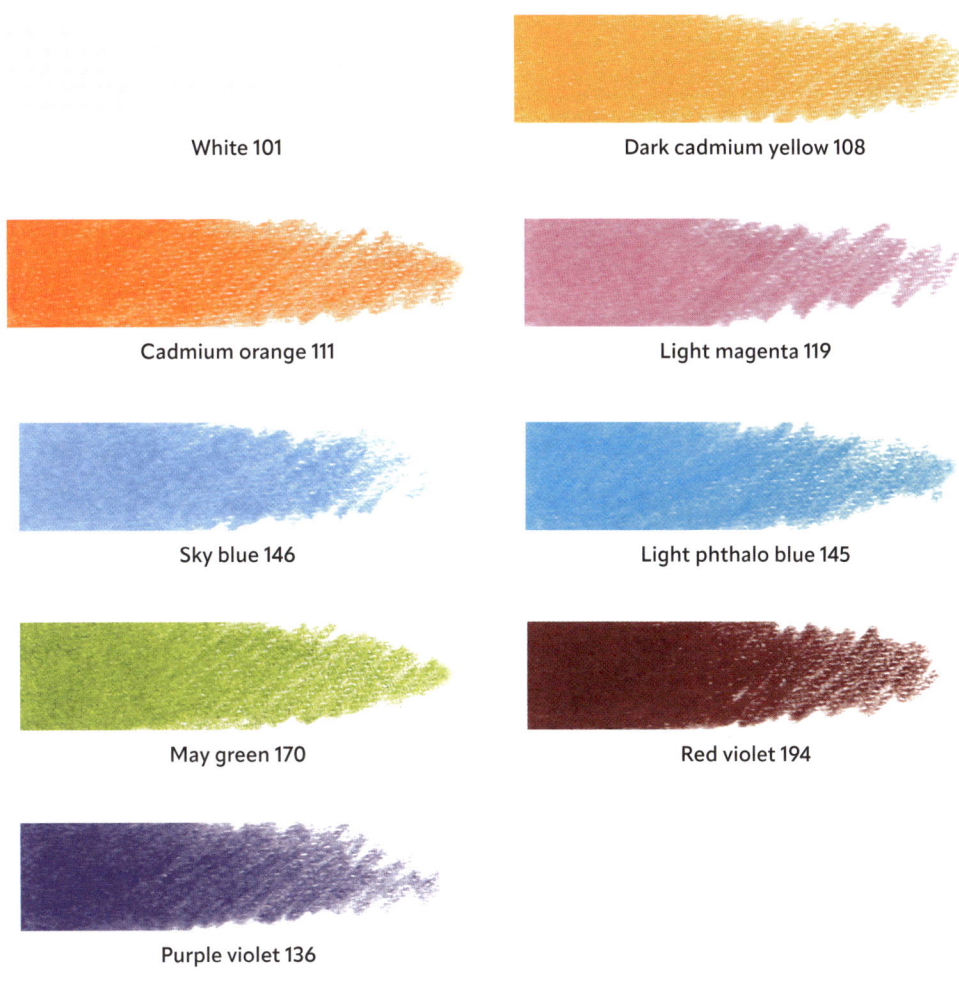

White 101

Dark cadmium yellow 108

Cadmium orange 111

Light magenta 119

Sky blue 146

Light phthalo blue 145

May green 170

Red violet 194

Purple violet 136

OTHER MATERIALS

Eraser • Brush • Pencil sharpener

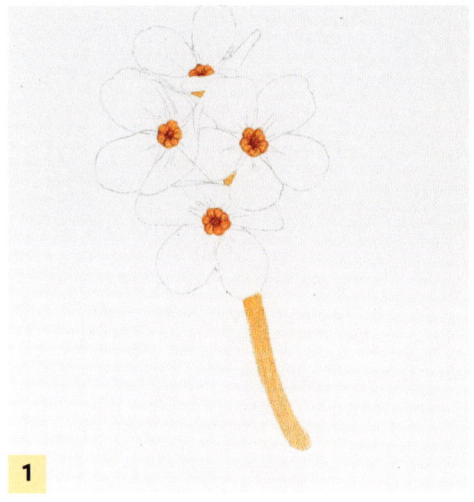

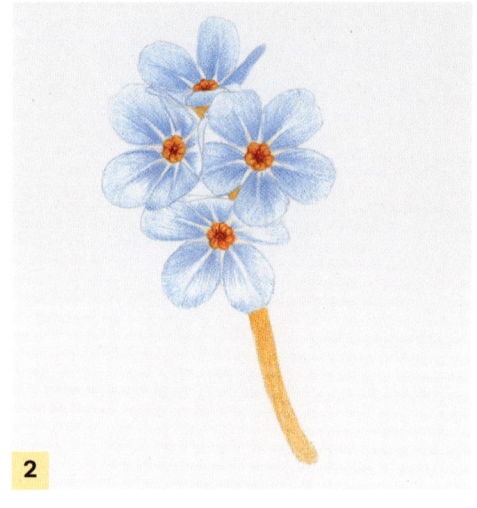

TIP

Pay special attention to each individual petal. It could easily look flat and boring if you color all the petals the same shade of blue. Mix the colors until you are happy with the end result. Experiment to find your favourite colors.

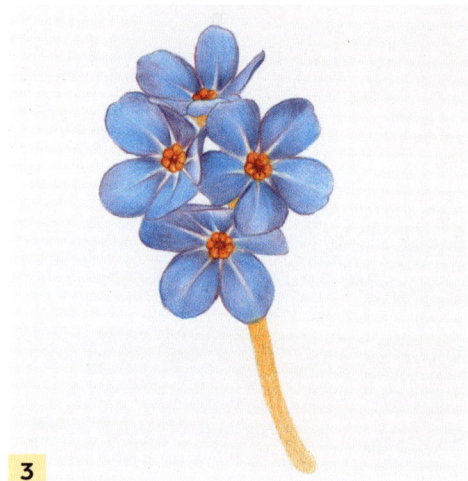

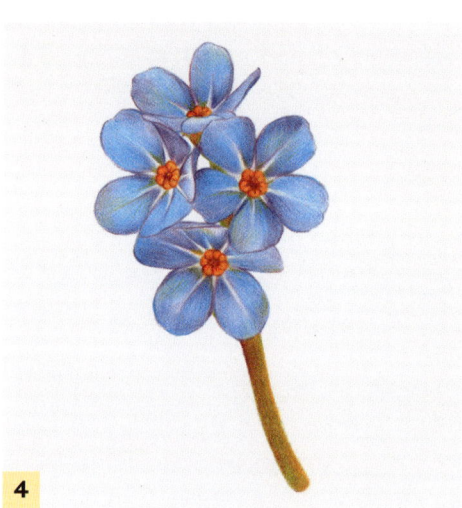

1 Make sure you have a sharp point on your pencil to draw in the middle details of the flowers, using 108. Using the same color, apply the first layer on the stem. Then use 111 and 194 to shape up the details in the middle of the flowers— it may look like a small flower itself.

2 Carefully map out the white lines of the petals with 101, starting from the yellow center. This process will help prevent the blue color application from covering the white line details when you start to color the petals.

Use 146 to color the individual petals carefully. Color the bright parts once lightly, and apply additional layers to give more definition while distinguishing between the lighter and darker areas. Leave the light parts for now, as you will build on these in the next step.

3 Add tones to create the areas of light and shade using 146 and 145. Use 119 to add warmth to the petals. Blend the colors with 101 as needed. Use 136 to color the petals darker, creating some of the shadows and deeper tones. Color the convex centers of the petals lightly and the edges darker to give a sense of their shape.

4 Use 170 to color the stem and 194 to color the darker parts close to the petals, creating the shadows. Don't forget to include the stem in between the petals of the flowers. Apply a gentle touch of 108 to the petals to give a hint of natural depth.

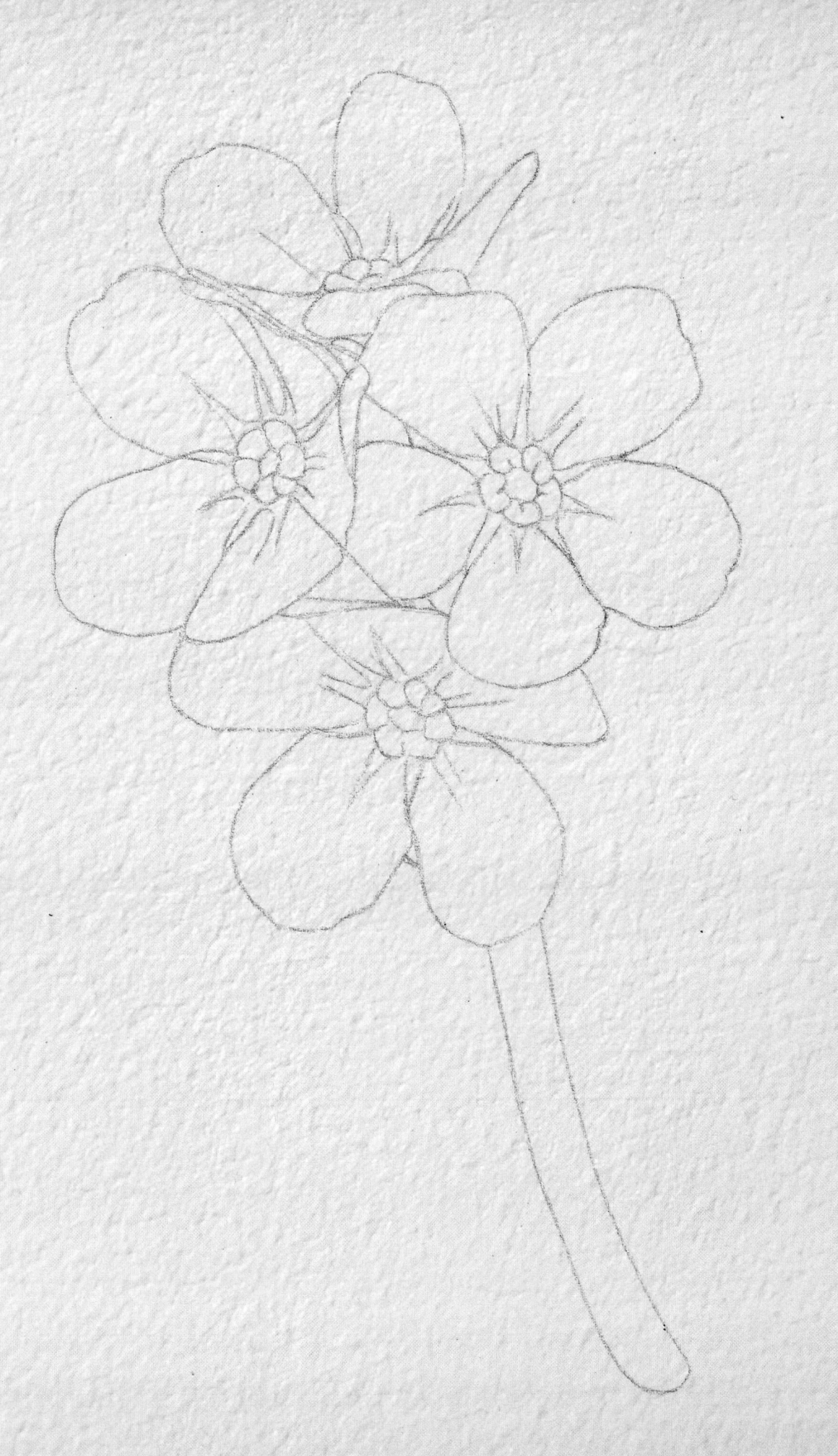

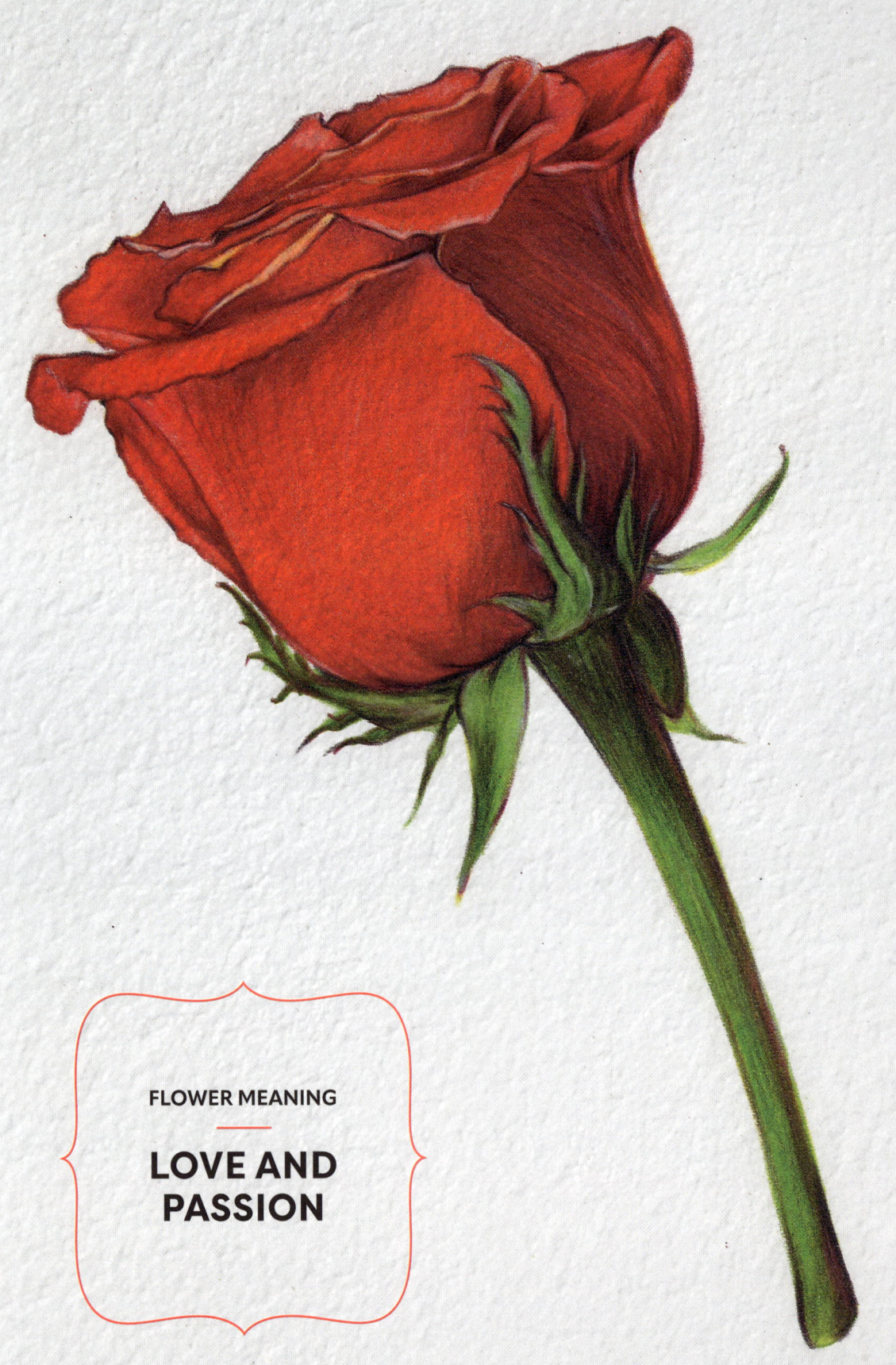

FLOWER MEANING

—

LOVE AND PASSION

ROSE

The red rose is known to symbolize love. The darker the color, the deeper the love. The rose has shown its links to true love through many stories and is still a Valentine's Day favorite. A true classical beauty.

SCAN TO WATCH
A SPED-UP VIDEO
OF THE STEPS.

COLOR PALETTE

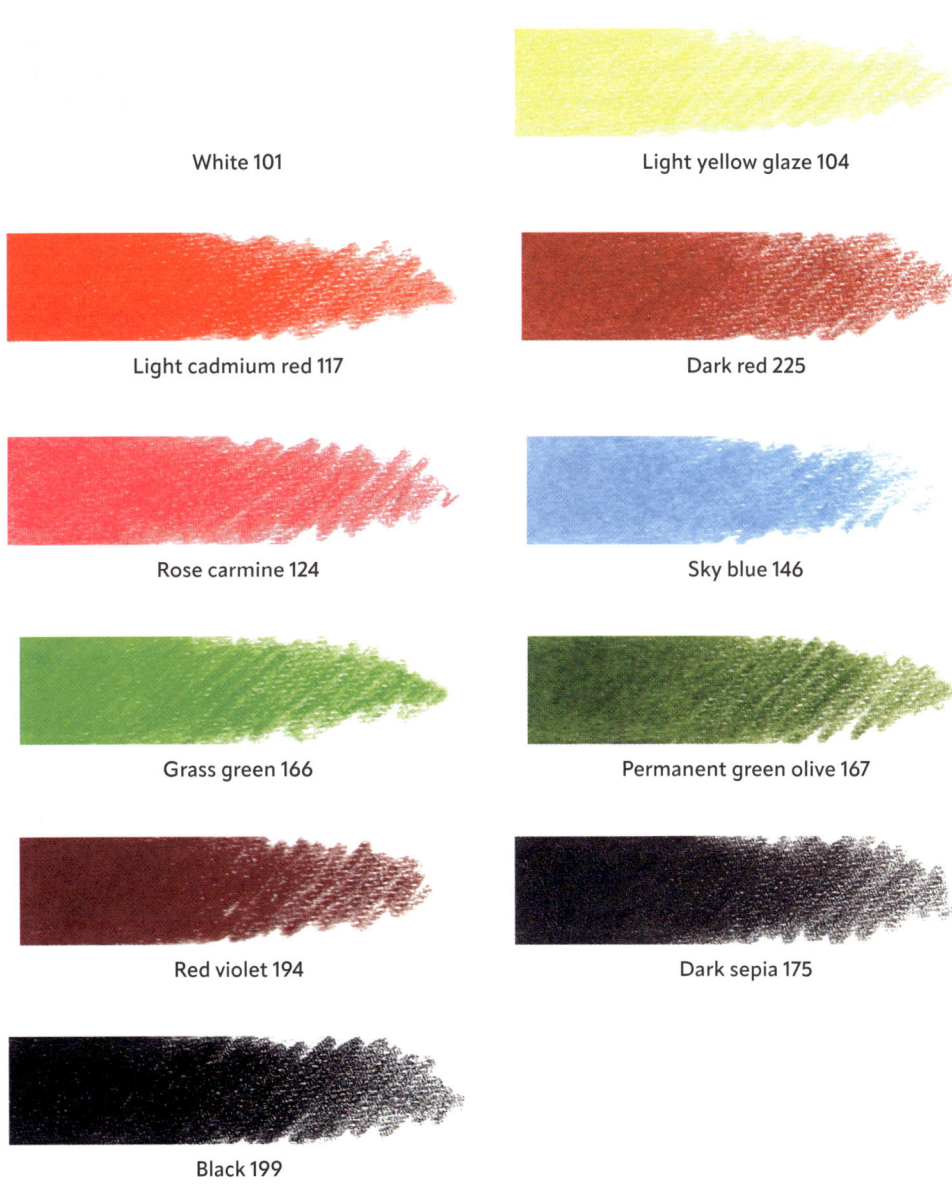

White 101

Light yellow glaze 104

Light cadmium red 117

Dark red 225

Rose carmine 124

Sky blue 146

Grass green 166

Permanent green olive 167

Red violet 194

Dark sepia 175

Black 199

OTHER MATERIALS

Eraser • Brush • Pencil sharpener

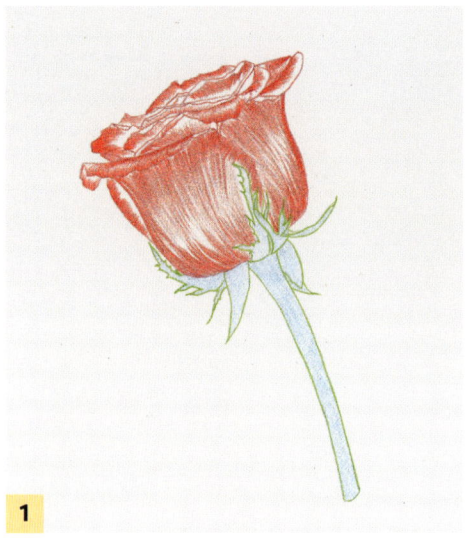

1

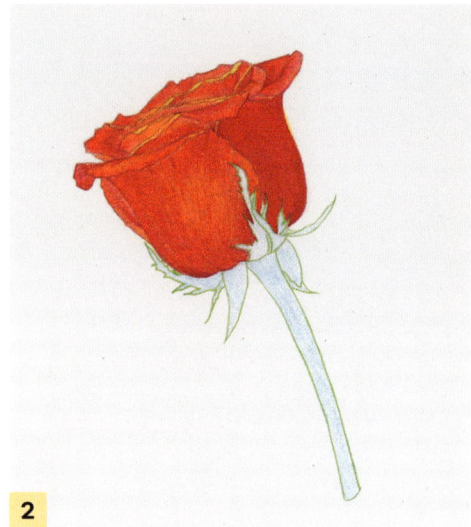

2

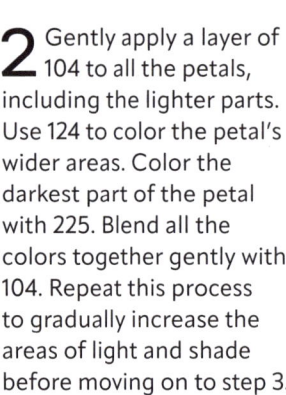

TIP
Pay attention to define the dried part of the flower petals to capture a more realistic look.

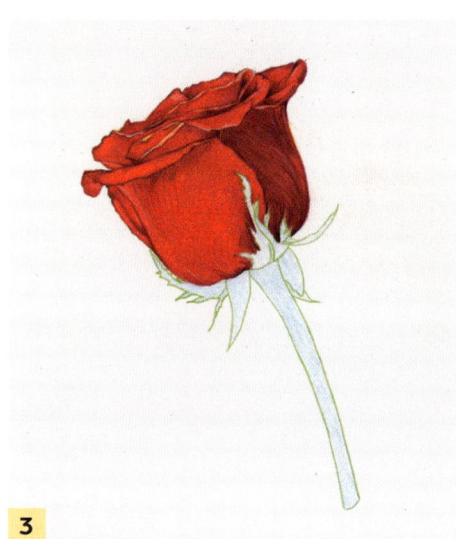

3

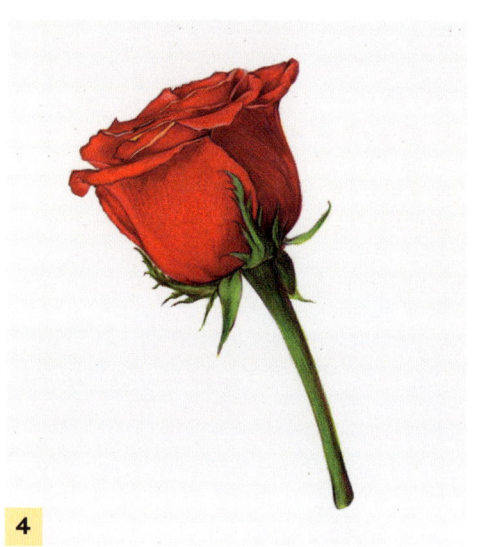

4

1 Study the direction of the petal flow. First, lightly color the wide surface of the petals using 117. Then color the dried tips of the petals using the little hooks technique (Line Practice, Exercise 5). This will create a good guide to follow for the remaining steps. Make an outline of the stem and leaves using 166, and give them a light first layer of color with 146.

2 Gently apply a layer of 104 to all the petals, including the lighter parts. Use 124 to color the petal's wider areas. Color the darkest part of the petal with 225. Blend all the colors together gently with 104. Repeat this process to gradually increase the areas of light and shade before moving on to step 3.

3 Use 225 and a light touch of 199 to express the darker tones of the flower, enhancing the details, including the dried and overlapping petals. Then use 101 to capture the lighter areas, highlighting the edges of the petals where needed.

4 To express the glossiness of the stem's surface, color the light parts with 104 and 166, then color the dark parts with 167 and 175. Draw the red line of the stem with 194, and color the shadows between the sepals with 194 to bring out their natural look and depth.

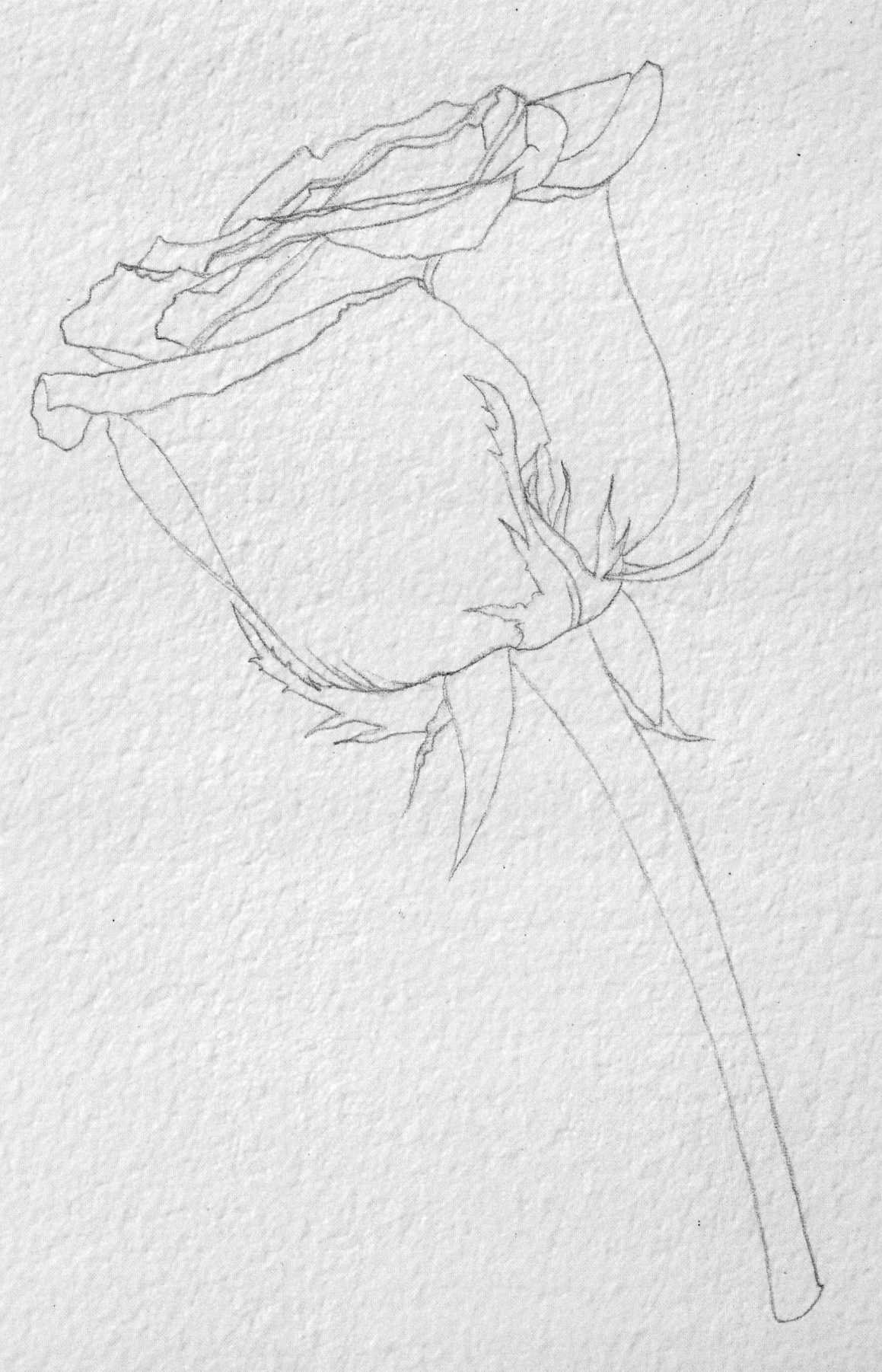

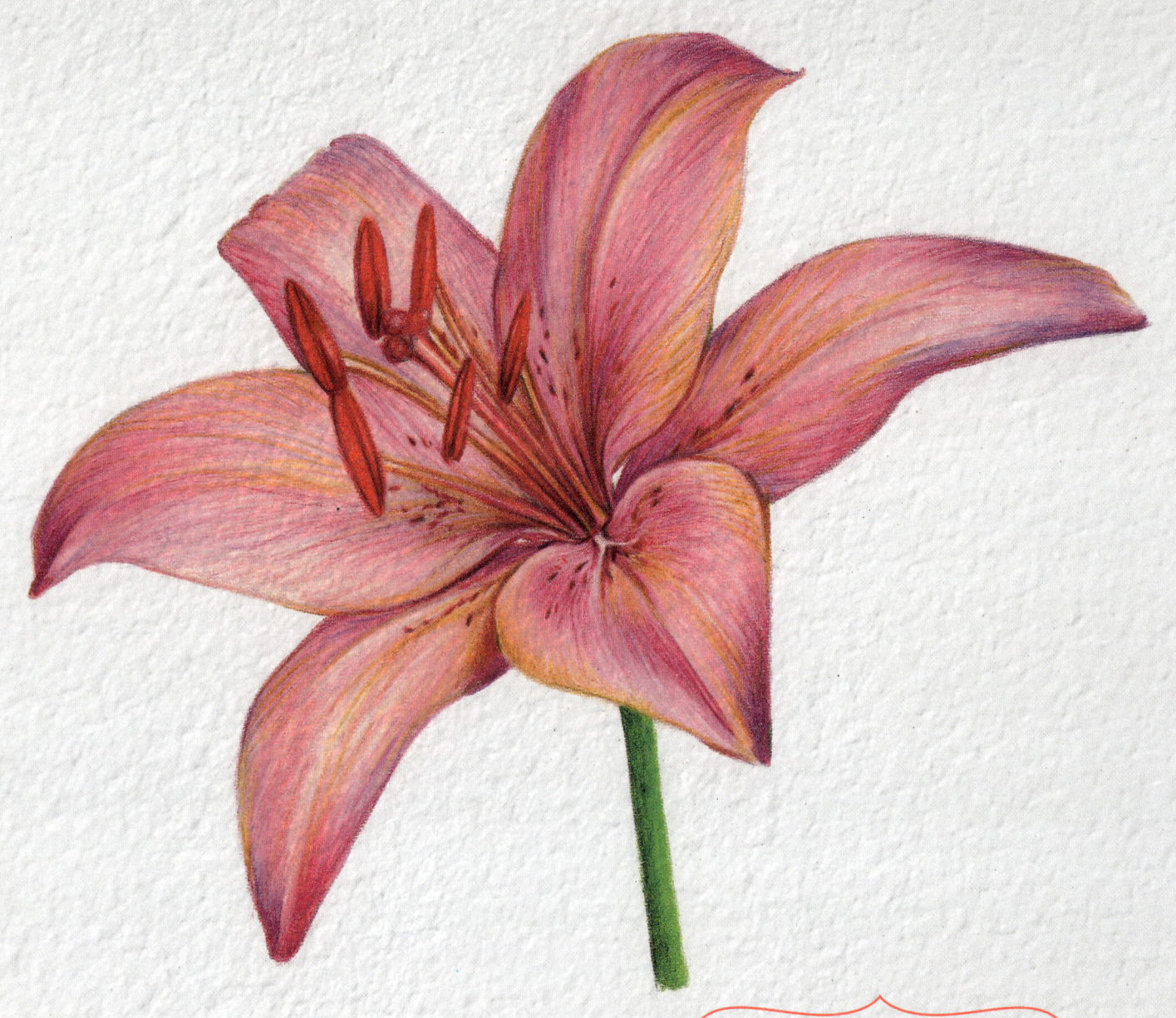

PURITY, REMEMBRANCE, AND FERTILITY

LILY

Each variety of lily holds a different meaning. They are often found in memorial arrangements, due to their link to remembrance, and are also a symbol of the circle of life.

SCAN TO WATCH
A SPED-UP VIDEO
OF THE STEPS.

COLOR PALETTE

Ivory 103

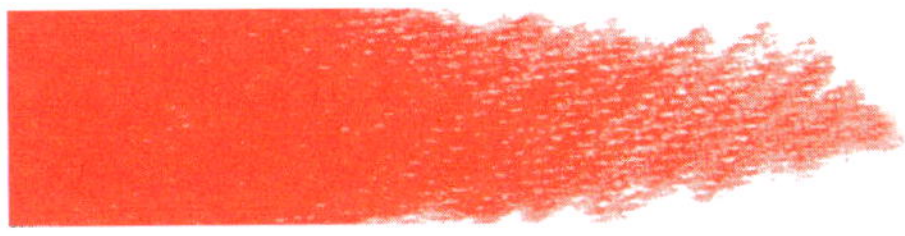

Light cadmium red 117

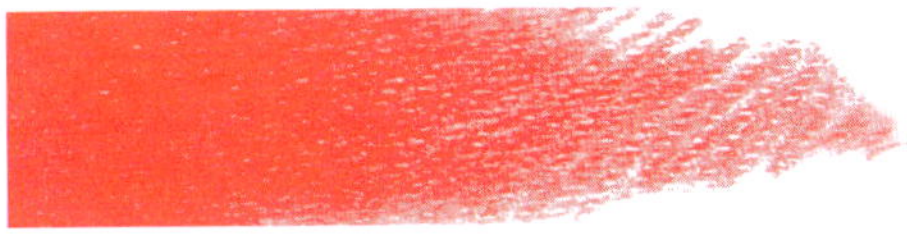

Pale geranium lake 121

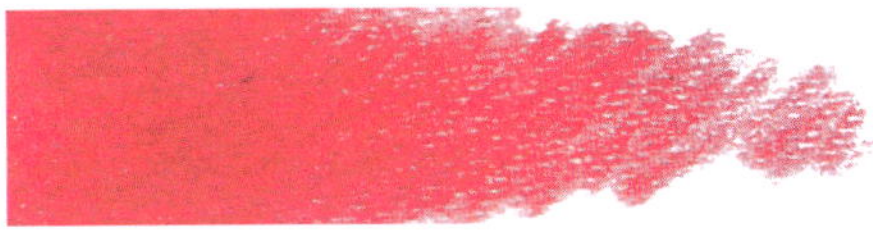

Fuchsia 123

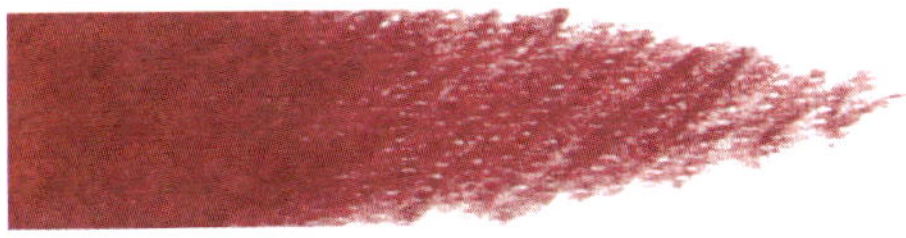

Magenta 133

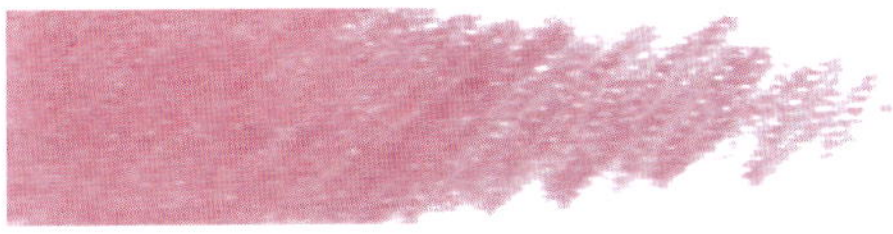

Light magenta 119

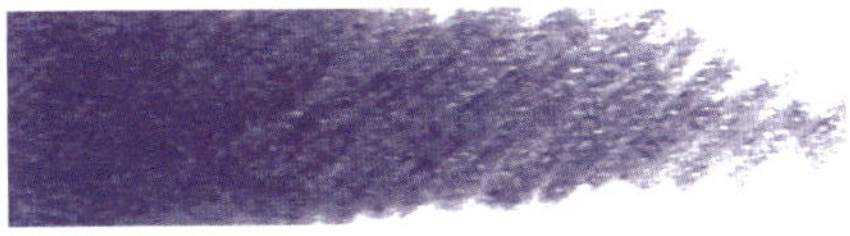

Purple violet 136

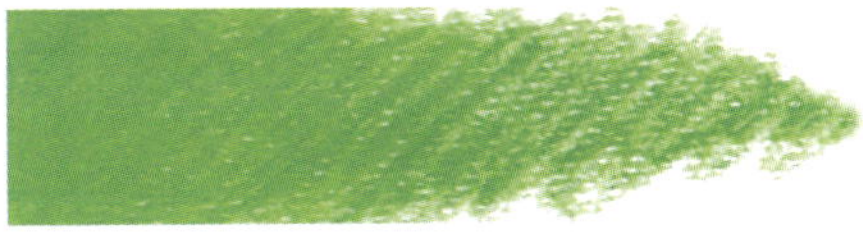

Grass green 166

Chrome oxide green 278

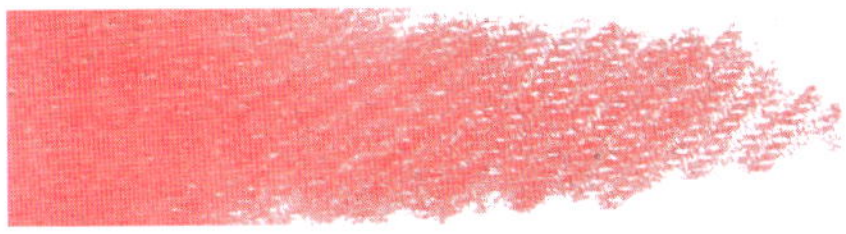

Dark flesh 130

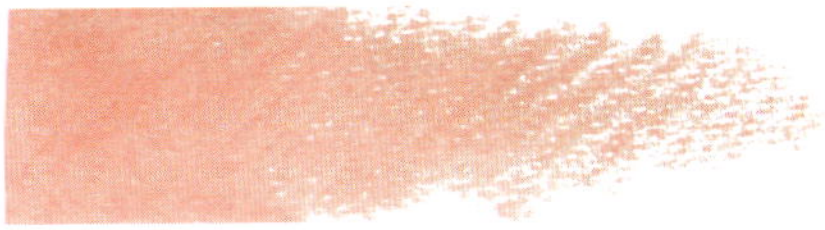

Light flesh 132

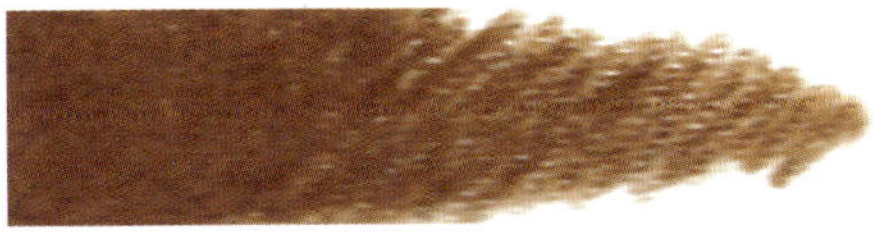

Raw umber 180

OTHER MATERIALS

Eraser • Brush • Pencil sharpener

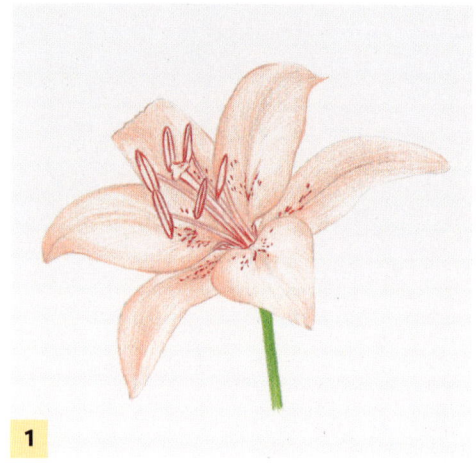

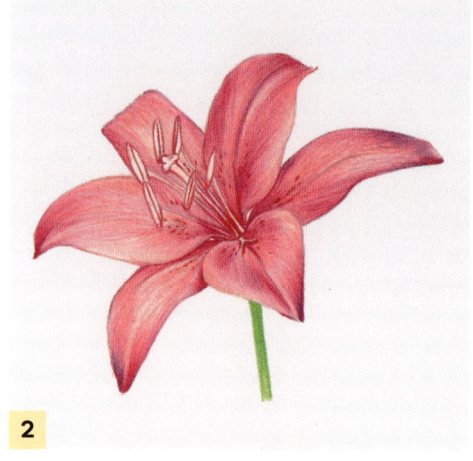

TIP
When the petal size is big, take your time to build and blend the colors. Pay attention to capture the small details as much as possible.

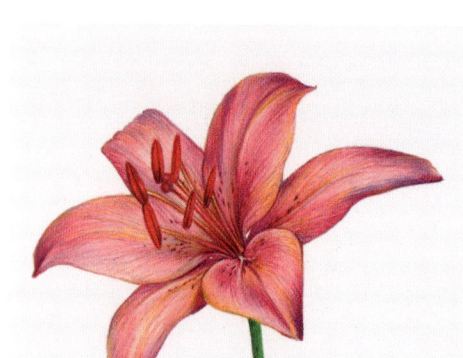

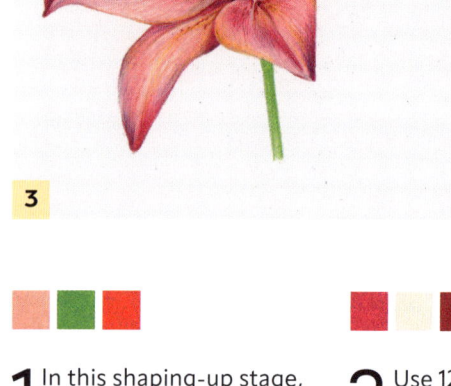

1 In this shaping-up stage, take your time to study the flow of petals, and map them out carefully using 132. Still using 132, apply the first layer to the petals. Apply additional layers to start building the shape of the petals and highlighting the darker areas, creating greater definition.

Use 166 to apply the first layer on the stem. Then use 121 to shape up the stamens and add the pollen to the petals.

2 Use 123 to carefully color the petals. As the petal size is big, take your time to color them building the layers up slowly. Use 103 to blend while coloring. Repeat the process until you achieve the color and texture you are happy with.

Lightly define the outline of the petals with 133 and add another layer of shadows. Also use 119 to emphasize the petals' volume, enhancing their shape. You can add 130 to give warmth to the petals.

3 It's time for the detail—the fun part! Emphasize the shadow and darker areas with 136 to create a richer tone. Now color the stamens with 117, using 133 for the outline. Use 180 to create a warm shadow where needed.

4 Shape up the stem with 278. Also use 278 to darken the areas between the stamens in the center of the flower, and add more shadow to the areas that need it. Remember, a little touch makes a big difference, so don't be afraid to add some extra touches.

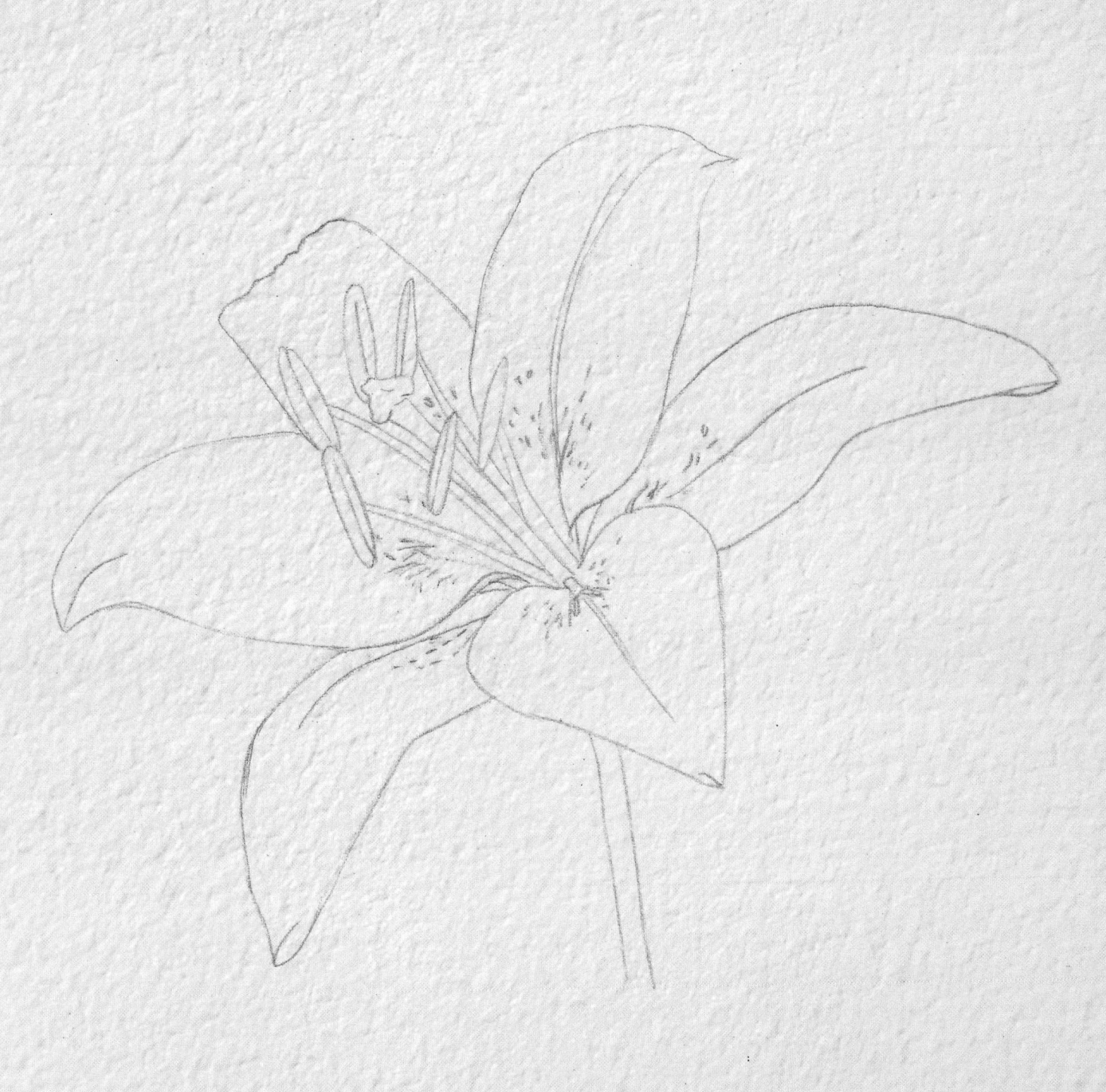

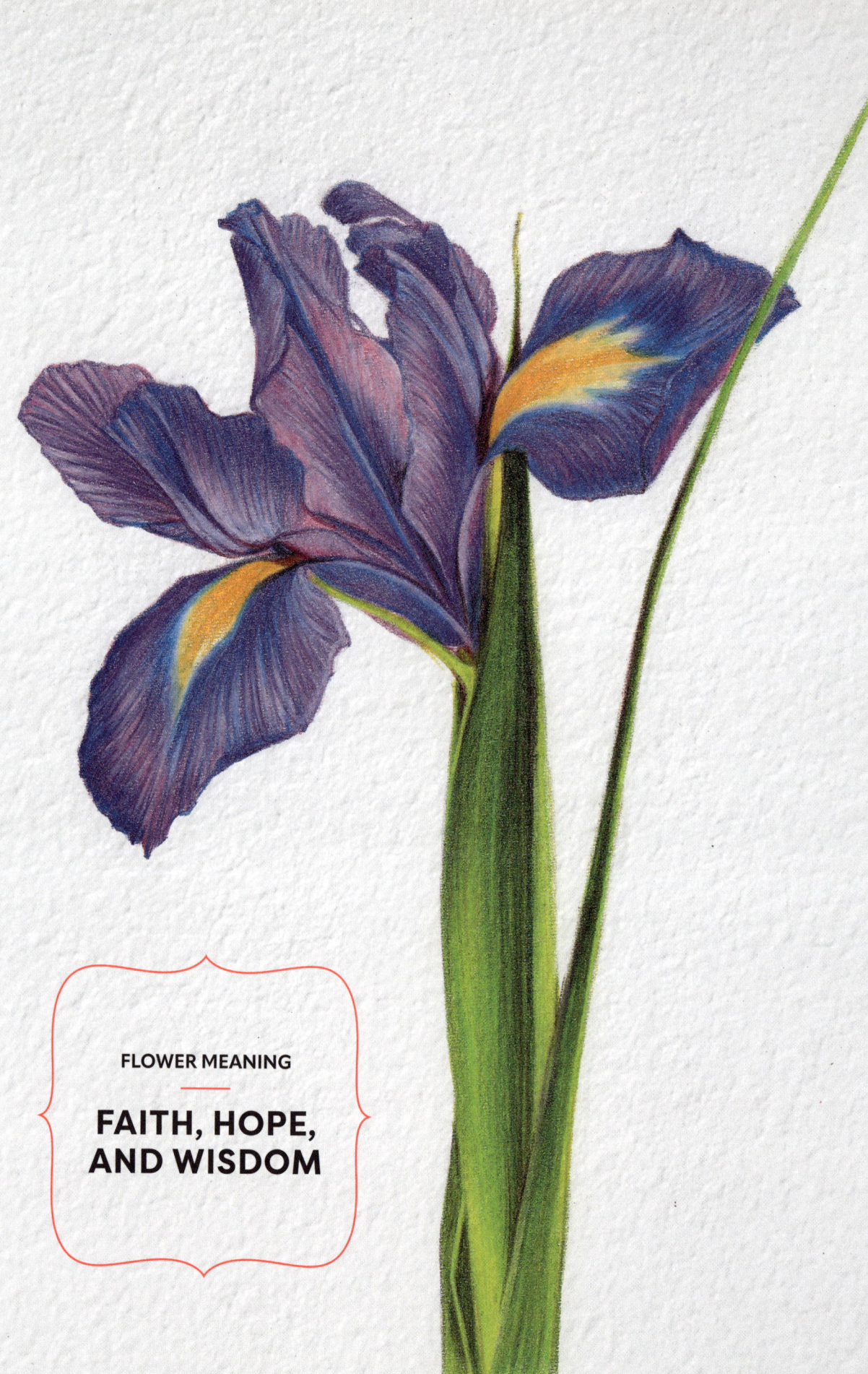

FLOWER MEANING

—

FAITH, HOPE, AND WISDOM

IRIS

The iris is named after the Greek goddess Iris, who is the embodiment of the rainbow. The iris grows in many colors and symbolizes everything from wisdom to hope through its flawless beauty.

SCAN TO WATCH A SPED-UP VIDEO OF THE STEPS.

COLOR PALETTE

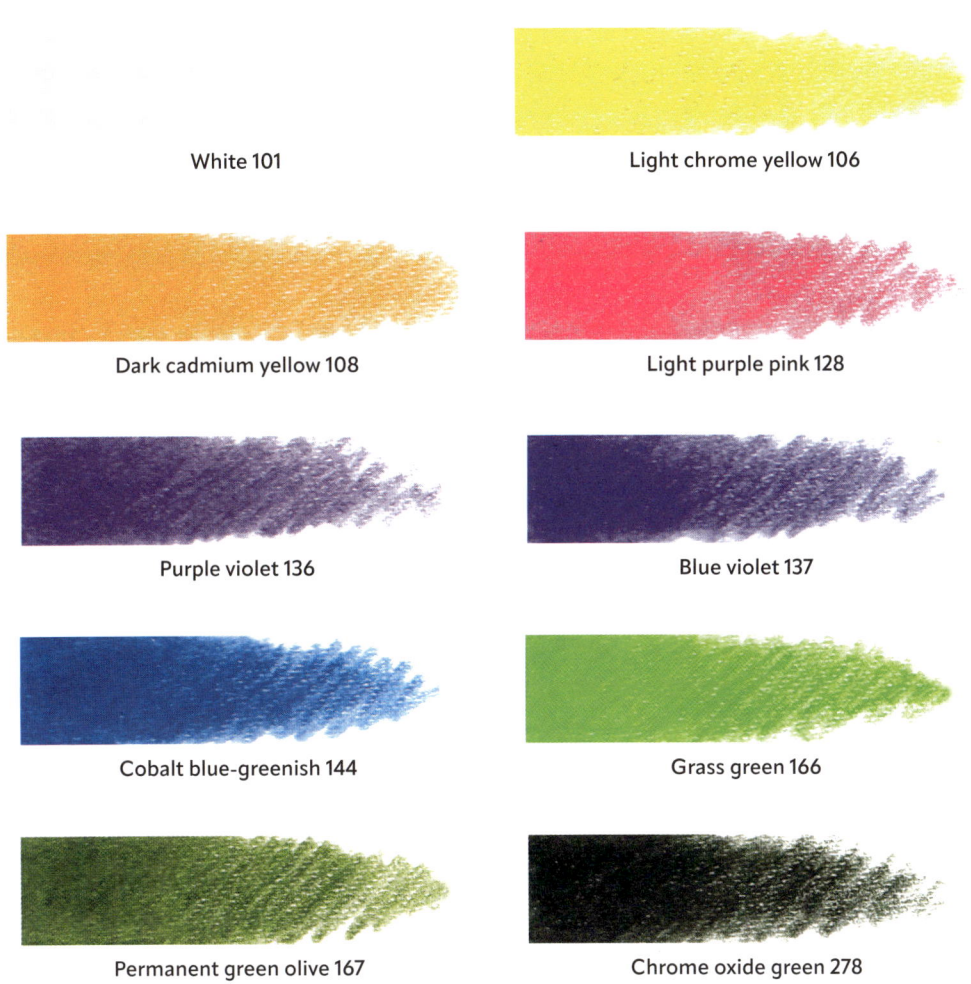

White 101

Light chrome yellow 106

Dark cadmium yellow 108

Light purple pink 128

Purple violet 136

Blue violet 137

Cobalt blue-greenish 144

Grass green 166

Permanent green olive 167

Chrome oxide green 278

OTHER MATERIALS

Eraser • Brush • Pencil sharpener

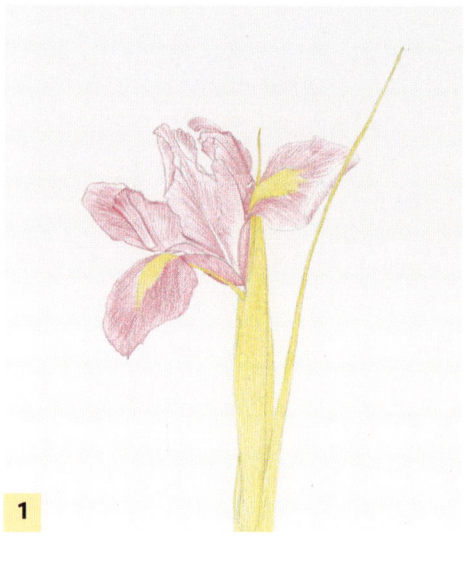

1

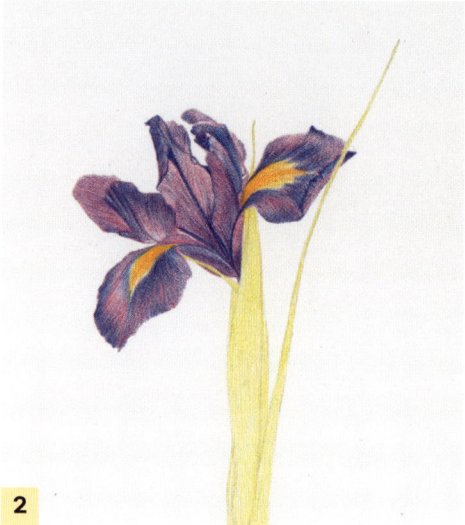

2

TIP

Where flowers overlap each other, you can create a sense of depth by slightly darkening the overlapping parts to better reflect the natural light.

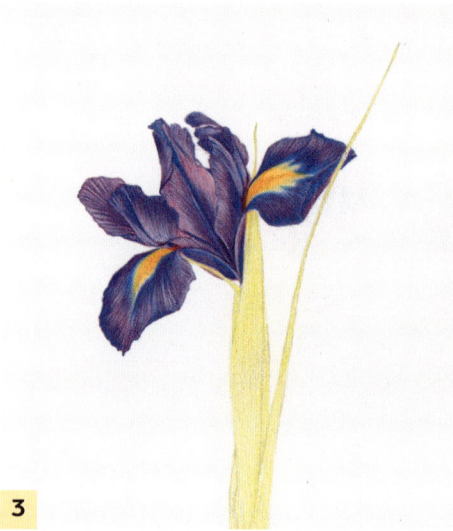

3

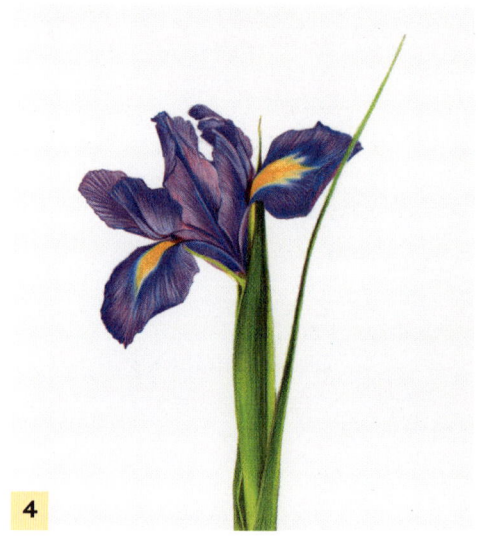

4

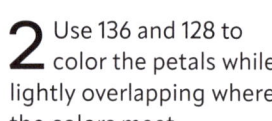

1 First apply a base layer on the stem and leaves with 106, making sure to include the inner part of the petals, as shown. Use 128 to color the rest of the petals. Pay attention to the direction of the petals and follow their flow as you apply the color.

2 Use 136 and 128 to color the petals while lightly overlapping where the colors meet.

Depending on the direction of the light, color the darkest area with 144 to create a sense of depth on the flower.

Increase the tone of the yellow part of the petals using 108, building on what you did in step 1.

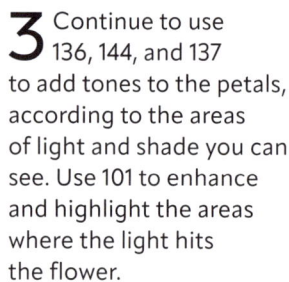

3 Continue to use 136, 144, and 137 to add tones to the petals, according to the areas of light and shade you can see. Use 101 to enhance and highlight the areas where the light hits the flower.

Express the texture and shape of the petal edges using the little hooks technique (Line Practice, Exercise 5), and use both curved and straight lines to define the flow of the petals.

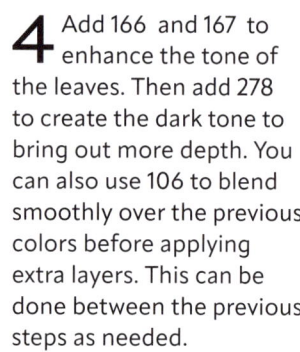

4 Add 166 and 167 to enhance the tone of the leaves. Then add 278 to create the dark tone to bring out more depth. You can also use 106 to blend smoothly over the previous colors before applying extra layers. This can be done between the previous steps as needed.

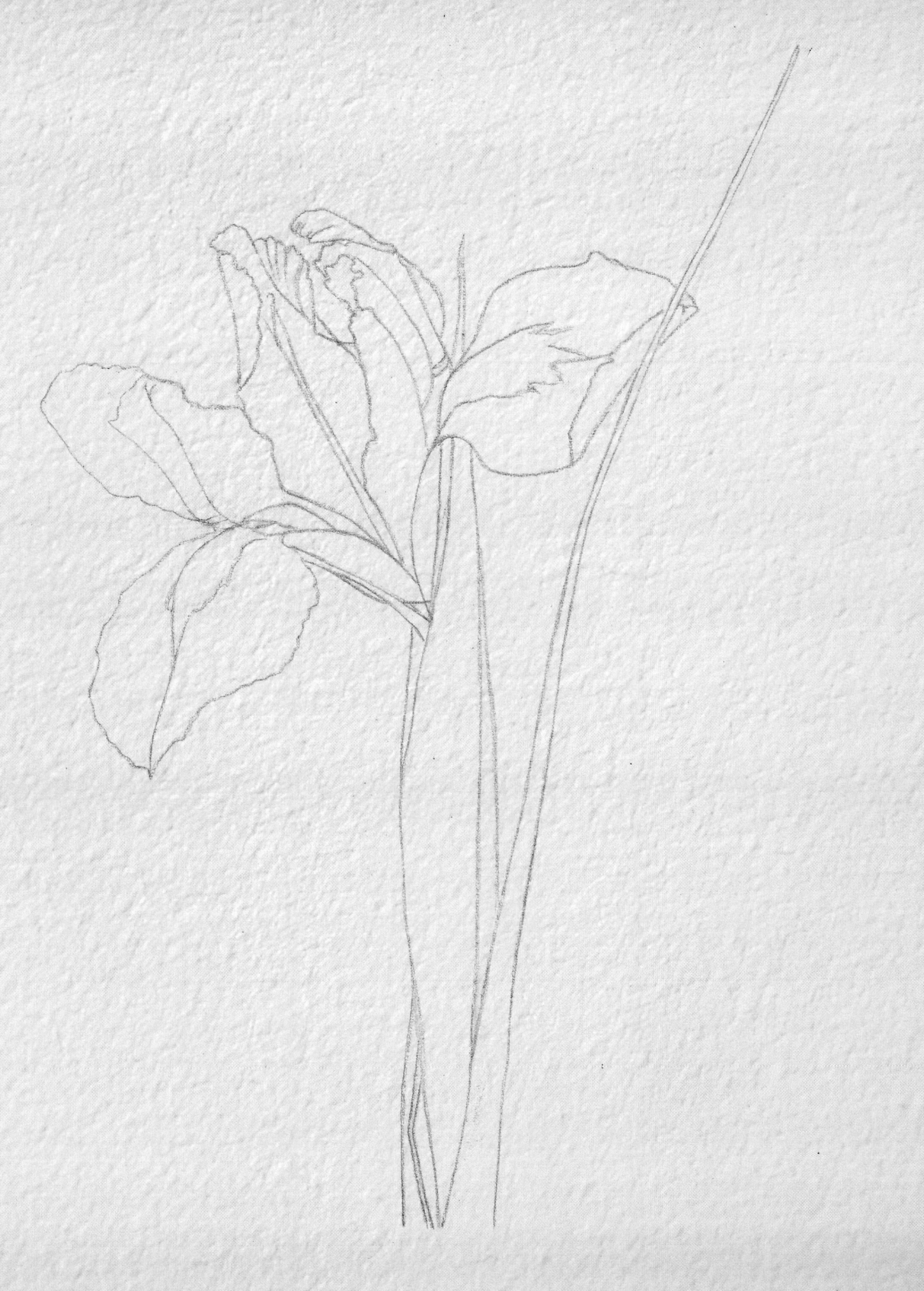

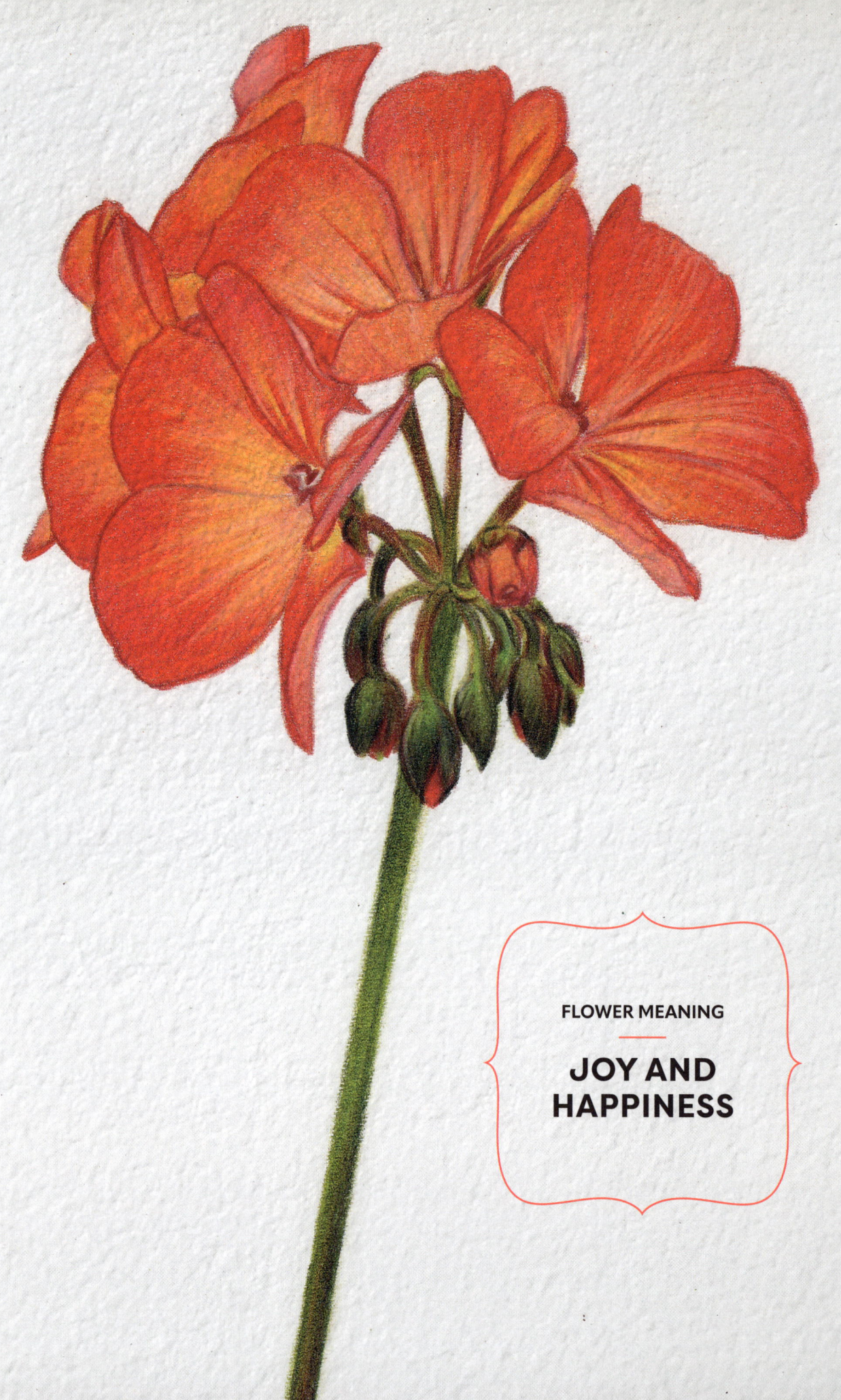

FLOWER MEANING

—

JOY AND HAPPINESS

GERANIUM

Geraniums are often found in bouquets, due to their cheerful appearance and positive energy. They symbolize friendship and show joy and appreciation to those who receive them.

SCAN TO WATCH A SPED-UP VIDEO OF THE STEPS.

COLOR PALETTE

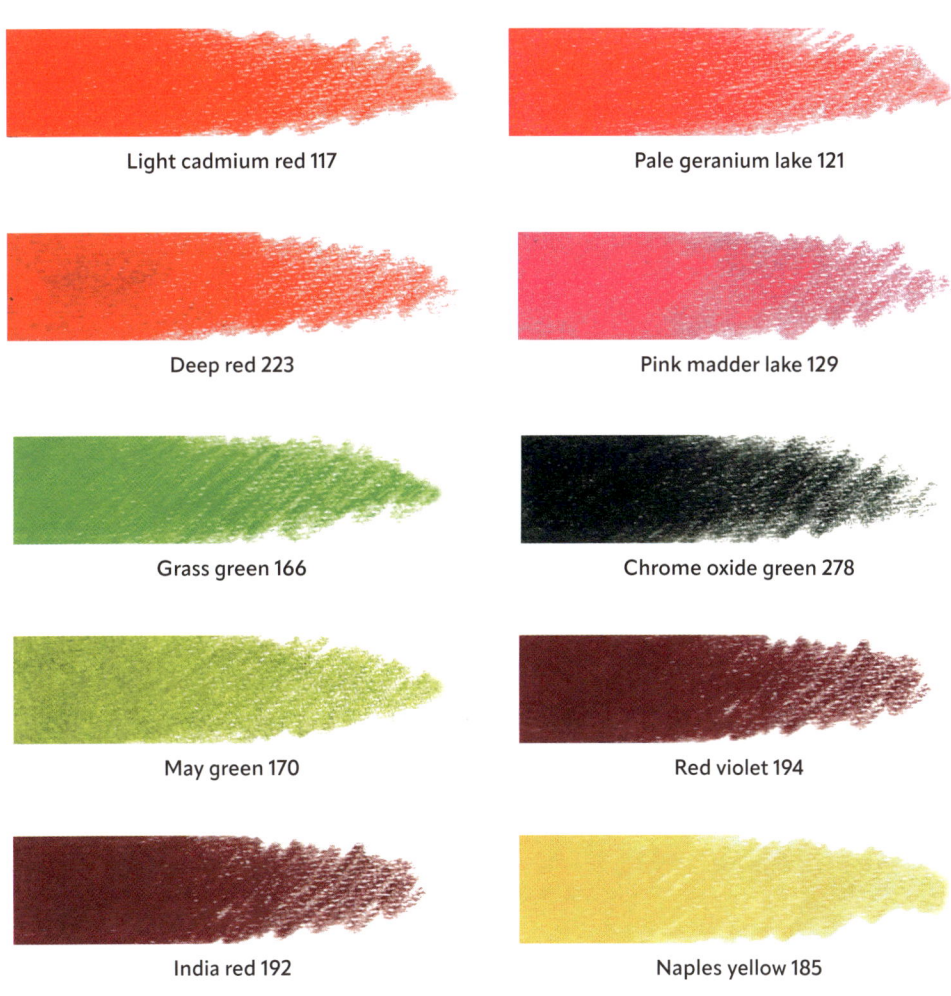

Light cadmium red 117

Pale geranium lake 121

Deep red 223

Pink madder lake 129

Grass green 166

Chrome oxide green 278

May green 170

Red violet 194

India red 192

Naples yellow 185

OTHER MATERIALS

Eraser • Brush • Pencil sharpener

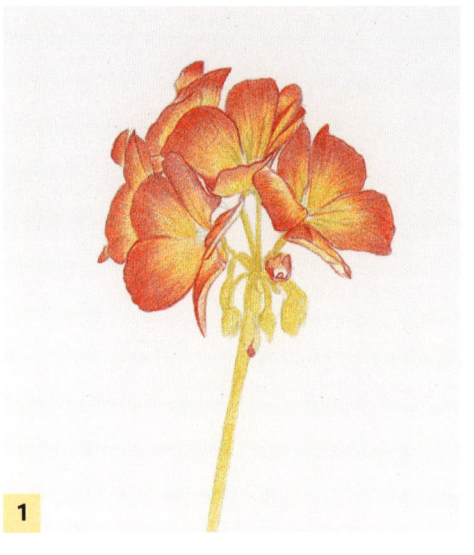

1

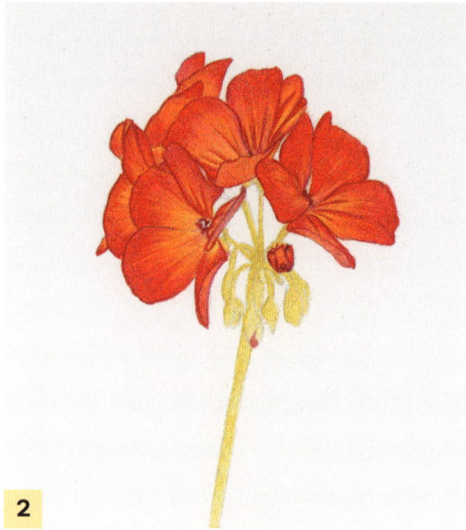

2

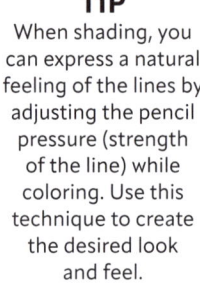

TIP
When shading, you can express a natural feeling of the lines by adjusting the pencil pressure (strength of the line) while coloring. Use this technique to create the desired look and feel.

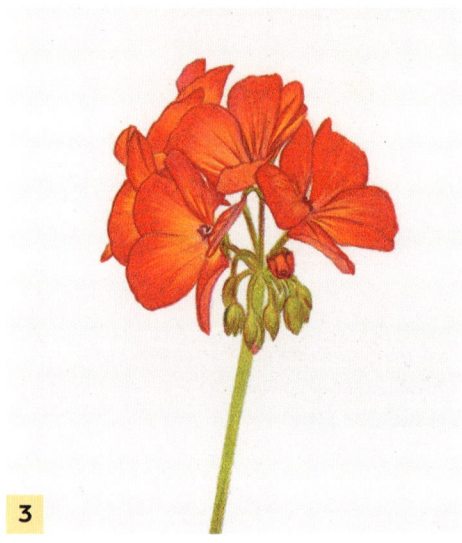

3

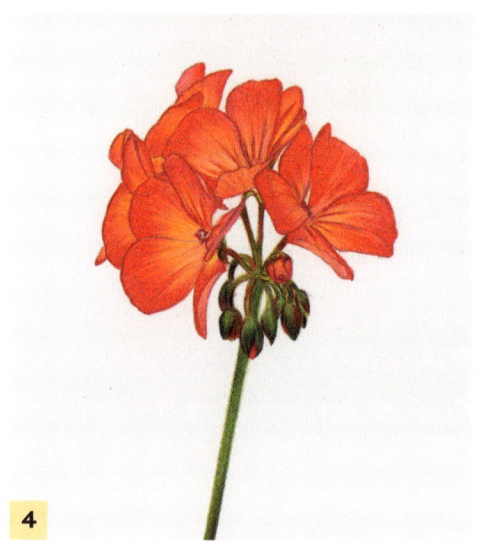

4

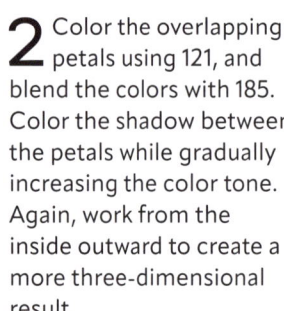

1 Lightly color from the center outward using 185. Using the same color, apply the first layer on the stem and buds. Lightly draw the edge of the petals with 117 and apply color from the edge of the petals, working inward. Gently blend the two colors together where they meet.

2 Color the overlapping petals using 121, and blend the colors with 185. Color the shadow between the petals while gradually increasing the color tone. Again, work from the inside outward to create a more three-dimensional result.

Now draw the small stamens in the middle of the flowers with 194. Redefine the petal outlines using 223. Add a light layer of 129 if you want some warm tones in the petals.

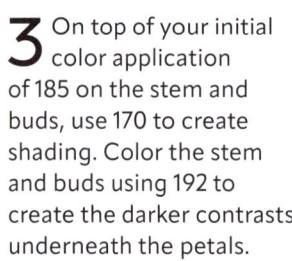

3 On top of your initial color application of 185 on the stem and buds, use 170 to create shading. Color the stem and buds using 192 to create the darker contrasts underneath the petals.

4 Bring definition to the buds and stem, paying close attention to their individual shape, using 278, 192, and 166. Take your time here and use the colors to give your drawing more shape and realism.

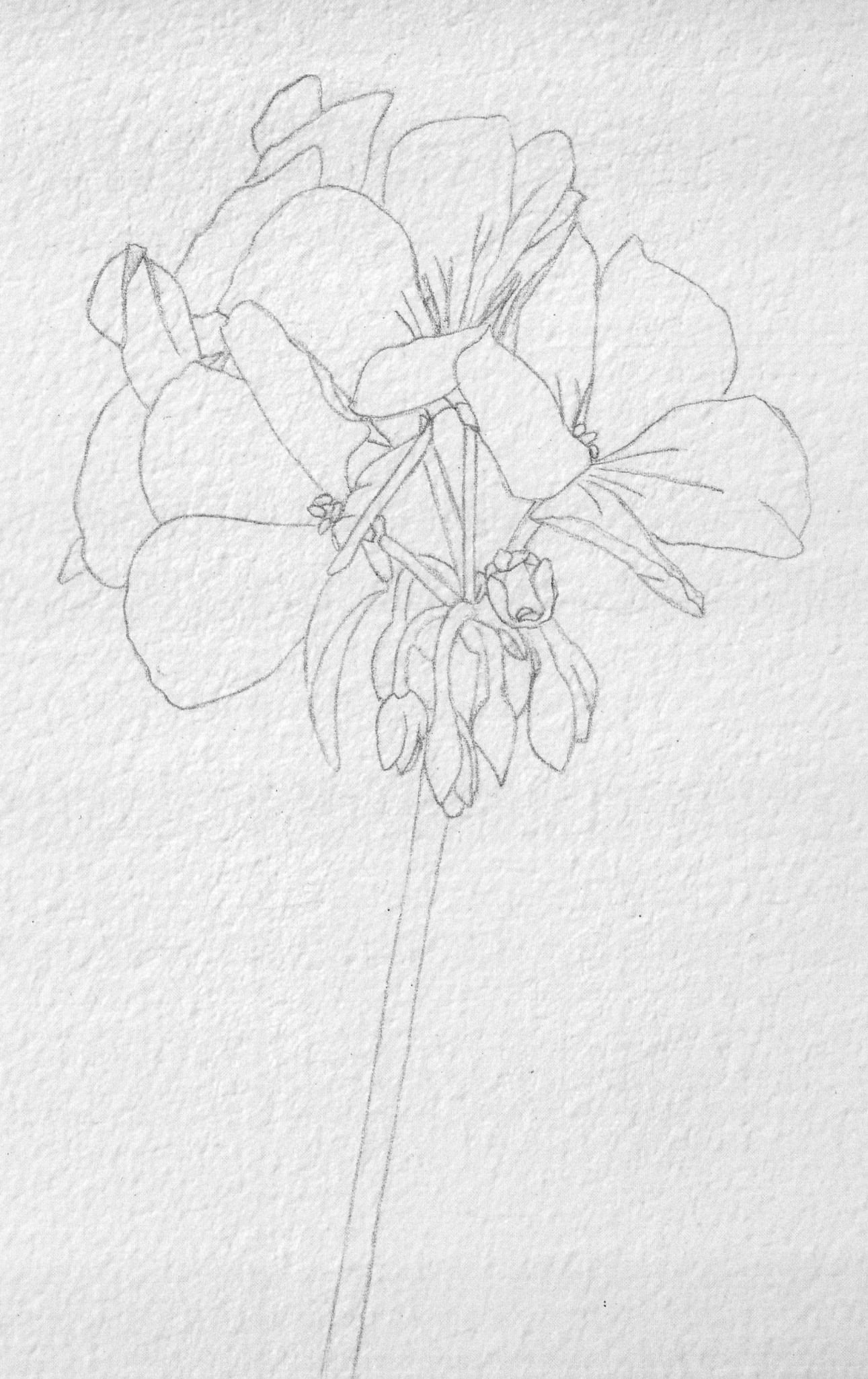

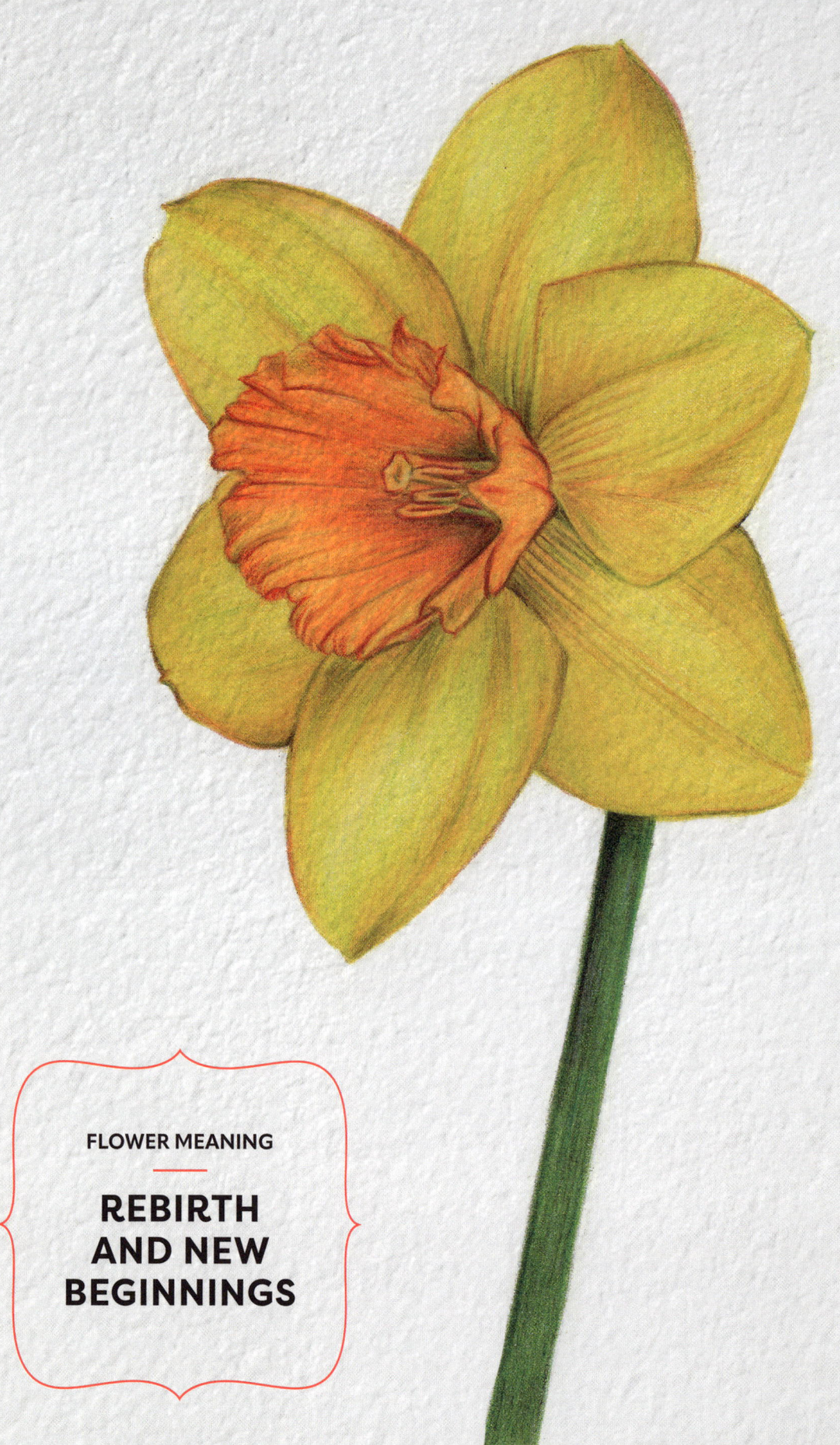

FLOWER MEANING

REBIRTH AND NEW BEGINNINGS

DAFFODIL

The daffodil is one of the first flowers I see following an often cold and wet Welsh winter. It lets me know spring and warmer weather are just around the corner. It is also the national flower of Wales and is called Cenhinen pedr in Welsh.

SCAN TO WATCH
A SPED-UP VIDEO
OF THE STEPS.

COLOR PALETTE

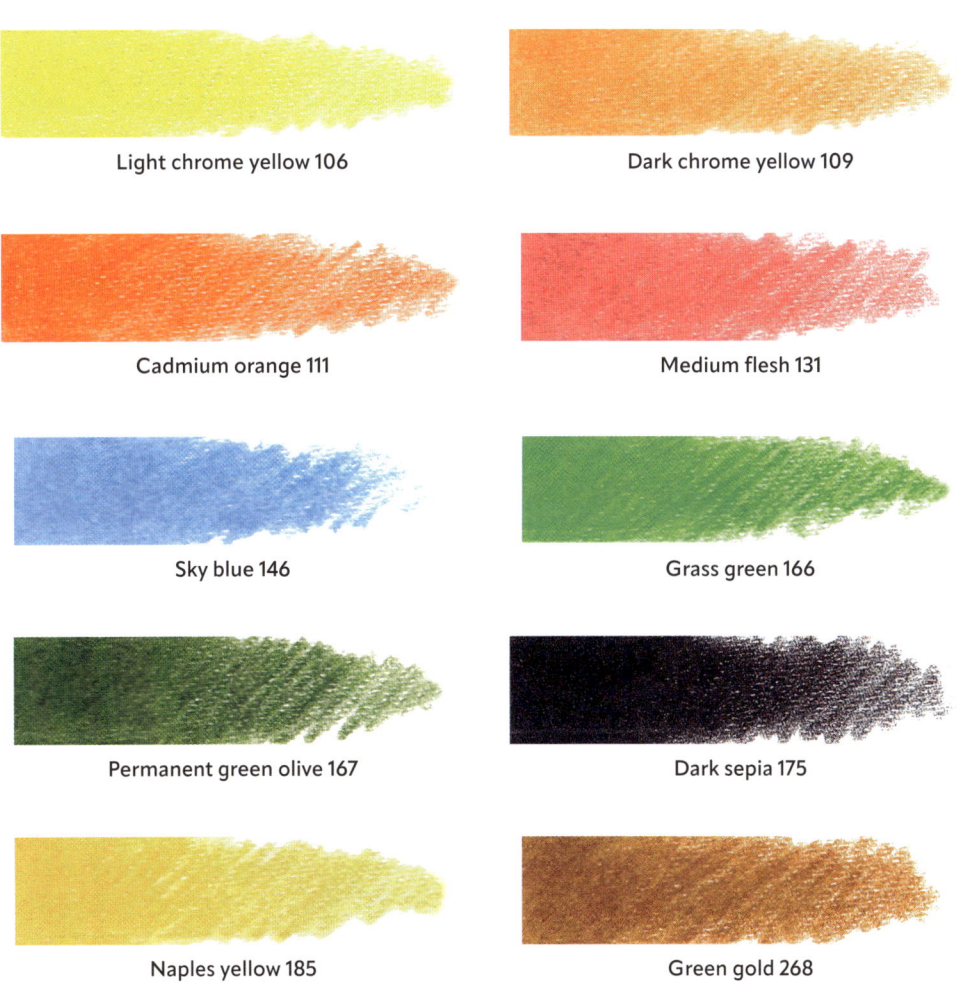

Light chrome yellow 106

Dark chrome yellow 109

Cadmium orange 111

Medium flesh 131

Sky blue 146

Grass green 166

Permanent green olive 167

Dark sepia 175

Naples yellow 185

Green gold 268

OTHER MATERIALS

Eraser • Brush • Pencil sharpener

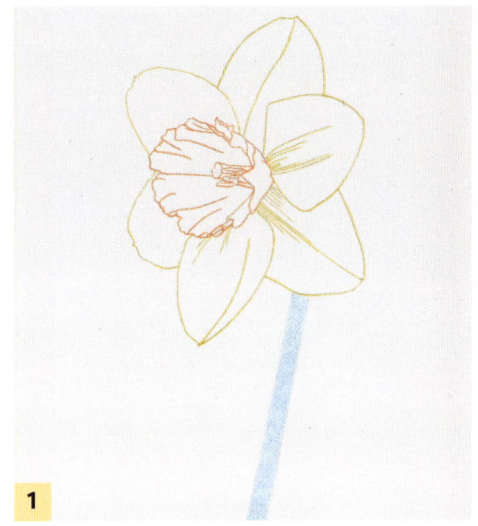

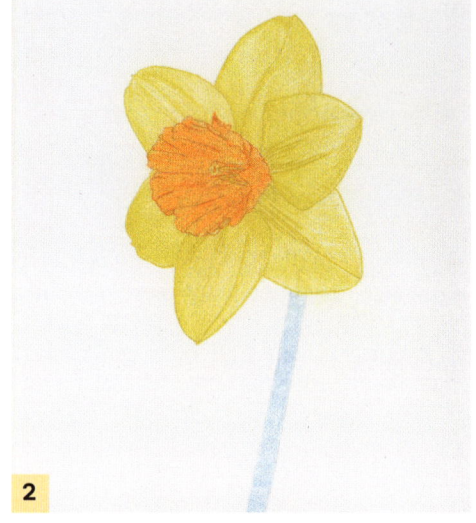

TIPS

As shown in Line Practice, Exercise 5, work from the edge of the petals inward to create the desired effect.

Focus your layers on building depth in the areas that require it, while leaving those that do not to show where the light hits the flower.

Remember, daffodil petals are not flat, so it's important to look at the direction of the petals and follow the natural lines.

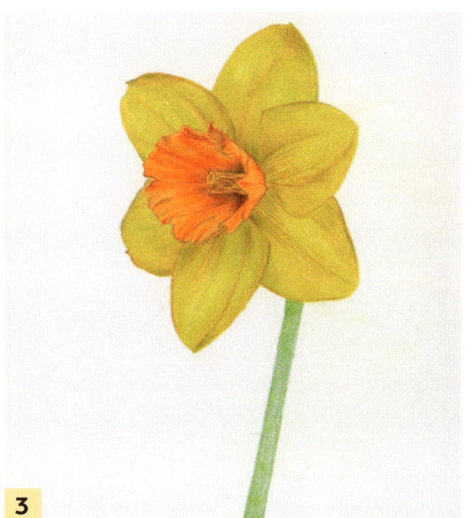

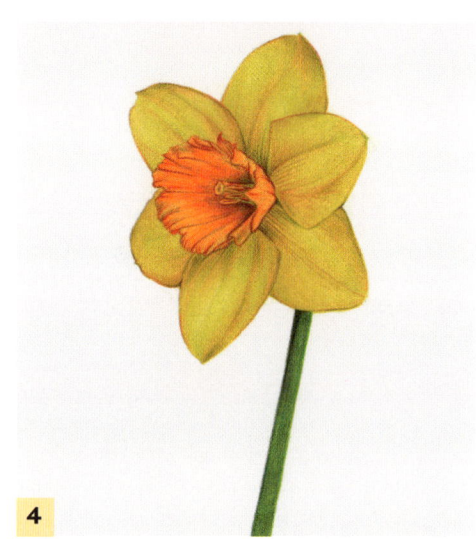

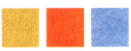

1 Start by mapping out the colors. Do this by outlining the petals with 185 and 111.

Apply a base layer of 146 to the stem.

2 Using 106, start coloring all six petals and the corona (center). Once the first layer is completed, start applying a second layer to the darker areas to show shadow and depth.

Now use 109 to color the corona, following the lines like frills on a dress to achieve the desired color and texture.

3 Now for the details. Use 111, 185, and 268 to gradually build up the layers, enhance the lines you have already laid, and create more depth in your shadows. Use 175 for the darkest areas, such as the center of the corona, the tips of some of the darker petals, and the bottom of the petals toward the inner part of the flower.

Use 106 to blend all the colors you have now laid. Repeat this process until you achieve the desired look. Now use 166 to add another layer of color to the stem.

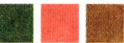

4 Gently use 167 to add volume to the daffodil and 131 to add some warmth to the petals. Ensure you leave the areas with less layers to create the reflection of light. Use 167 and 268 to complete the stem, using your layers to create darker areas, as shown in the picture.

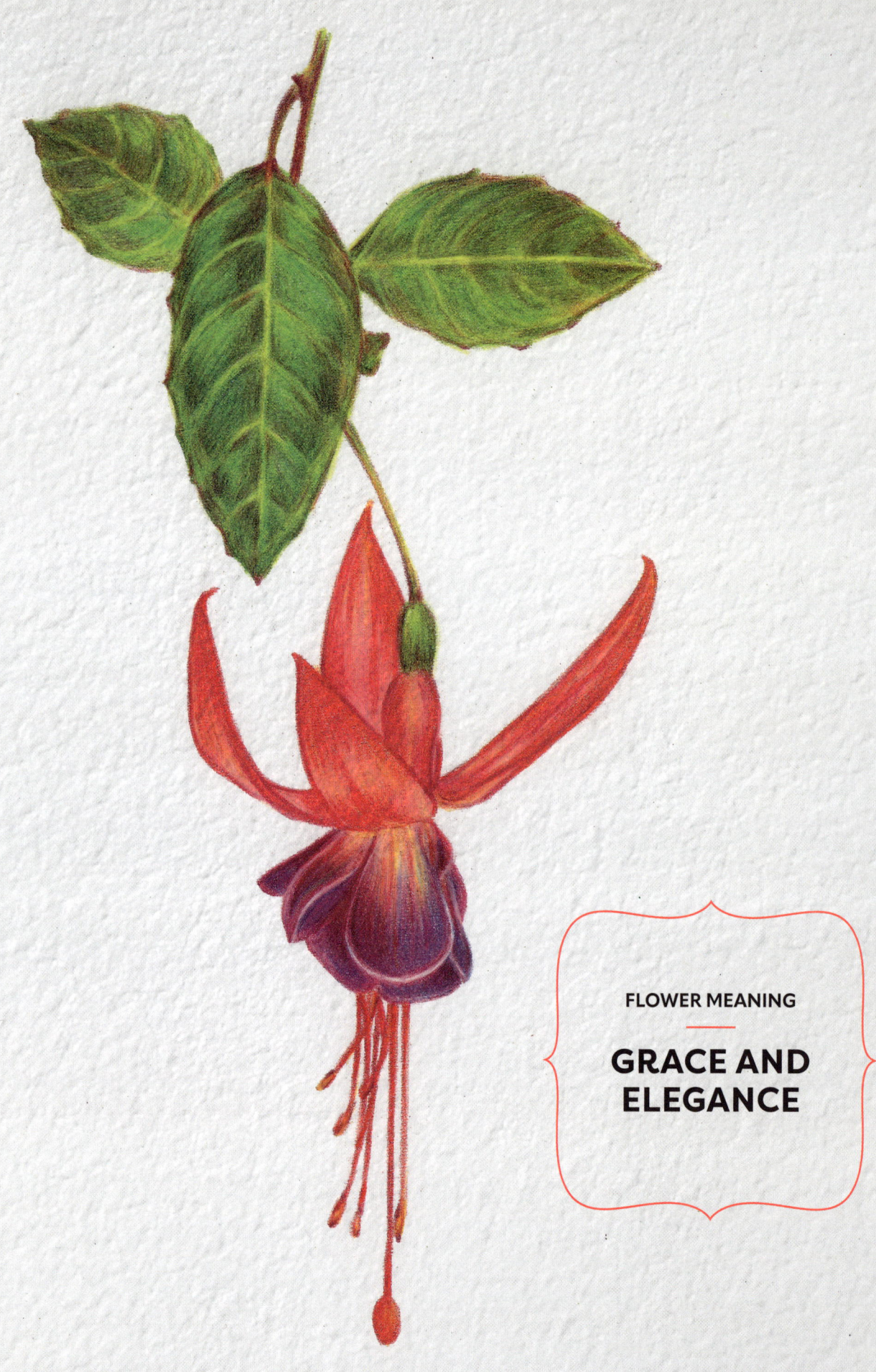

FLOWER MEANING

GRACE AND ELEGANCE

FUCHSIA

In many cultures, the fuchsia is a symbol of grace and elegance. It is also believed to represent prosperity and is associated with beauty and harmony in many traditions, making them a perfect gift. To me the fuchsia will always be a dancing fairy delicately displaying its whimsical moves.

SCAN TO WATCH A SPED-UP VIDEO OF THE STEPS.

COLOR PALETTE

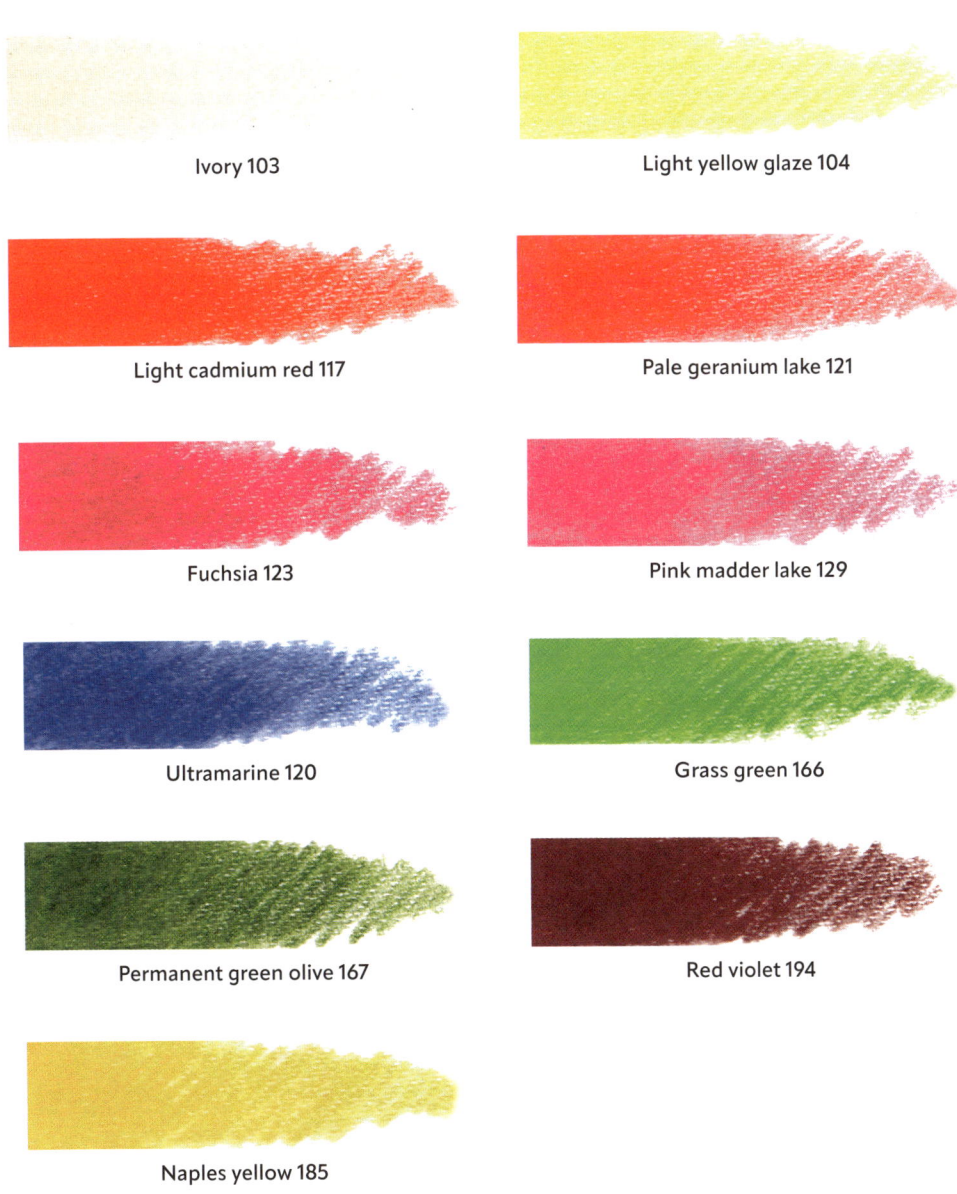

Ivory 103

Light yellow glaze 104

Light cadmium red 117

Pale geranium lake 121

Fuchsia 123

Pink madder lake 129

Ultramarine 120

Grass green 166

Permanent green olive 167

Red violet 194

Naples yellow 185

OTHER MATERIALS

Eraser • Brush • Pencil sharpener

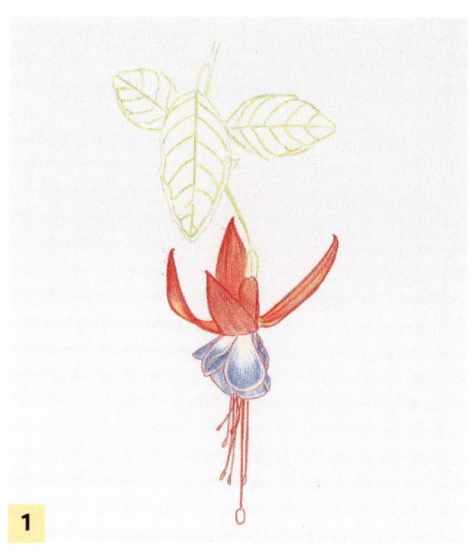

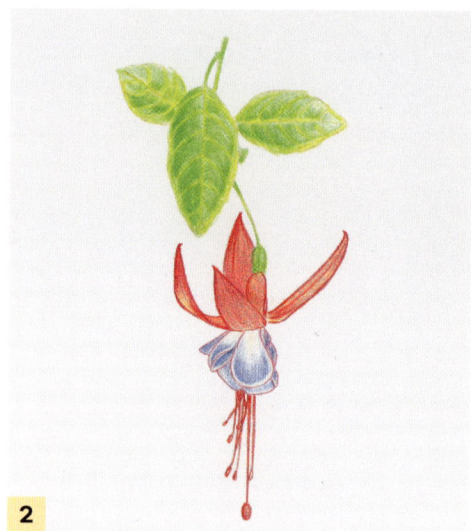

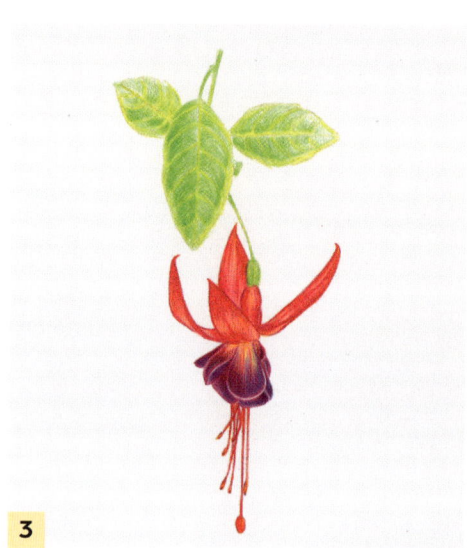

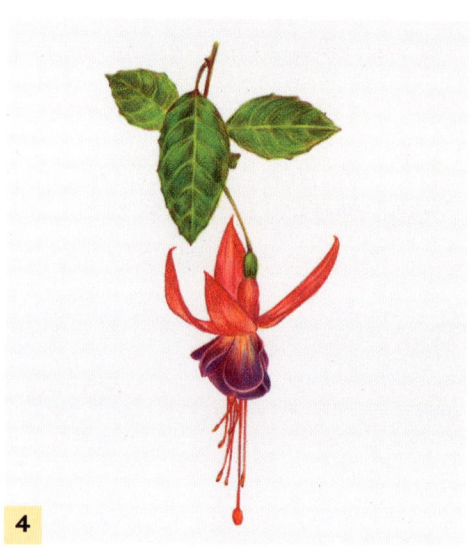

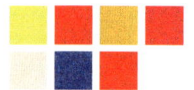

1 For the outline, use 104 to draw the vein and outline of the leaves, using hard pressure to indent the paper. Use 117 for the sepals, followed by a light layer of 185 and 121 to create the dark shadows. Then, using 103, draw inside the edge of the petals to create a gap before applying a light layer of 120. Map out the stamens using 117.

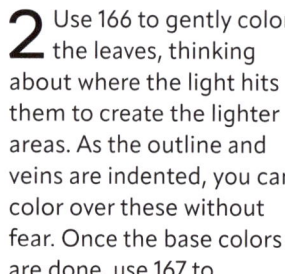

2 Use 166 to gently color the leaves, thinking about where the light hits them to create the lighter areas. As the outline and veins are indented, you can color over these without fear. Once the base colors are done, use 167 to enhance the volume on the dark part of the leaves.

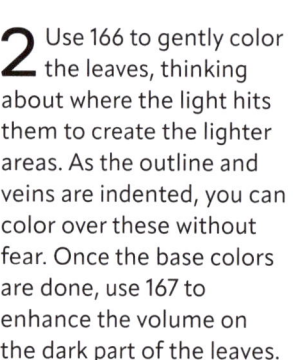

3 Gently layer the color 123 on the top of 120 to create the deep purple. Continue coloring until you achieve the desired color. If you want a deeper color on the petal, add a light layer of 117.

Use 185, 129, and 121 to color the outer petals. Use 103 to blend the colors when needed. Lastly, sharpen your pencil and define the stamen details using 117 and 194.

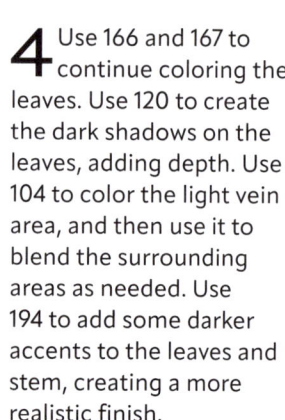

4 Use 166 and 167 to continue coloring the leaves. Use 120 to create the dark shadows on the leaves, adding depth. Use 104 to color the light vein area, and then use it to blend the surrounding areas as needed. Use 194 to add some darker accents to the leaves and stem, creating a more realistic finish.

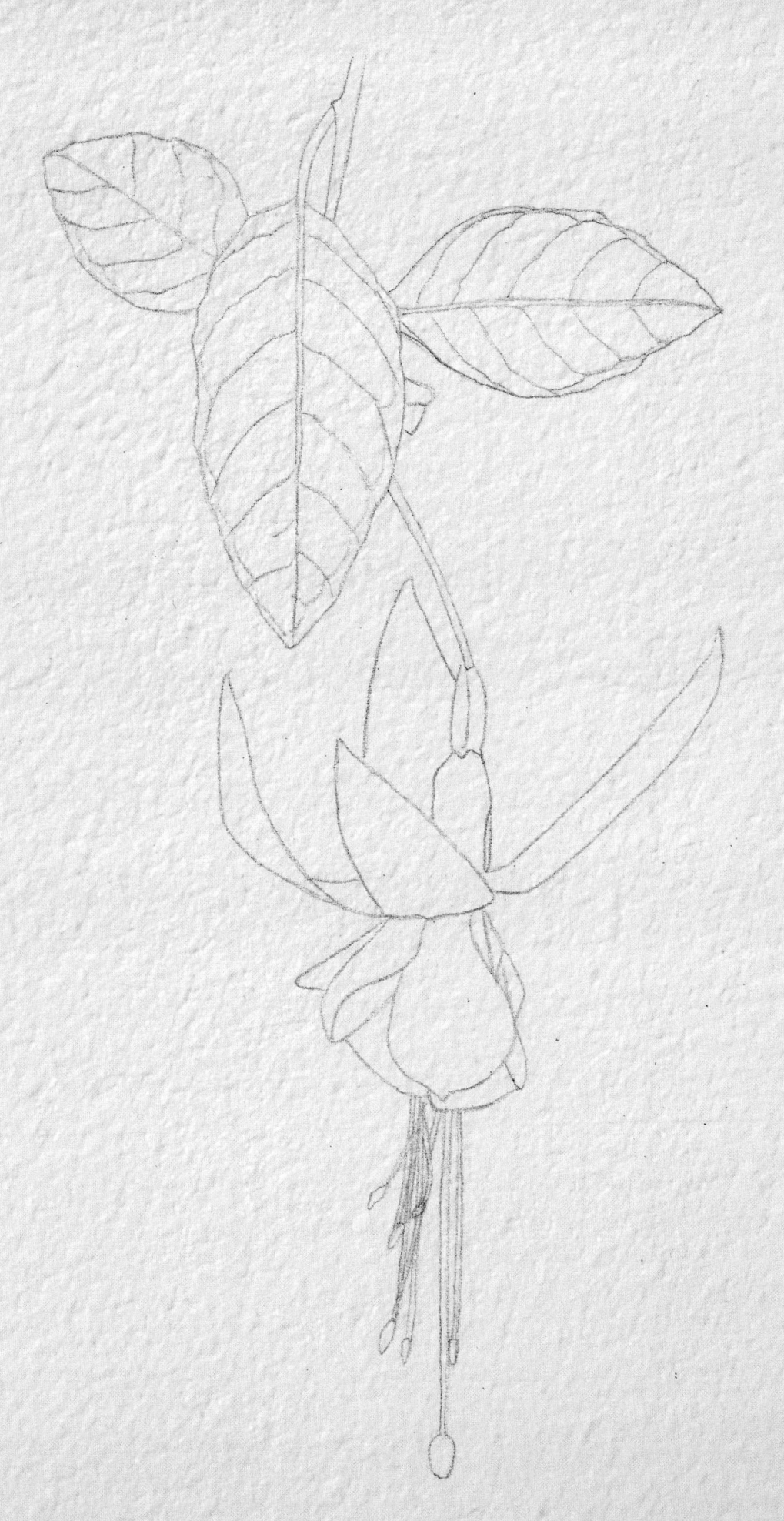

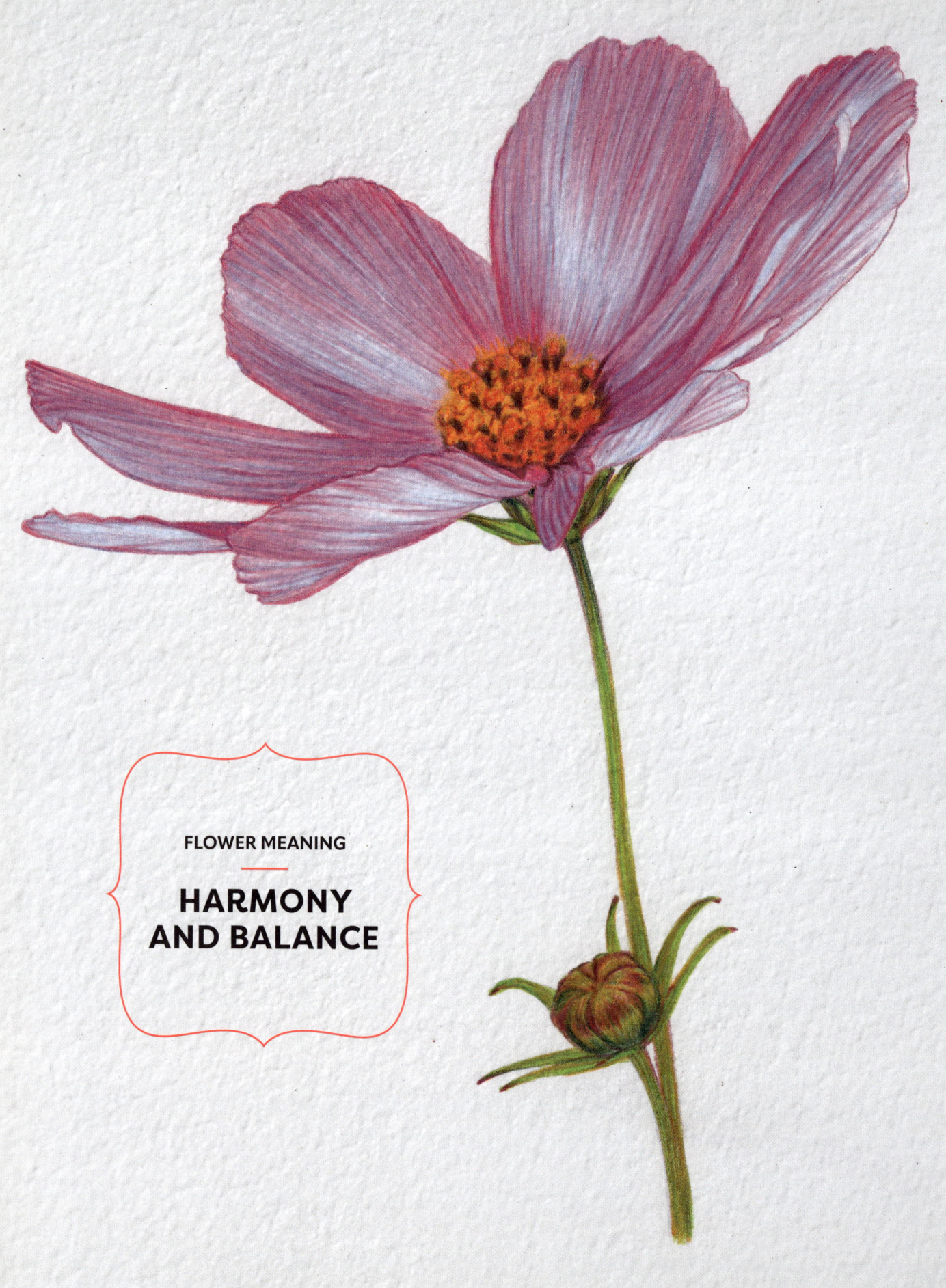

FLOWER MEANING

HARMONY AND BALANCE

COSMOS

Have you ever seen a field full of cosmos flowers? Their elegant, slim bodies with colorful flowers dancing in an autumn breeze bring harmony to the world.

SCAN TO WATCH
A SPED-UP VIDEO
OF THE STEPS.

COLOR PALETTE

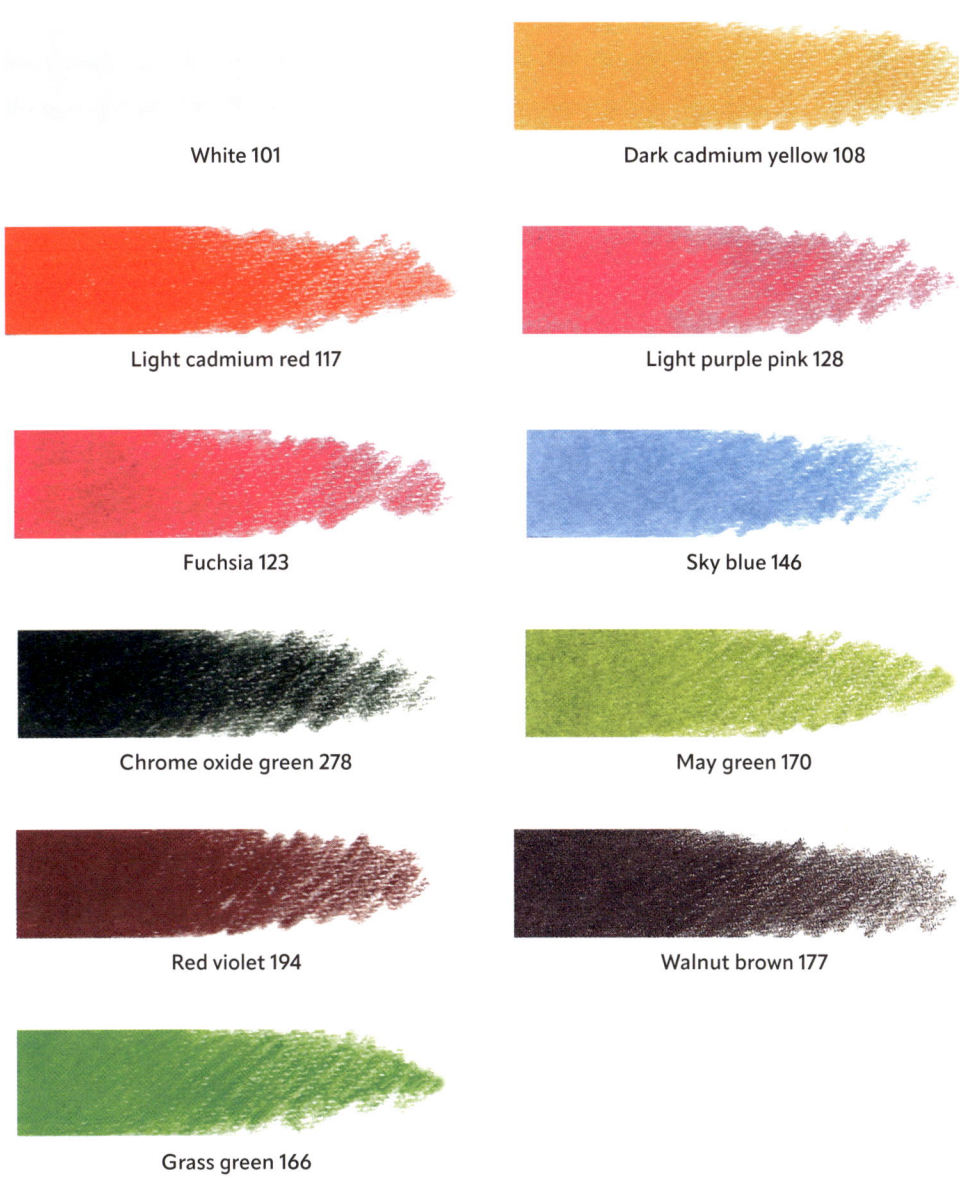

White 101

Dark cadmium yellow 108

Light cadmium red 117

Light purple pink 128

Fuchsia 123

Sky blue 146

Chrome oxide green 278

May green 170

Red violet 194

Walnut brown 177

Grass green 166

OTHER MATERIALS

Eraser • Brush • Pencil sharpener

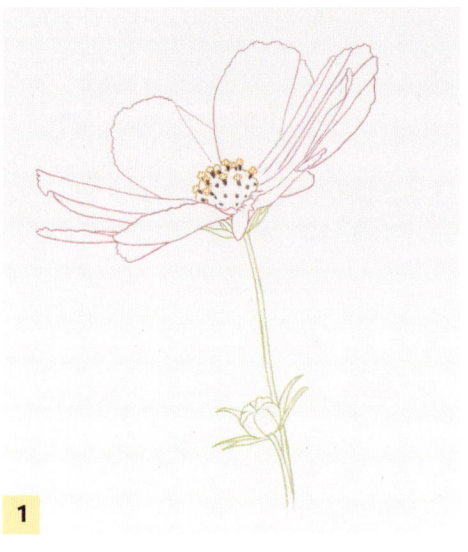

1

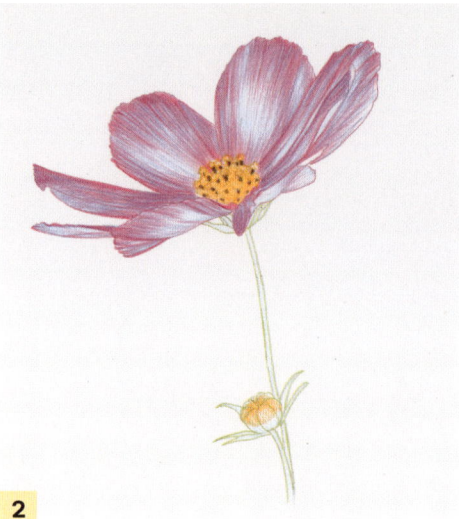

2

TIP
When coloring thin leaves or stems, it is best to color horizontally. You can turn your paper on its side if needed.

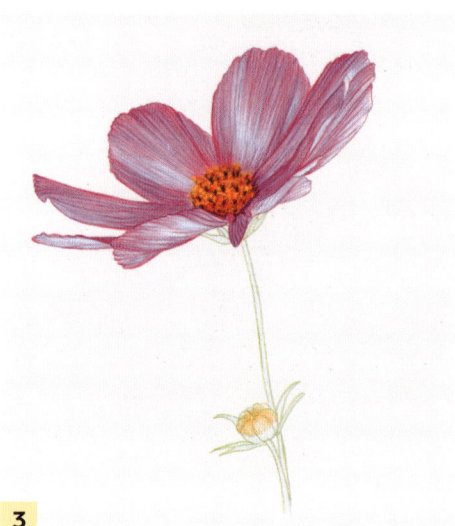

3

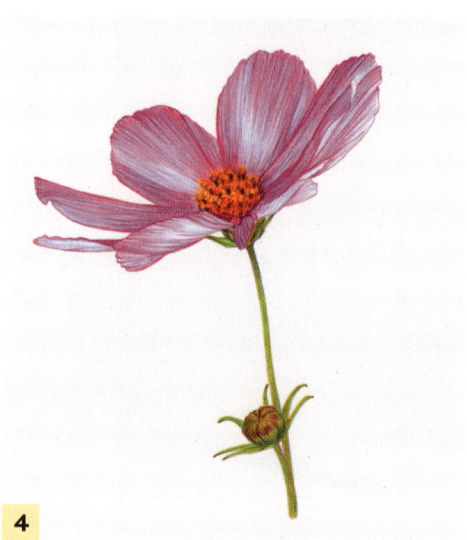

4

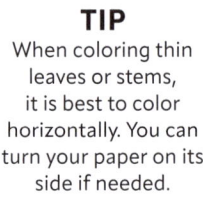

1 A cosmos has many small details to capture. Take your time to map out the outline of the petals using 123. Define the stamens with 108 and 177. Lastly, outline the stem and bud with 170.

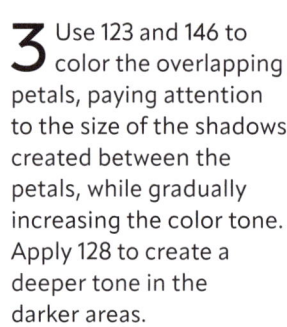

2 Lightly apply the first layer along the curved surface of the petals with 146. At this time, color the center stamens with 108. Use 123 to lightly draw the pointed shape of the petal edges with a line, and color from the edge inward. Let the two colors blend and meet naturally. Use 101 to blend and smooth the surface when needed. Apply a light layer to the stem, using 146 and 108 on the top of the bud.

3 Use 123 and 146 to color the overlapping petals, paying attention to the size of the shadows created between the petals, while gradually increasing the color tone. Apply 128 to create a deeper tone in the darker areas.

Define the details of the flowers. Pay attention to the shape of the shadow cast on the curved petals. Use 117 and 108 to further define the detail of the stamens and create the three-dimensional feel.

4 Use 166 and 108 to color the stem and the bud.

Add 278 and 194 to create the darkest areas, completing the look.

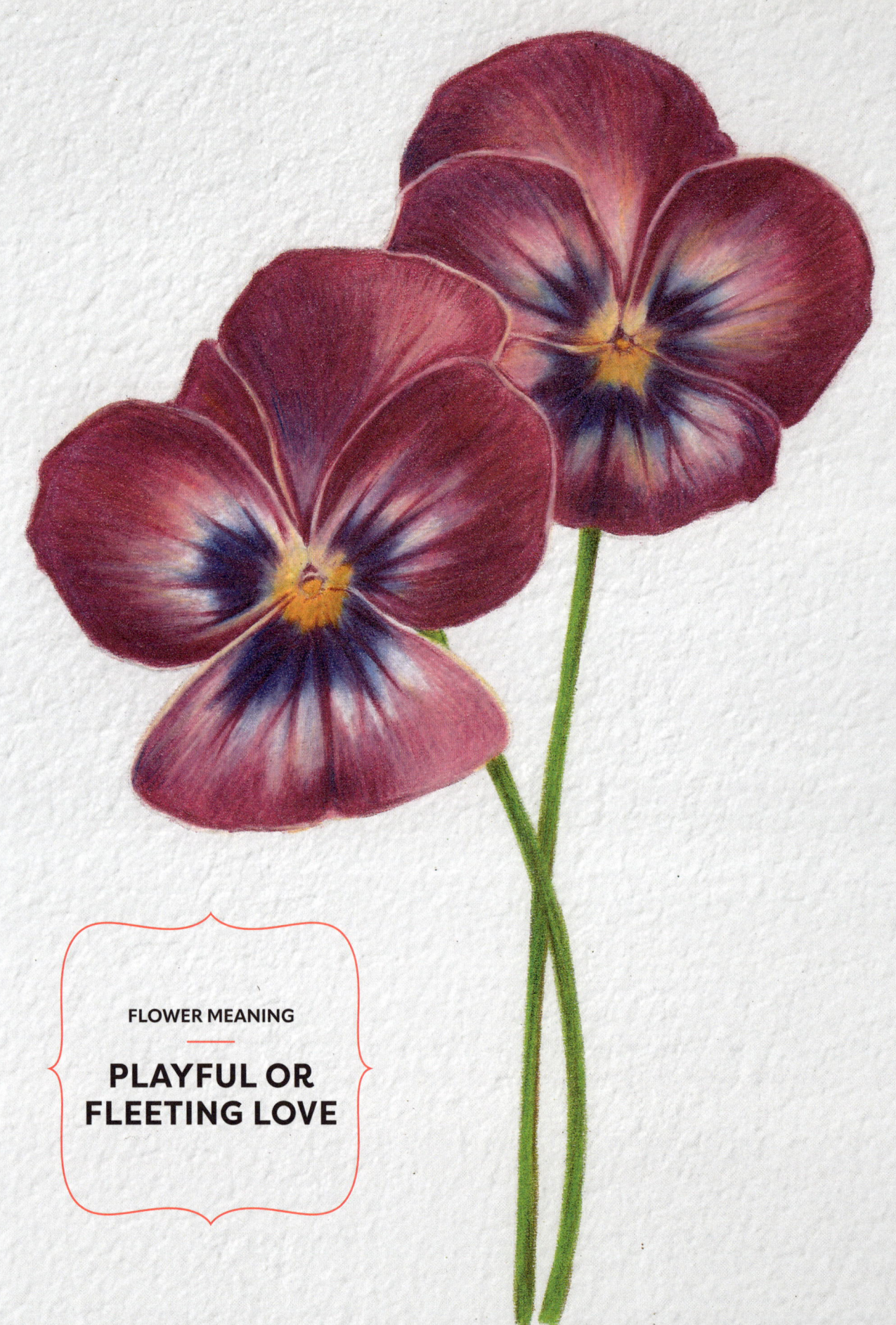

FLOWER MEANING

PLAYFUL OR FLEETING LOVE

PANSY

The English term "pansy" is derived from the French *pensée*, meaning "thought." The flowers are often associated with virtuous humility and tender, playful, or fleeting love. Did you know that pansies were used in love potions during the Victorian era?

SCAN TO WATCH
A SPED-UP VIDEO
OF THE STEPS.

COLOR PALETTE

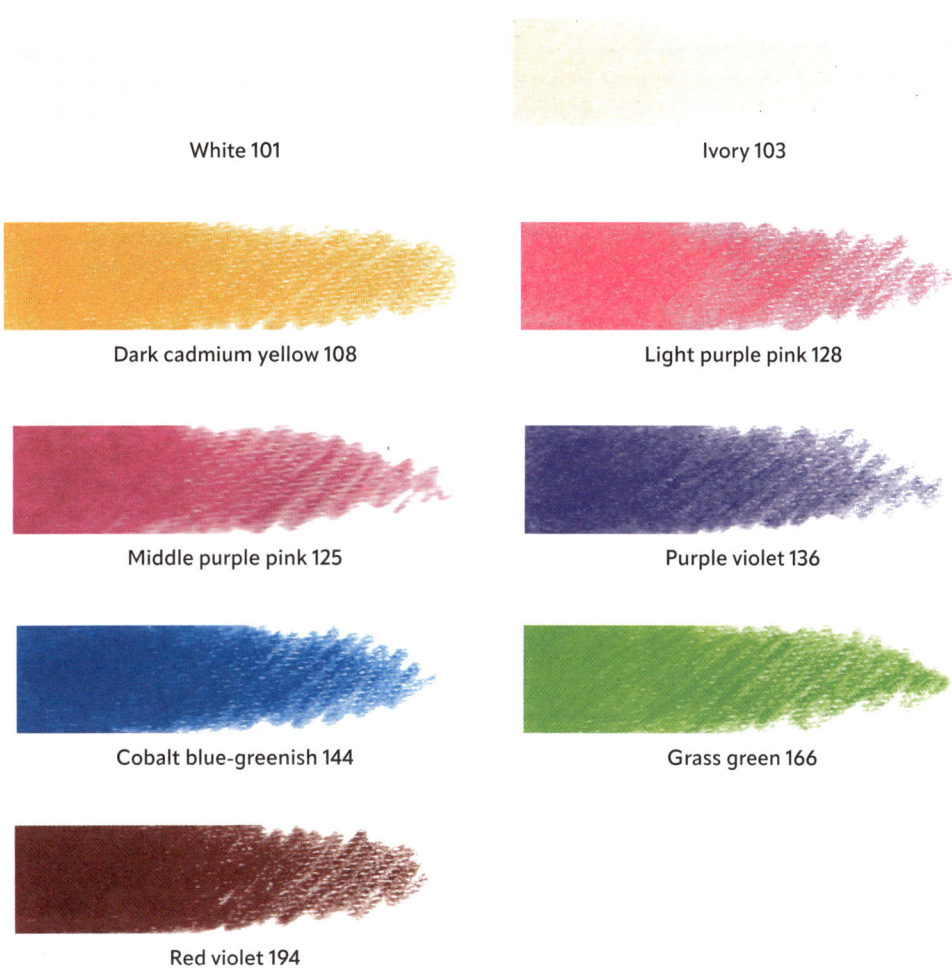

White 101

Ivory 103

Dark cadmium yellow 108

Light purple pink 128

Middle purple pink 125

Purple violet 136

Cobalt blue-greenish 144

Grass green 166

Red violet 194

OTHER MATERIALS

Eraser • Brush • Pencil sharpener

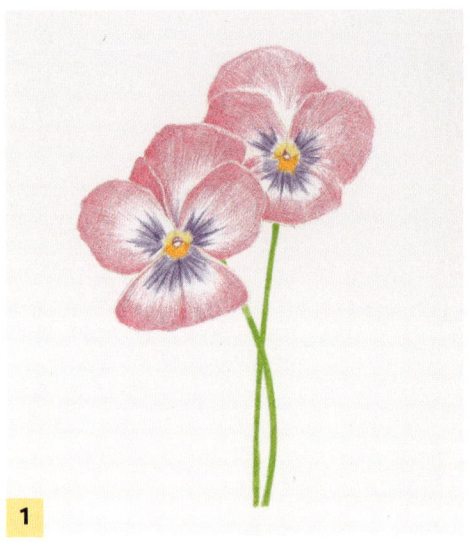

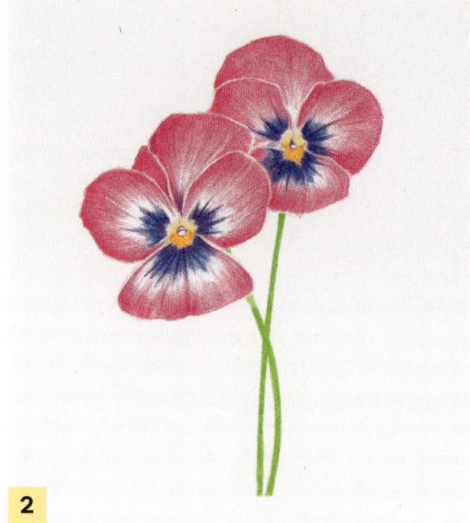

TIP

In order to achieve the realism in this drawing, you need to learn how to naturally blend the colors. Use 103 to smooth the surface and gradually connect the colors together. Take your time and don't rush.

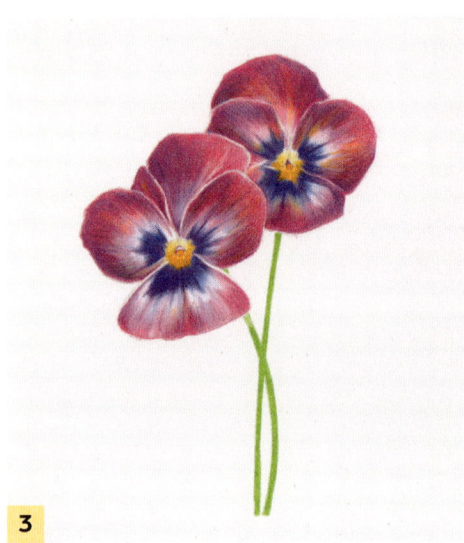

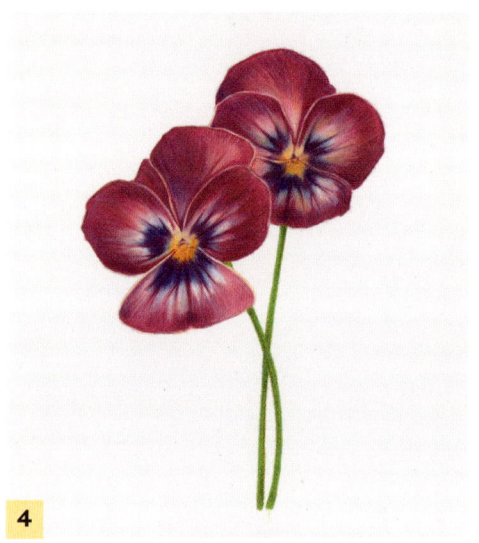

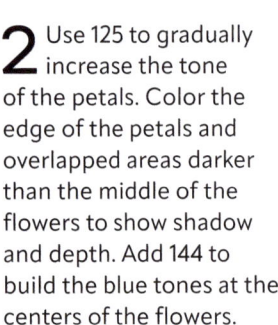

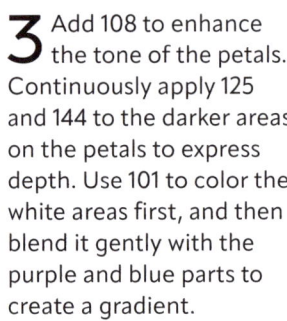

1 Before coloring the flowers, apply hard pressure to the edge of the petals with 103, creating an indent in the paper. Color gently, thinking of the wrinkles of the petals and applying the first layer from the edge, working inward with 128. Color the centers of the flowers with 108. Then use 136, working from the center outward. Also, add a base layer to the stems with 166.

2 Use 125 to gradually increase the tone of the petals. Color the edge of the petals and overlapped areas darker than the middle of the flowers to show shadow and depth. Add 144 to build the blue tones at the centers of the flowers.

3 Add 108 to enhance the tone of the petals. Continuously apply 125 and 144 to the darker areas on the petals to express depth. Use 101 to color the white areas first, and then blend it gently with the purple and blue parts to create a gradient.

4 This stage is all for the details. Use 194 to redefine the edge of the petals while enhancing the dark areas. Also draw the pattern lines in the middle of each petal, working outward. Use 103 to gently blend each color together. Apply extra layers of colors on the petals if needed. Add 128 to give a warm feeling to the petals where needed. Finish the stem using 166 and 194.

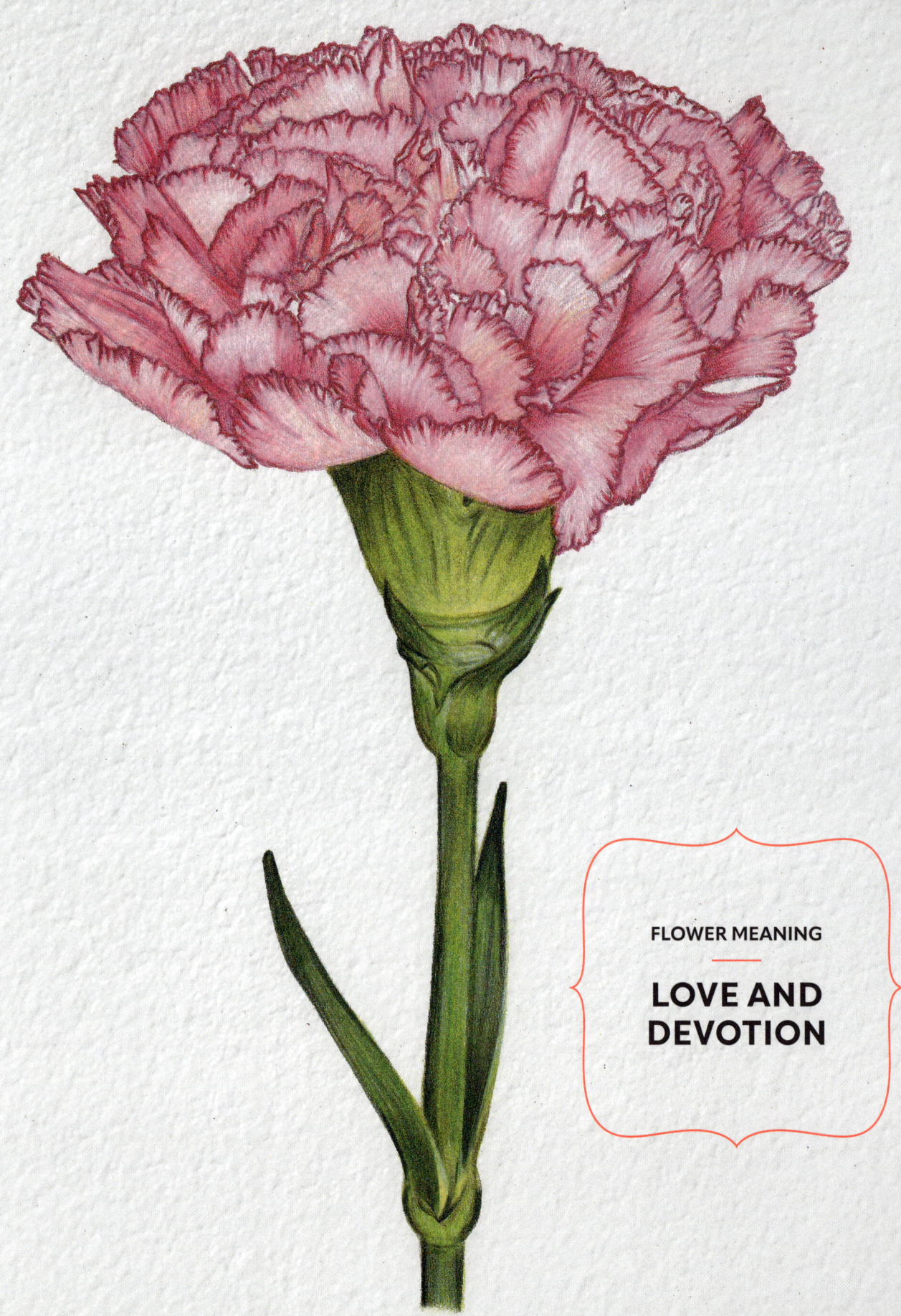

FLOWER MEANING
—
LOVE AND DEVOTION

CARNATION

Carnations are the symbol of love. Love for your family, your friends, or your partner. The pink carnation is linked to the love for your mother. Who would you like to give a carnation to?

SCAN TO WATCH
A SPED-UP VIDEO
OF THE STEPS.

COLOR PALETTE

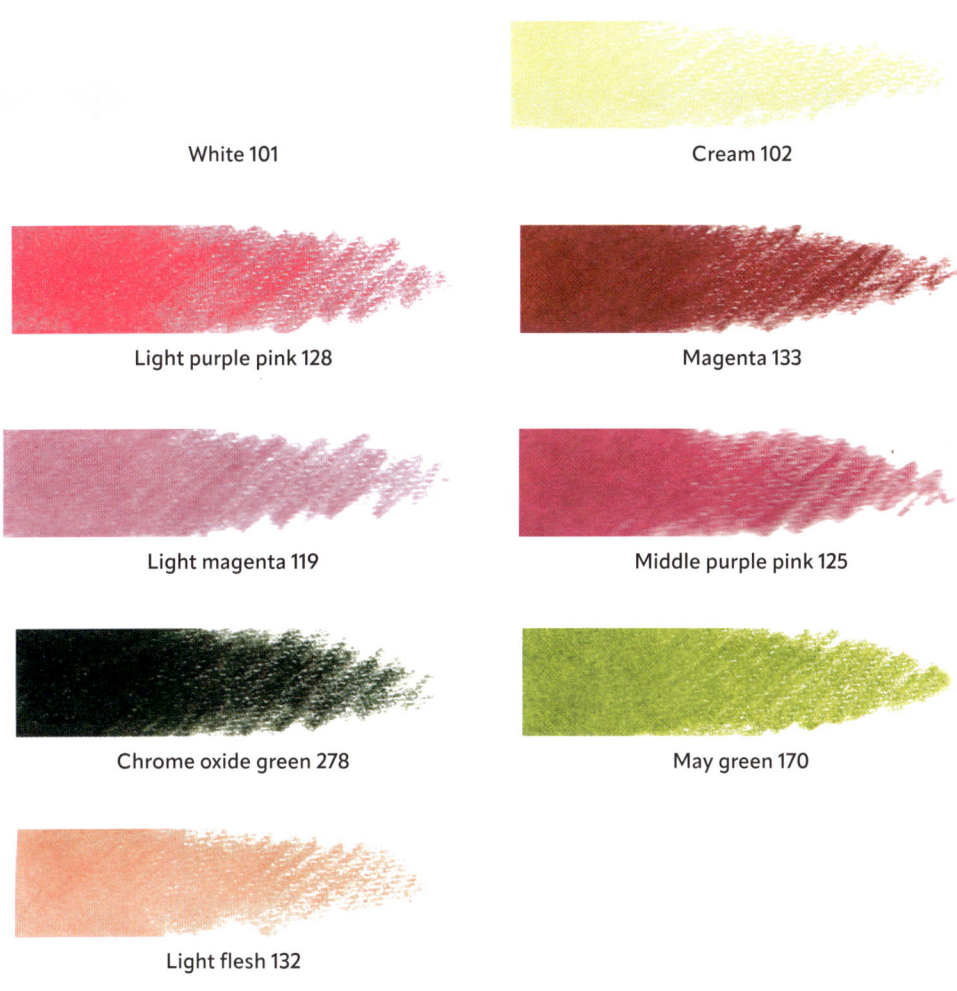

White 101

Cream 102

Light purple pink 128

Magenta 133

Light magenta 119

Middle purple pink 125

Chrome oxide green 278

May green 170

Light flesh 132

OTHER MATERIALS

Eraser • Brush • Pencil sharpener

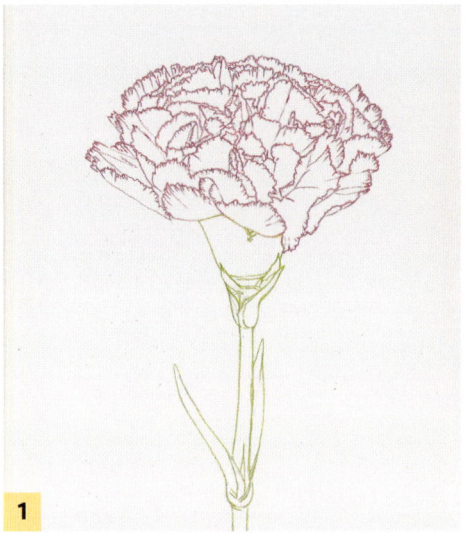
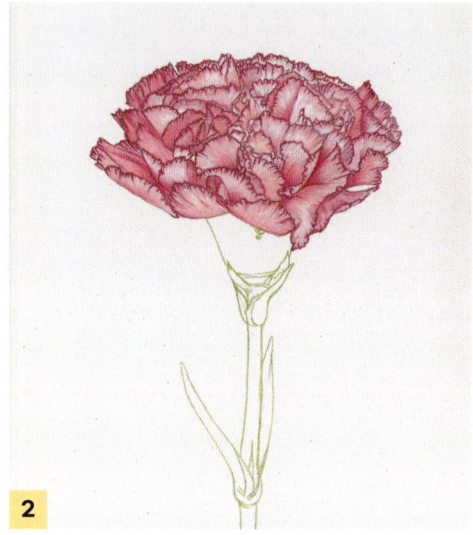
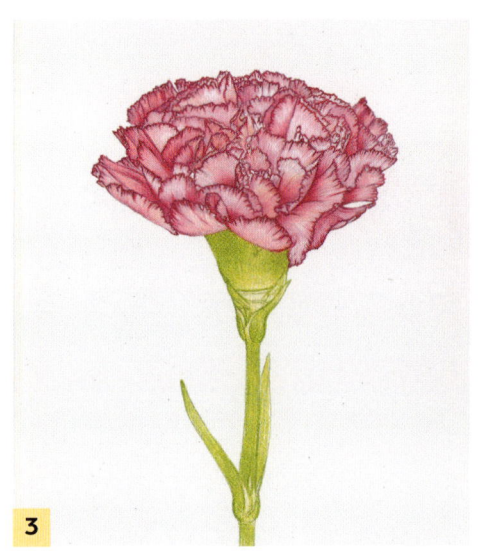
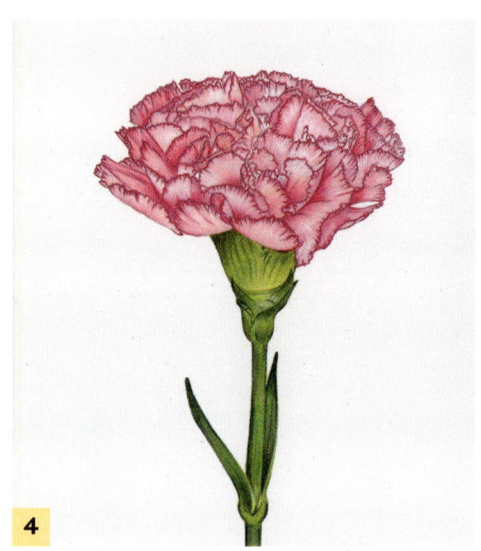

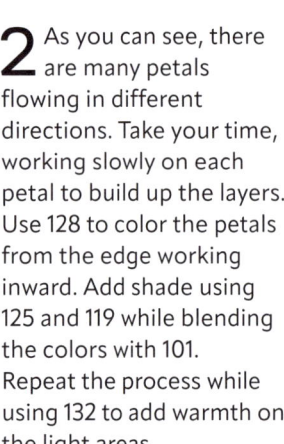

TIP

When there are so many little petals overlapping each other, it can quickly become overwhelming. Take your time and study the petals before you create the outlines. Work slowly and check the reference image often to ensure you capture every petal.

1 Use 125 to map out the edge of the flower petals. Pay attention to the little details that make up the frills. Take your time on this step to capture all the little details. Draw the outline of the stem and leaves using 170. Ensure you keep your pencils sharp throughout.

2 As you can see, there are many petals flowing in different directions. Take your time, working slowly on each petal to build up the layers. Use 128 to color the petals from the edge working inward. Add shade using 125 and 119 while blending the colors with 101. Repeat the process while using 132 to add warmth on the light areas.

3 Color in the shadows between the overlapping petals with 125 and redefine the color and detail on the edge of the petals using 133. Pay particular attention to the folds and shadows to add depth and make the drawing look more three-dimensional.

Color the entire stem with 102 as a base layer. Add 170 to enhance the tone of the green.

4 Use 170 to add texture and shape to the stem and leaves, paying particular attention to the darker areas. To bring the leaves to life, use 278 on the dark areas where the leaves overlap. Continue to define the outline of the leaves and edges of the stem. Use 146 to create highlights and show where the light hits the stem. Between layers use 102 to blend the colors when needed.

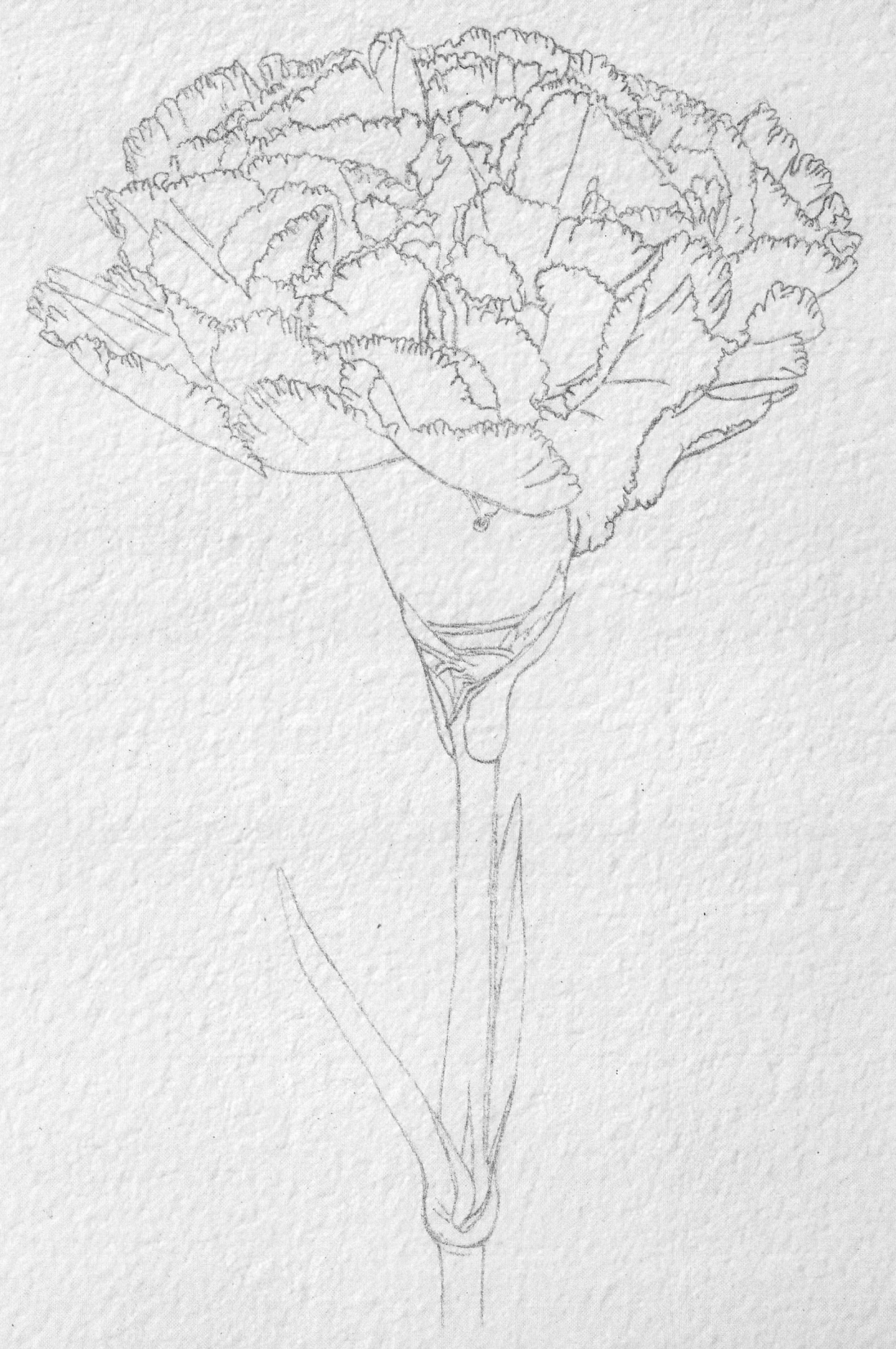

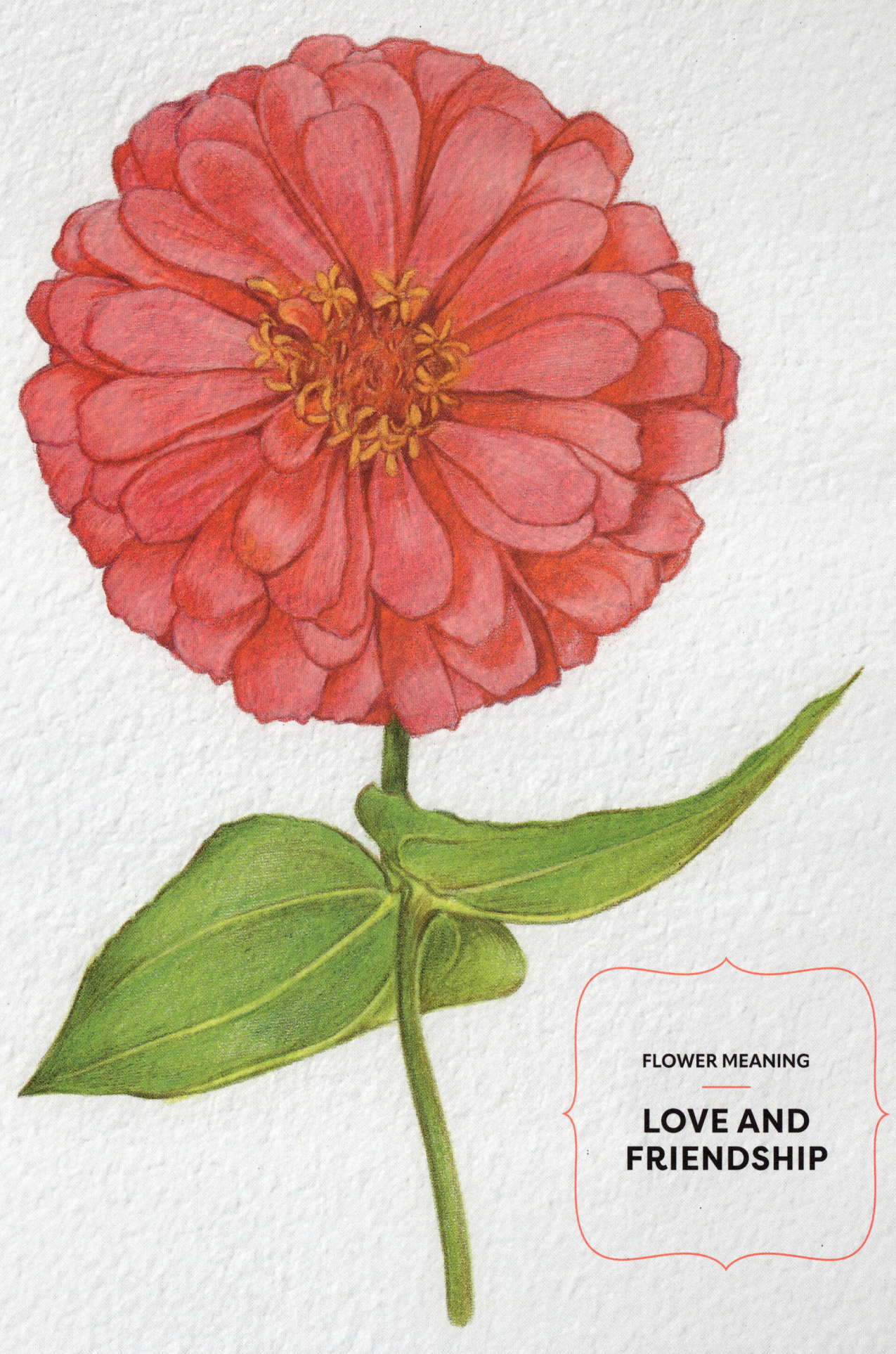

FLOWER MEANING

LOVE AND FRIENDSHIP

ZINNIA

The zinnia is now a symbol of spiritual growth and transformation. During the Victorian era, a bouquet of zinnias was often sent to absent friends to show you were still thinking of them. It just goes to show that flowers convey thoughts and emotions no matter the distance.

SCAN TO WATCH A SPED-UP VIDEO OF THE STEPS.

COLOR PALETTE

White 101

Light yellow glaze 104

Light chrome yellow 106

Light cadmium red 117

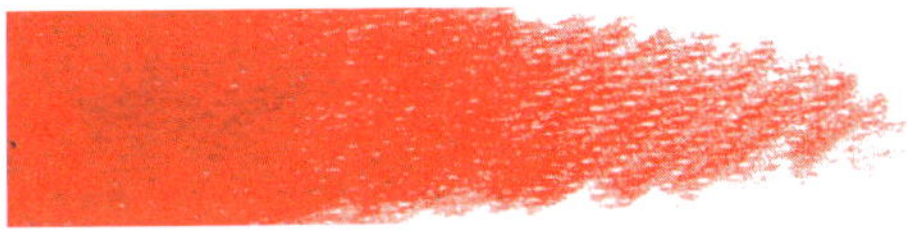

Deep red 223

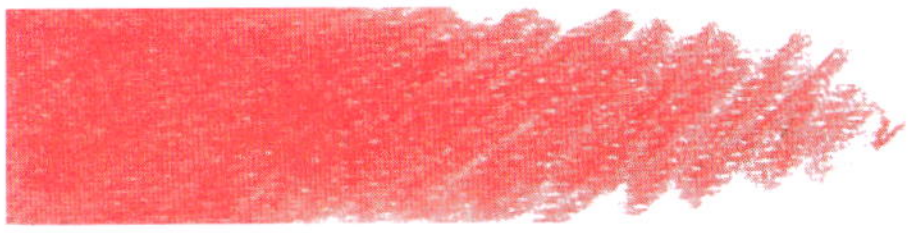

Rose carmine 124

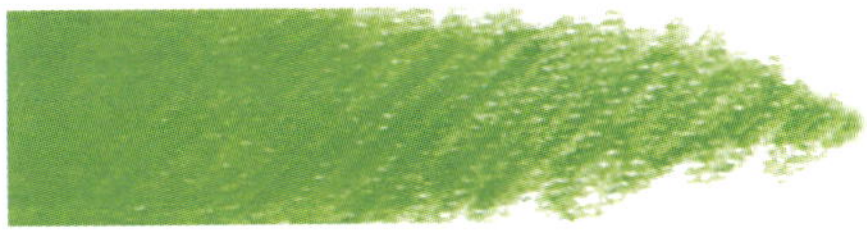

Grass green 166

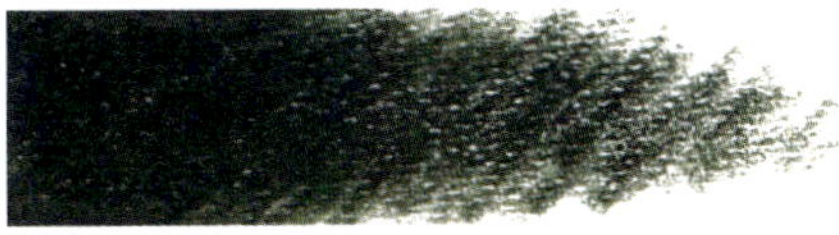

Chrome oxide green 278

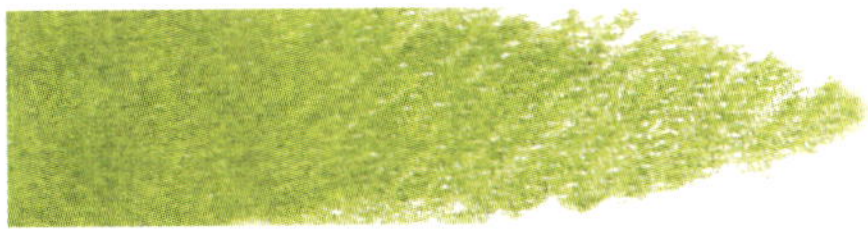

May green 170

Dark flesh 130

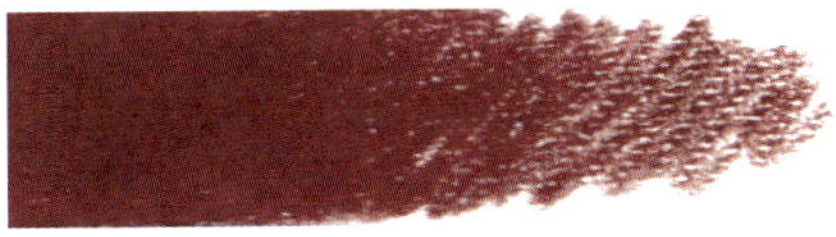

India red 192

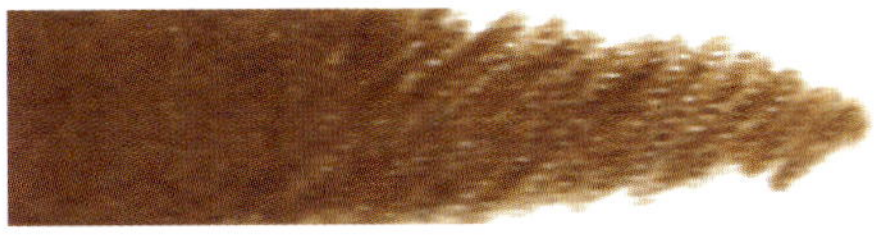

Raw umber 180

OTHER MATERIALS

Eraser • Brush • Pencil sharpener

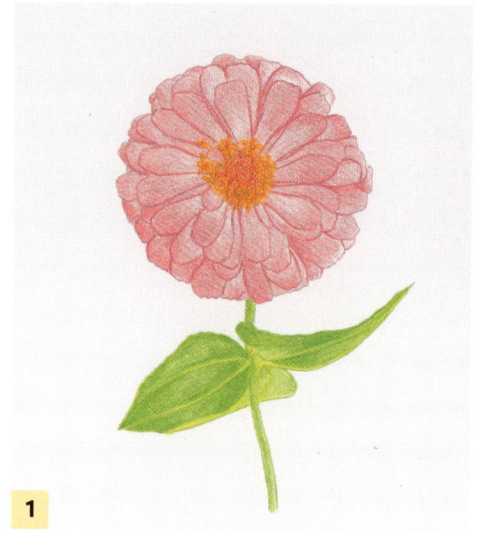

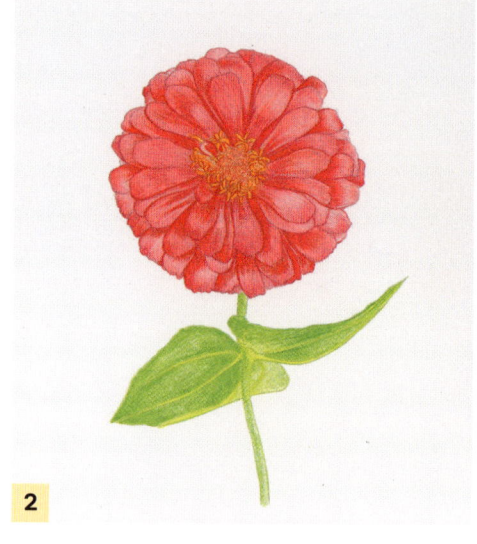

TIPS

Take your time and pay special attention to the individual petals.

Don't forget, all the petals have their own different shades of colors, depending on the light and shadows. Don't color them in all the same shade, as this will make your drawing appear flat.

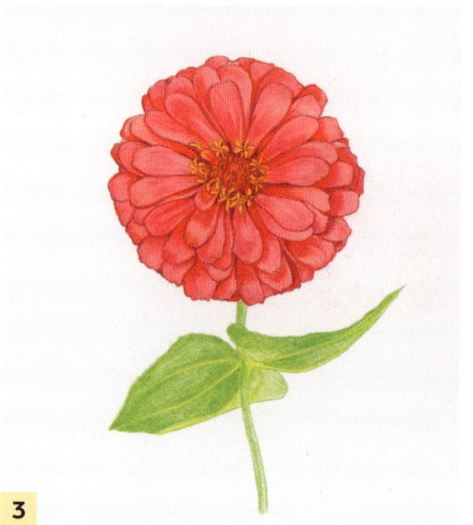

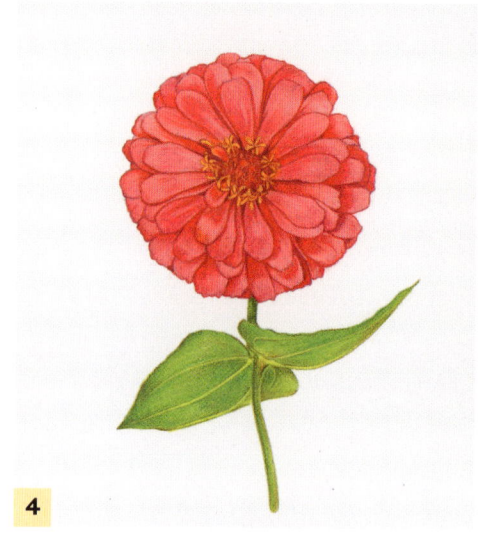

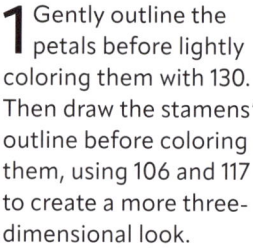

1 Gently outline the petals before lightly coloring them with 130. Then draw the stamens' outline before coloring them, using 106 and 117 to create a more three-dimensional look.

Apply hard pressure using 104 to create the leaf veins. Start coloring the leaves to balance out the flowers with 166.

2 Color the light area of the petals with 124, and create the shadow where the petals overlap with 117. Also, use 101 to smooth the petal surface where the light hits. Once the petal surface is smooth, apply more layers to give them a sense of shape.

3 Repeat step 2 to build the tones of the petals, while using 223 and 192 to add the darker shadows. Use 117, 192, and 106 to color the center of the flower and stamens.

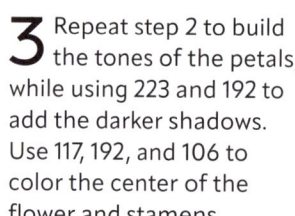

4 On top of the base colors on the stem and leaves, add light and dark tones using 170 and 278. Don't forget to add the shadows where the two leaves meet to create a more realistic finish. Use 180 to tidy up the edges of the stem and leaves.

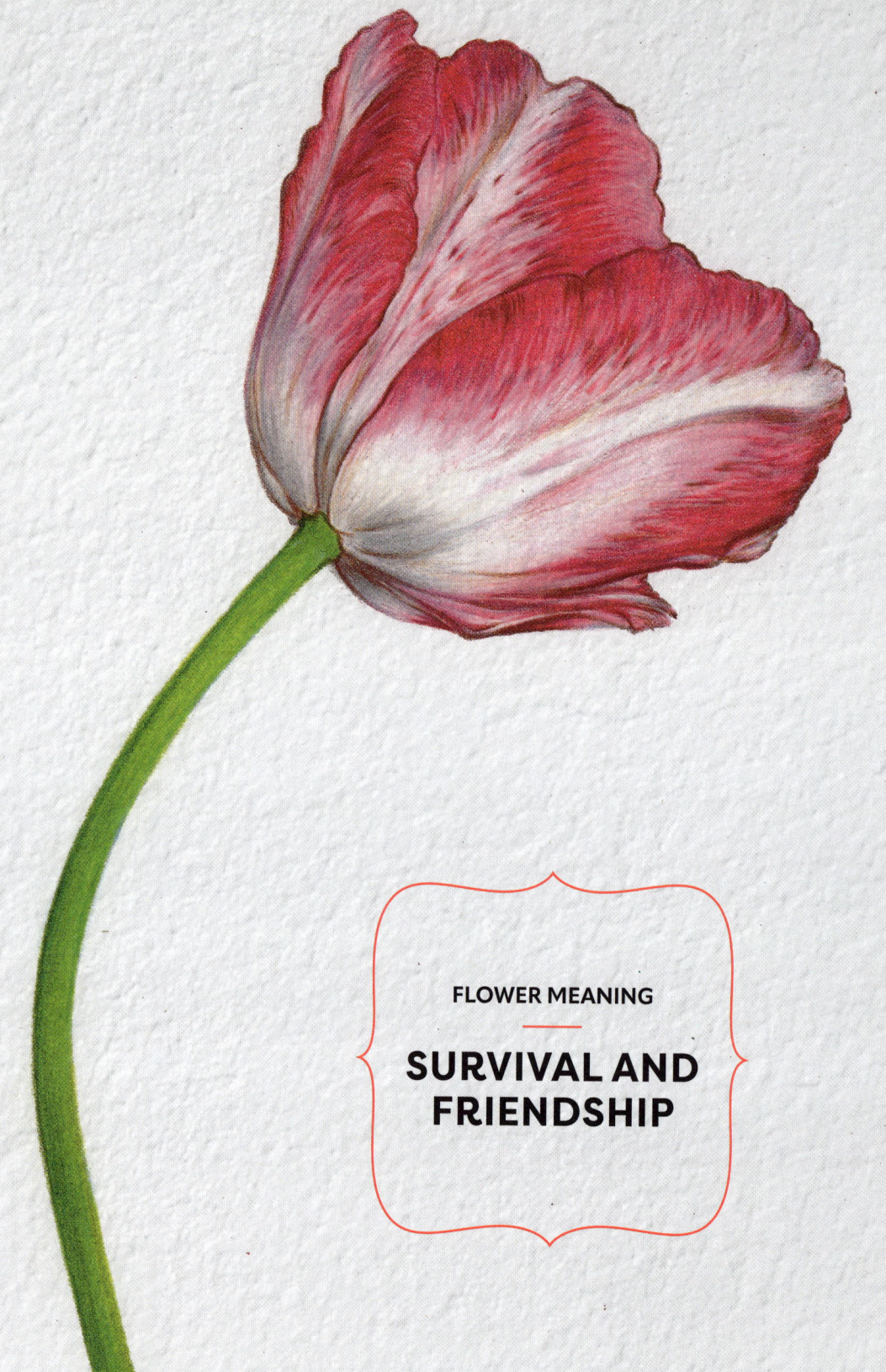

FLOWER MEANING
—
SURVIVAL AND FRIENDSHIP

PARROT TULIP

Parrot tulips are simply stunning, with wide-ranging colors, and often symbolize love and survival. I cannot help but see the passionate Spanish flamenco dresses with their vibrant colors elegantly twirling through the air every time I draw them.

SCAN TO WATCH A SPED-UP VIDEO OF THE STEPS.

COLOR PALETTE

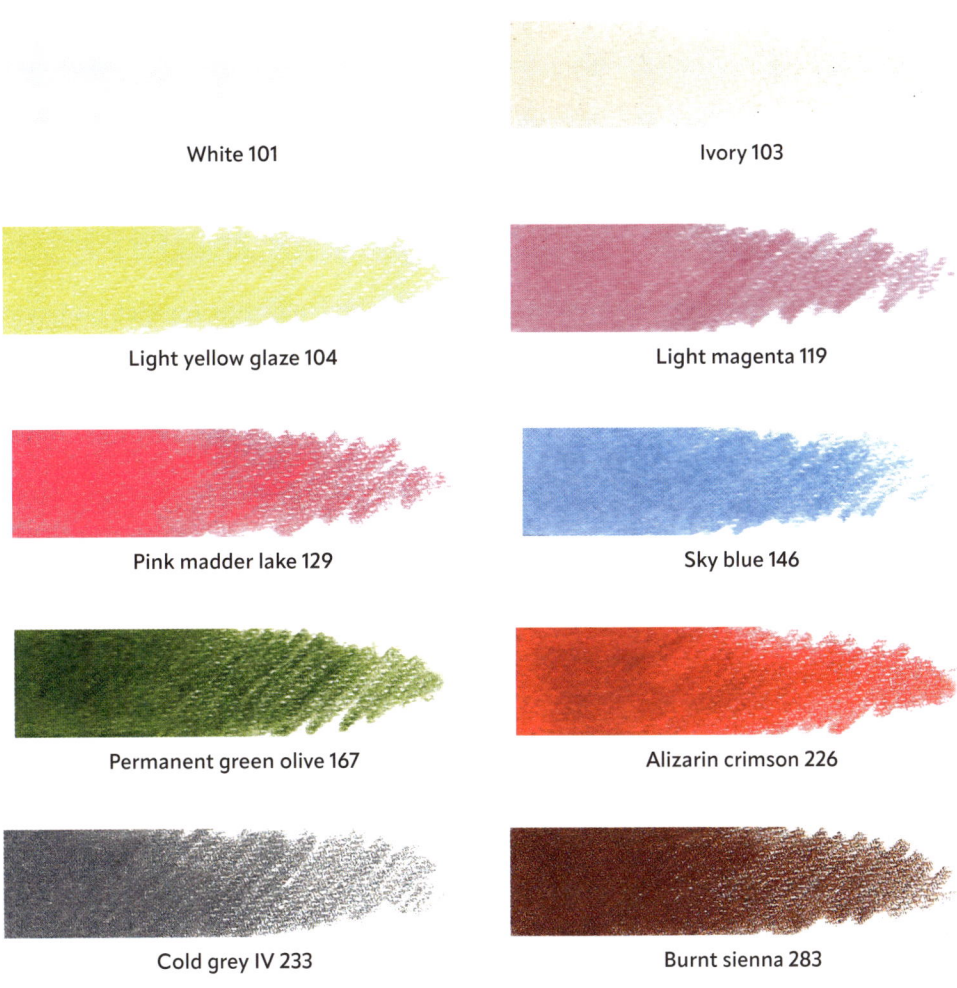

White 101

Ivory 103

Light yellow glaze 104

Light magenta 119

Pink madder lake 129

Sky blue 146

Permanent green olive 167

Alizarin crimson 226

Cold grey IV 233

Burnt sienna 283

OTHER MATERIALS

Eraser • Brush • Pencil sharpener

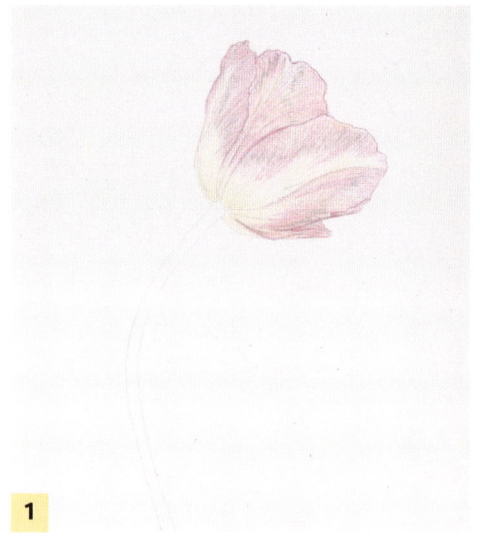

1

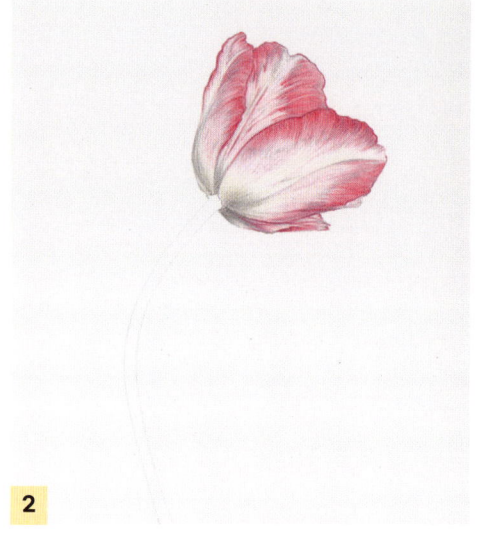

2

TIP
This project contains a number of repeated steps (i.e. 1–3), so take your time and believe in the process. Gentle pressure and light layers are the key here.

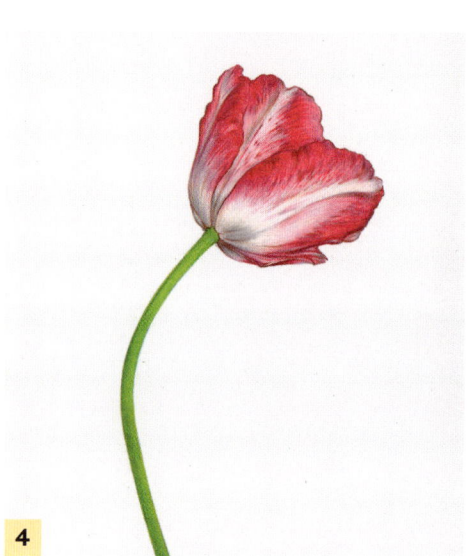

3

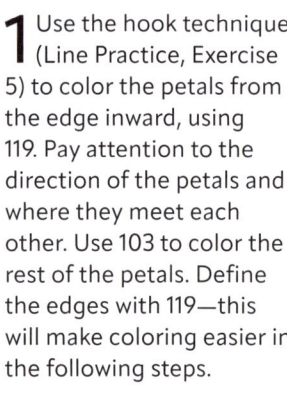

4

1 Use the hook technique, (Line Practice, Exercise 5) to color the petals from the edge inward, using 119. Pay attention to the direction of the petals and where they meet each other. Use 103 to color the rest of the petals. Define the edges with 119—this will make coloring easier in the following steps.

2 Apply 129 to increase the tone on the edges of the petals. Pay particular attention when creating the curves of the petals and follow their natural flow from the edge inward. Use 233 to create the shadows at the bottom of the flower. Now blend the flower petals following their natural direction, using 101. This process helps achieve the smooth surface for the next step.

3 Use 226 to express dark tones on the petals and overlapping areas. Use 103, 129, 226, and 233 to repeat steps 1–3 to gradually build up the colors and texture of the flower until you are happy with the overall look. Use 283 to define the edges of the petals while adding some shadows on the flower.

4 Apply a base layer on the entire stem with 146. Don't worry— it's supposed to be blue. Apply 167 to add green tone on the stem, then use 104 to gently blend the two colors. Use 167 to add shading and darken the outside area where needed.

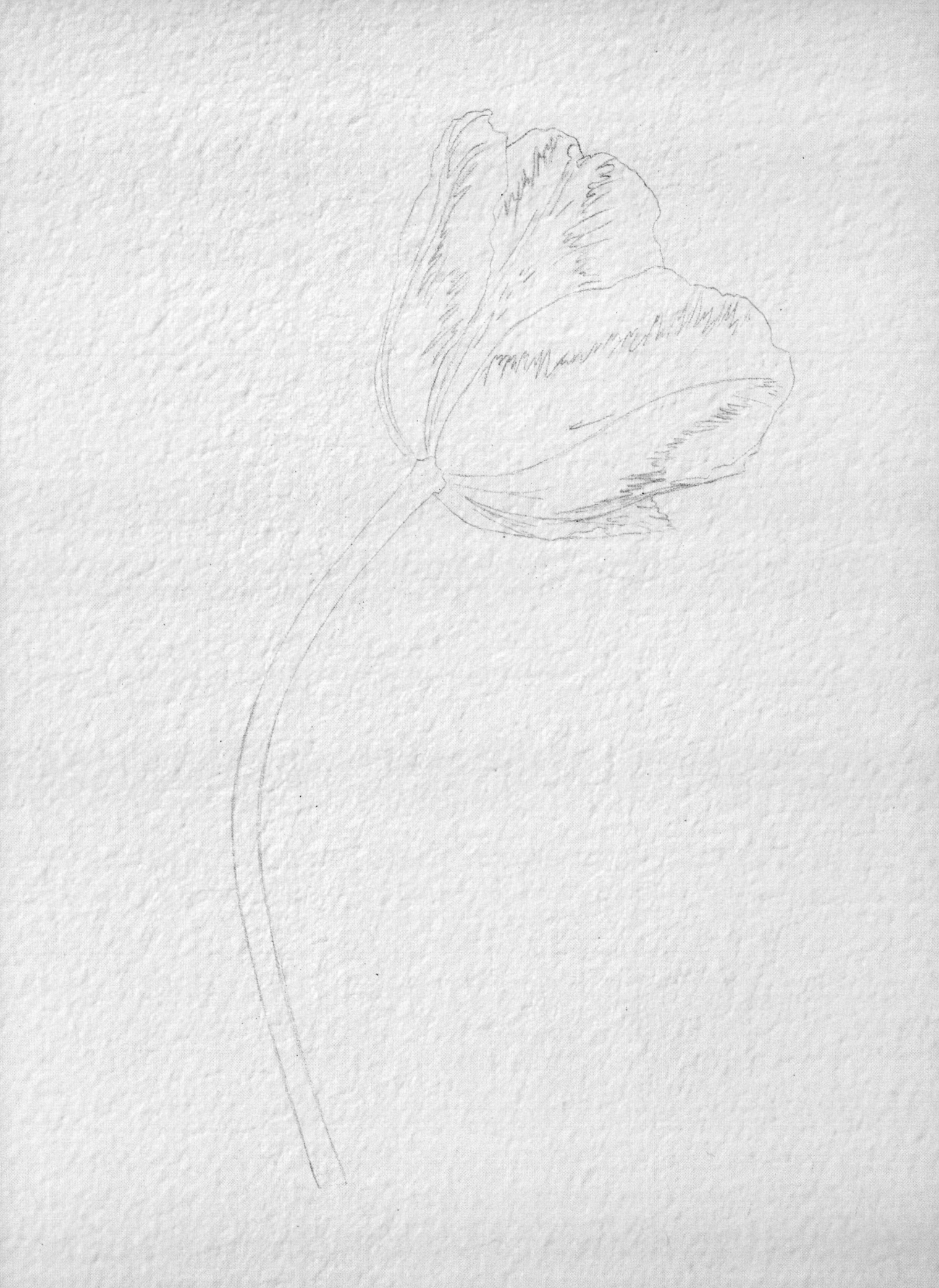

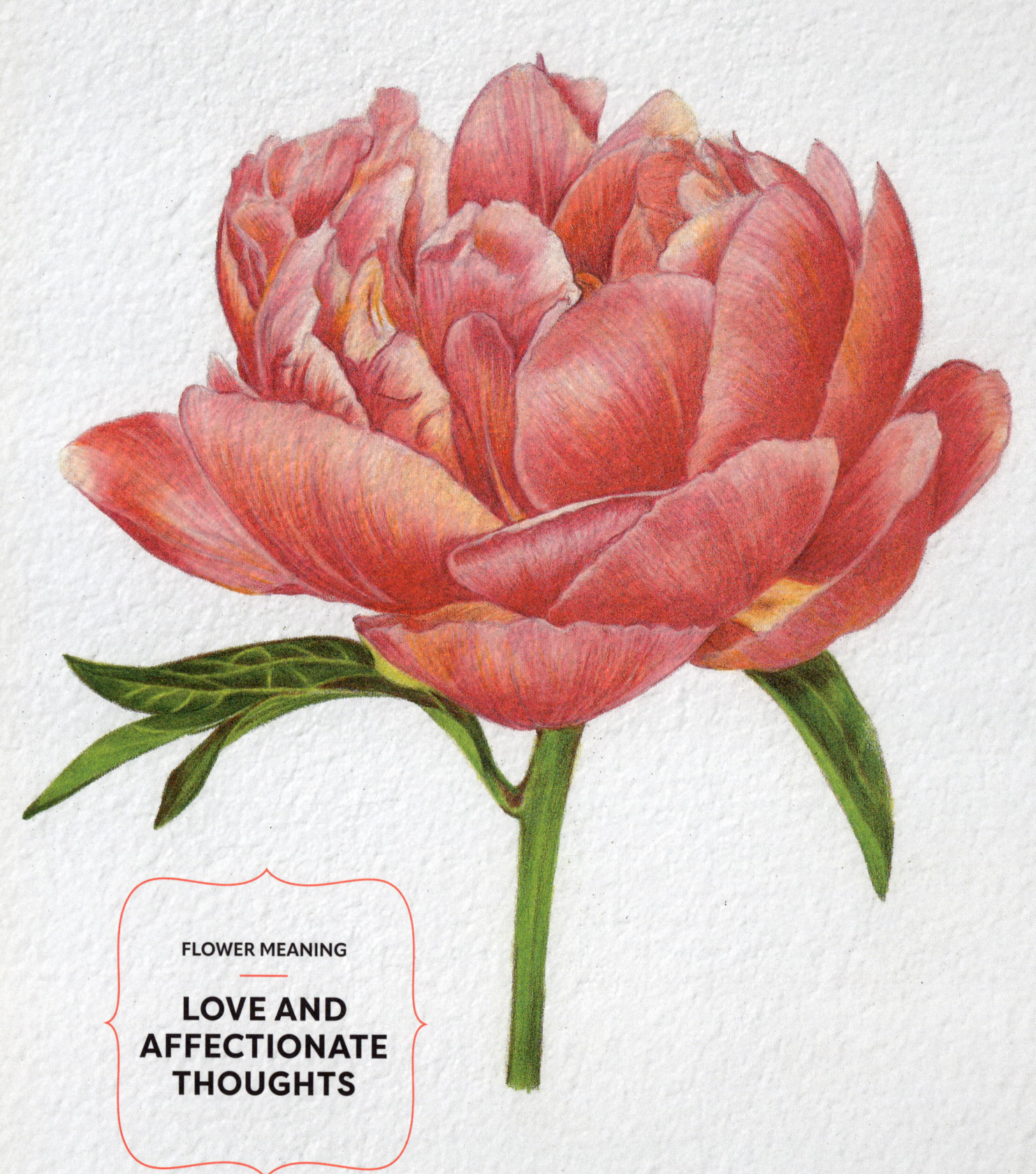

FLOWER MEANING

LOVE AND AFFECTIONATE THOUGHTS

PEONY

The peony always reminds me of a nineteenth-century ballroom dress elegantly flowing across the dance floor. You cannot help but be mesmerized by its beauty. Maybe that is why the peony is known as the wedding flower and symbolizes happiness and romance.

SCAN TO WATCH
A SPED-UP VIDEO
OF THE STEPS.

COLOR PALETTE

White 101

Ivory 103

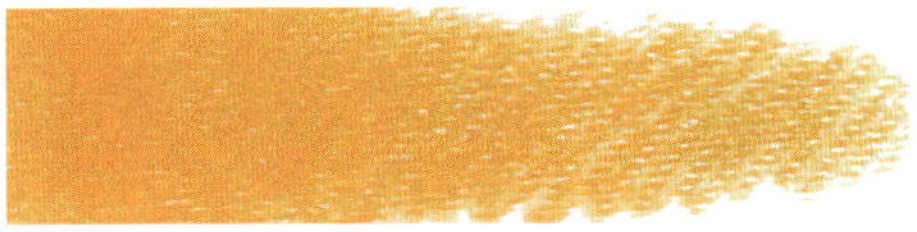

Dark cadmium yellow 108

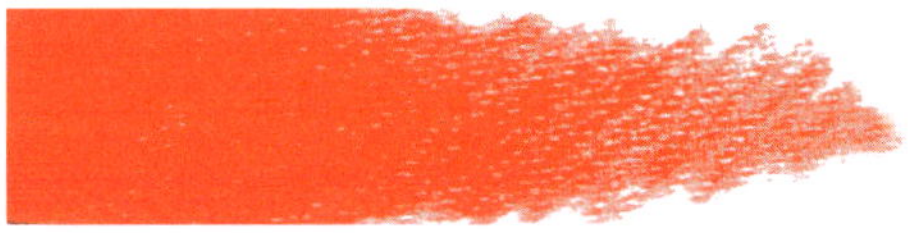

Light cadmium red 117

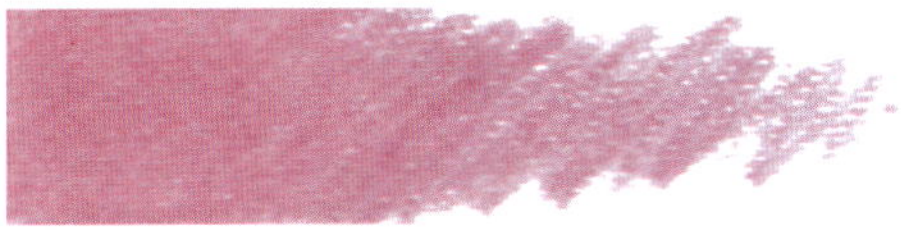

Light magenta 119

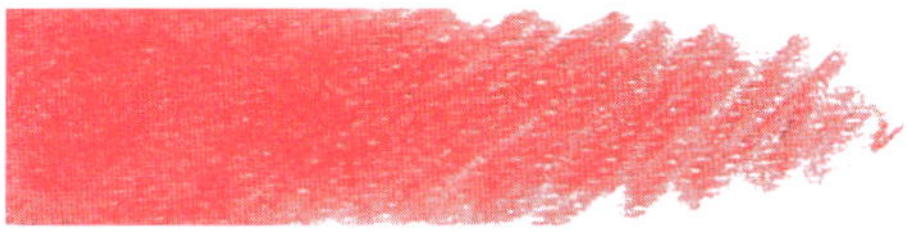

Rose carmine 124

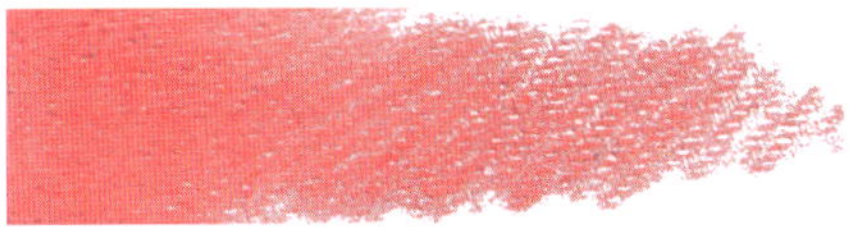

Dark flesh 130

Grass green 166

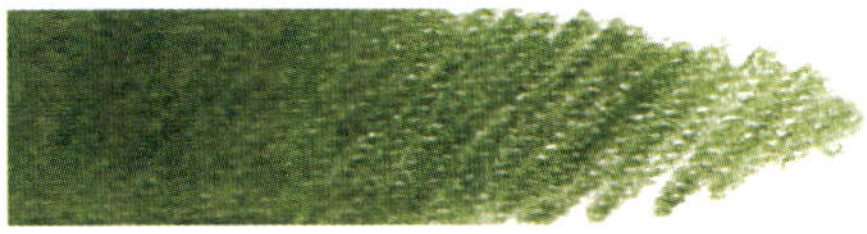

Permanent green olive 167

Cadmium yellow lemon 205

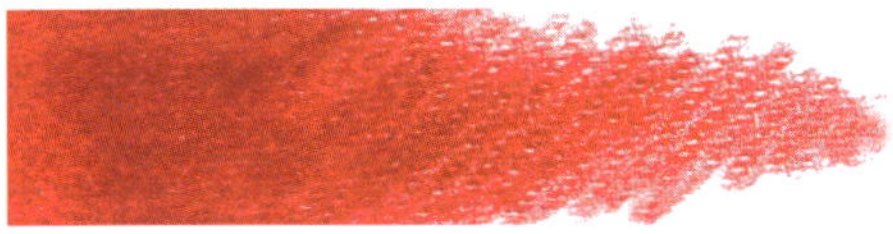

Alizarin crimson 226

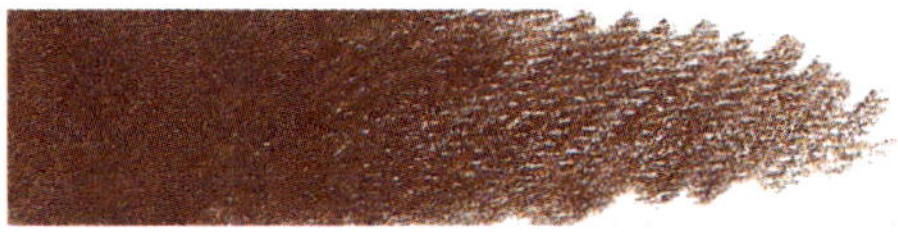

Burnt sienna 283

OTHER MATERIALS

Eraser • Brush • Pencil sharpener

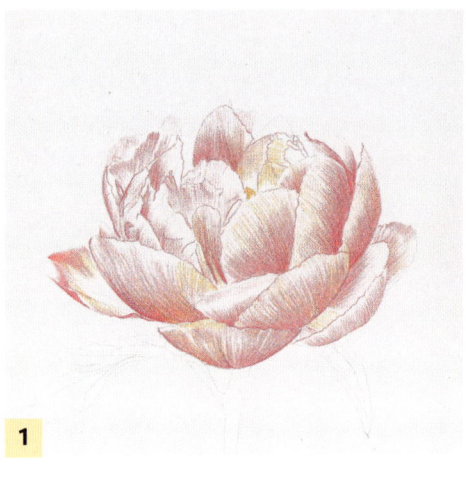

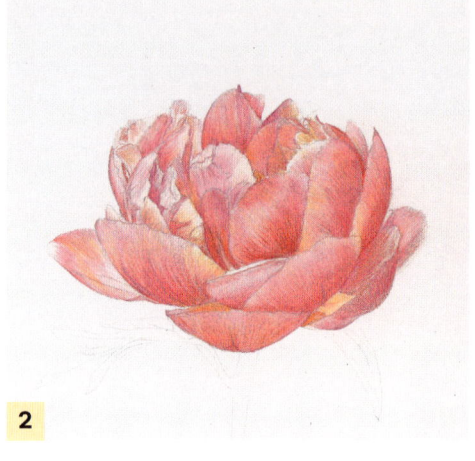

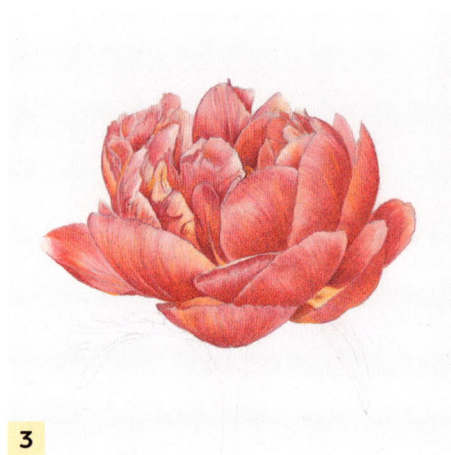

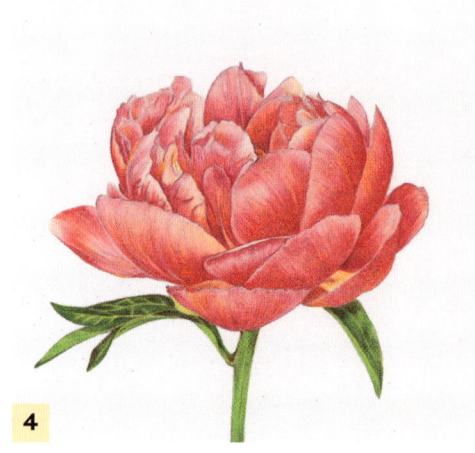

1 Use 130 and 108 to start defining and mapping out the individual petals. Take your time and don't be overwhelmed by the number of petals. Focus on one at a time and they will become easier. Pay attention to the direction of the petals and follow the natural lines as shown in the picture. Use Line Practice, Exercise 5 to help with this step. Use 103 to create a base color for the petal edges and deeper areas.

2 Use 124 and 117 to start coloring in the area, using your shading and layering techniques. Make sure you continue to follow the direction of the petals, building on step 1. Also look at the curves of the petals, leaving more light in certain areas to give more definition. Use 101 to blend the colors you just layered and apply 119 to start introducing another color into your drawing.

3 Use 226 to create the darker parts of the image (e.g., where the petals meet). Repeat step 2 and 3 to layer and shade each petal until you are happy with the depth of color. Use 101 to blend each color between steps. To do this, first blend the color and then add a new layer to achieve a smoother surface.

4 Use 205 to gently map out the veins of the leaves and act as a base. Once you have colored the base of the stem and leaves use 166 and 167 to color in the leaves and stem. Pay attention to the light and how this affects the color and brightness of the greens to give some more contrast. Use 283 to highlight the brown areas shown, adding more depth and shading.

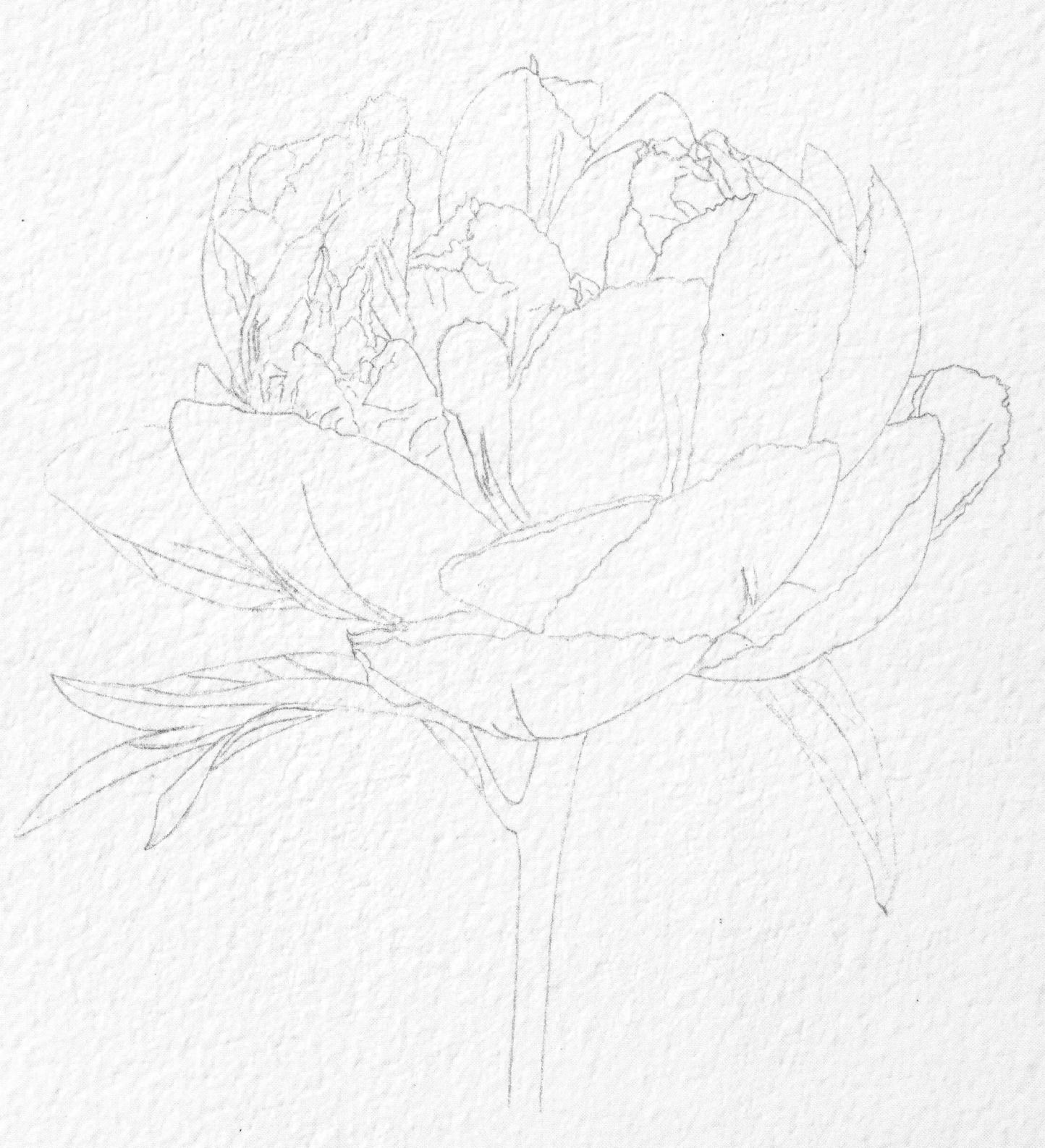

PHOTO REFERENCES

FOR THE PROJECTS IN THIS BOOK, I worked from photos. On these pages are the photo references I used. It might be helpful for you to study these to help you as you recreate the projects in this book.

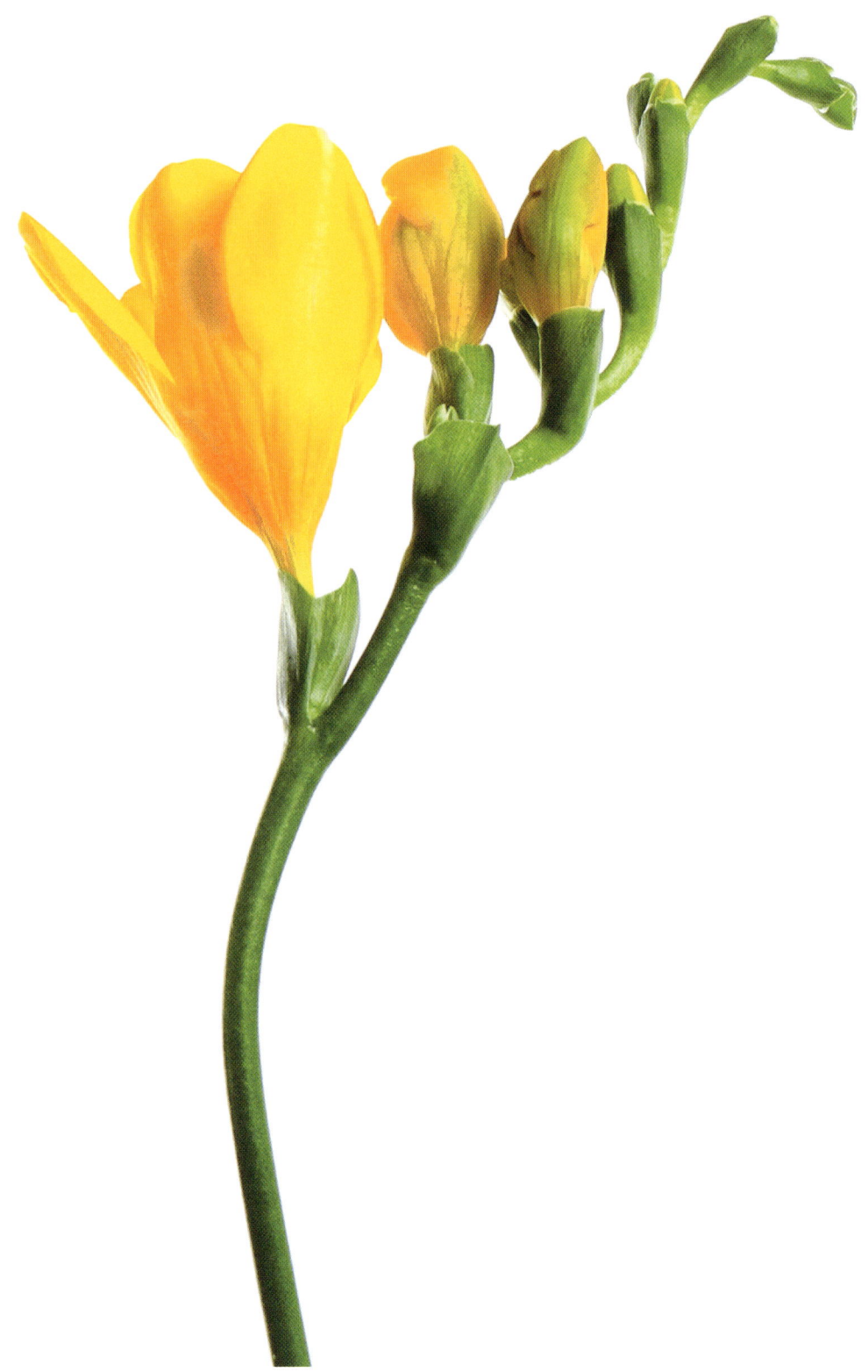

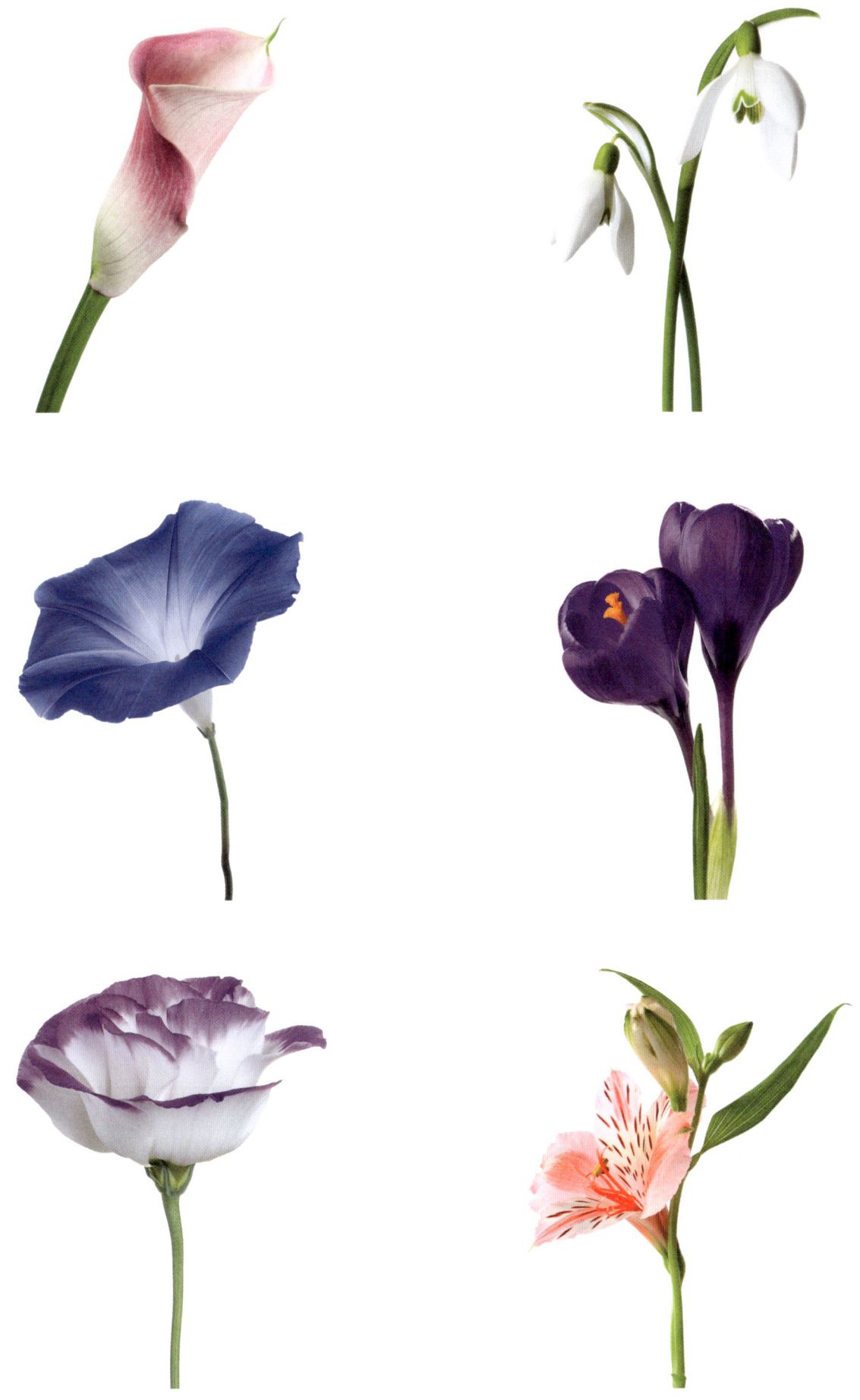

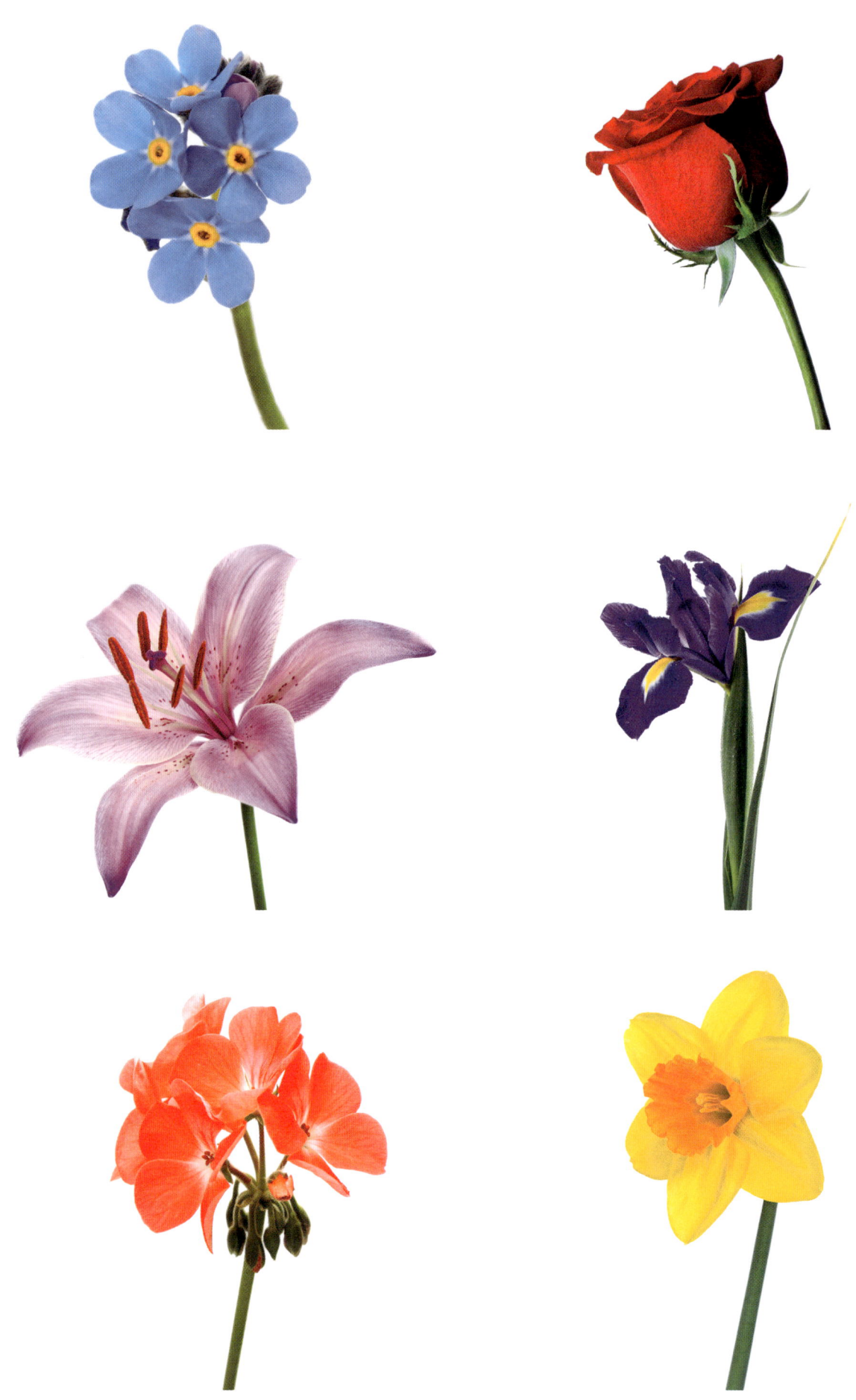

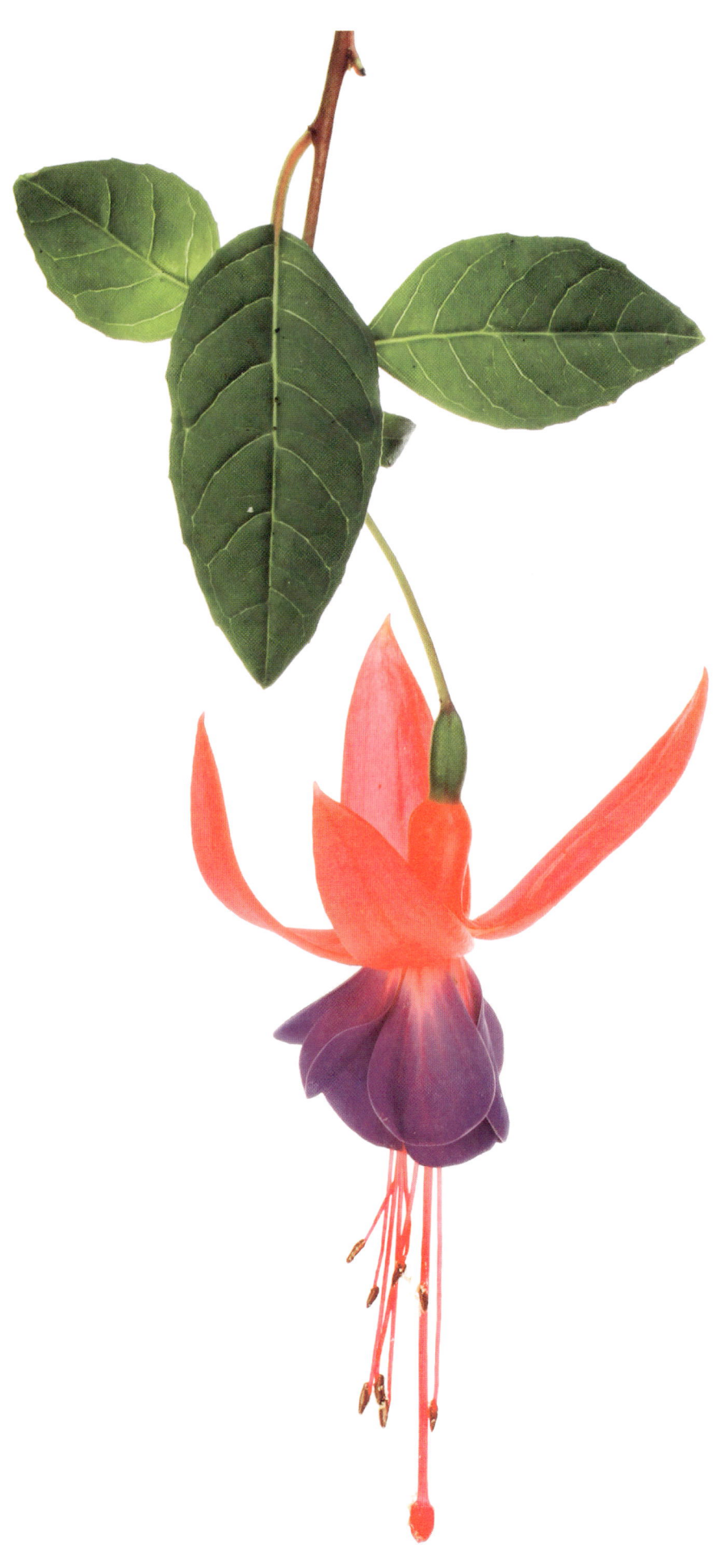

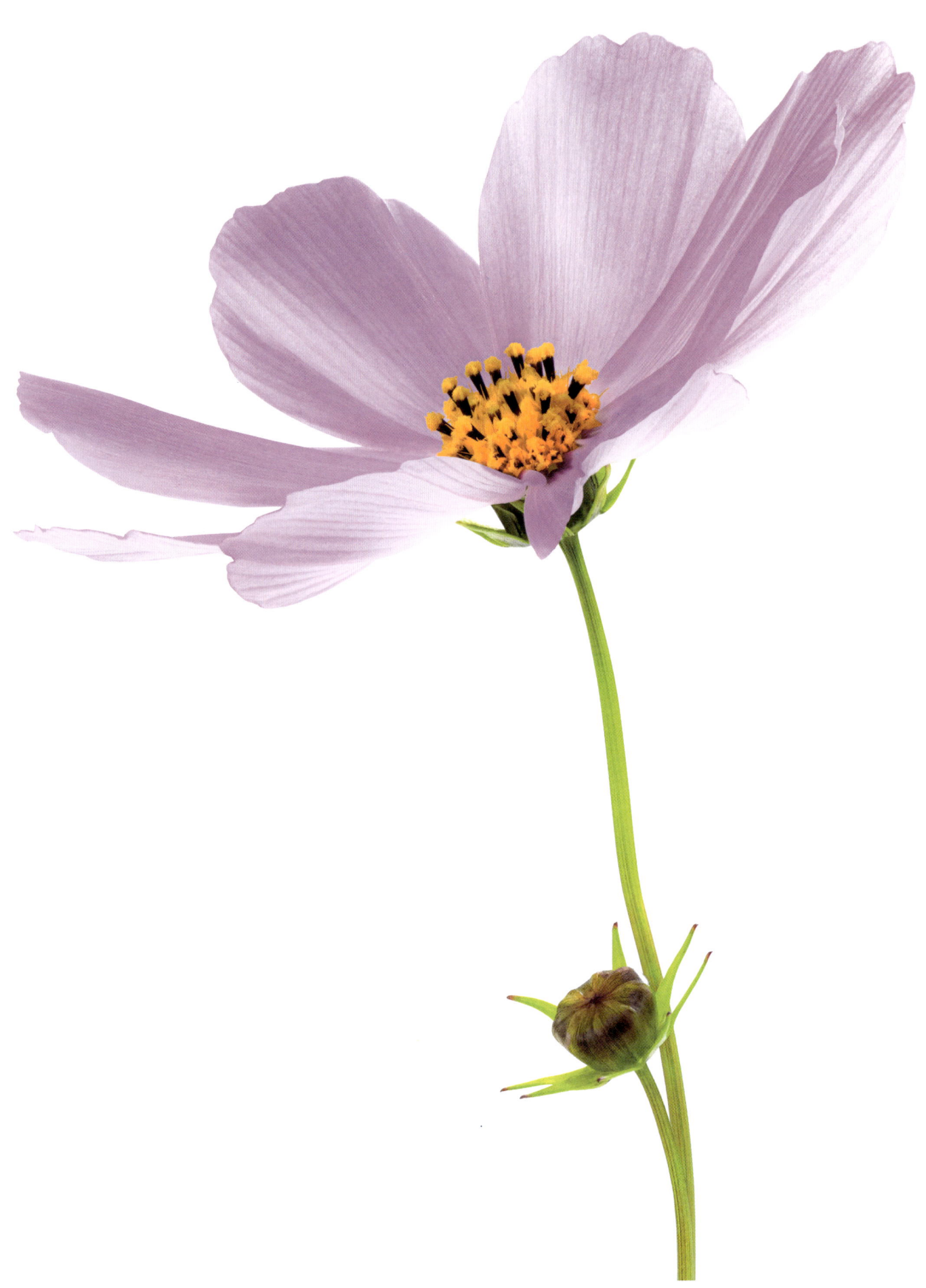

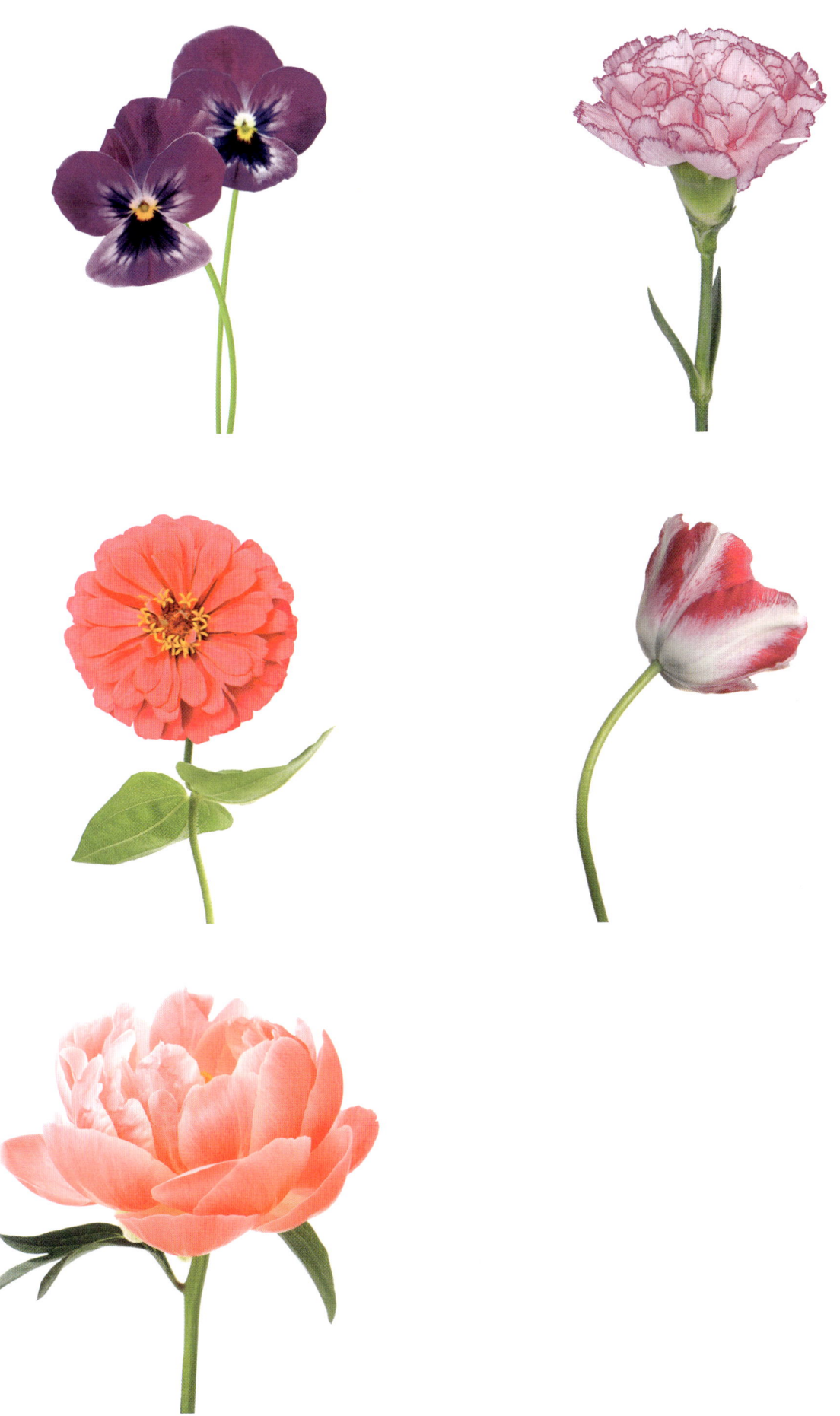

INSPIRATION GALLERY

ON THESE PAGES are some examples of my colored pencil artwork. I generally work very large. Most of my finished pieces are 20" x 30" (50.8 x 76.2 cm). You can see just how rich colored pencil artwork can be. If you are just starting out working with colored pencils, I hope these images will be inspirational to you and encourage you to develop your colored pencil skills.

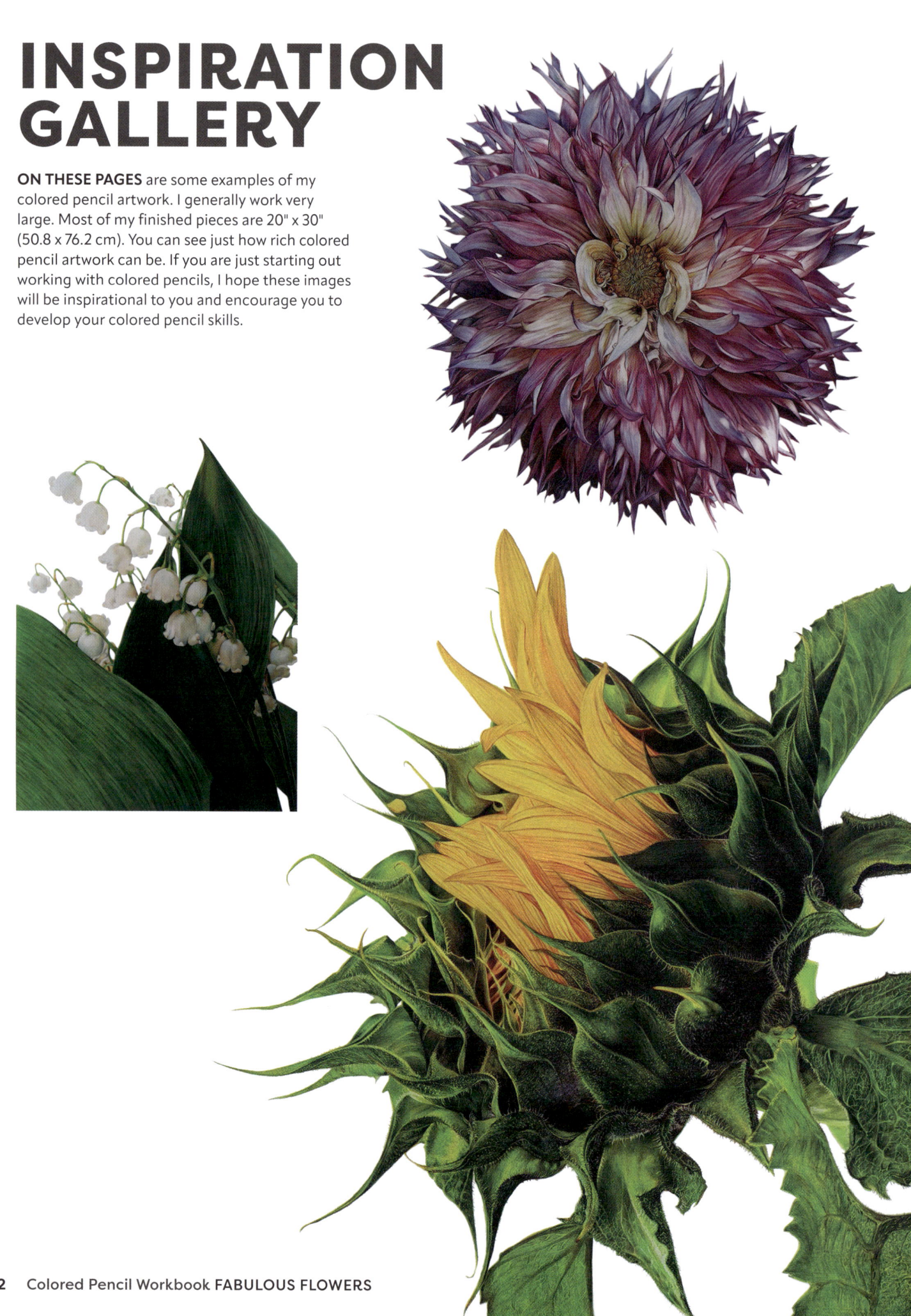

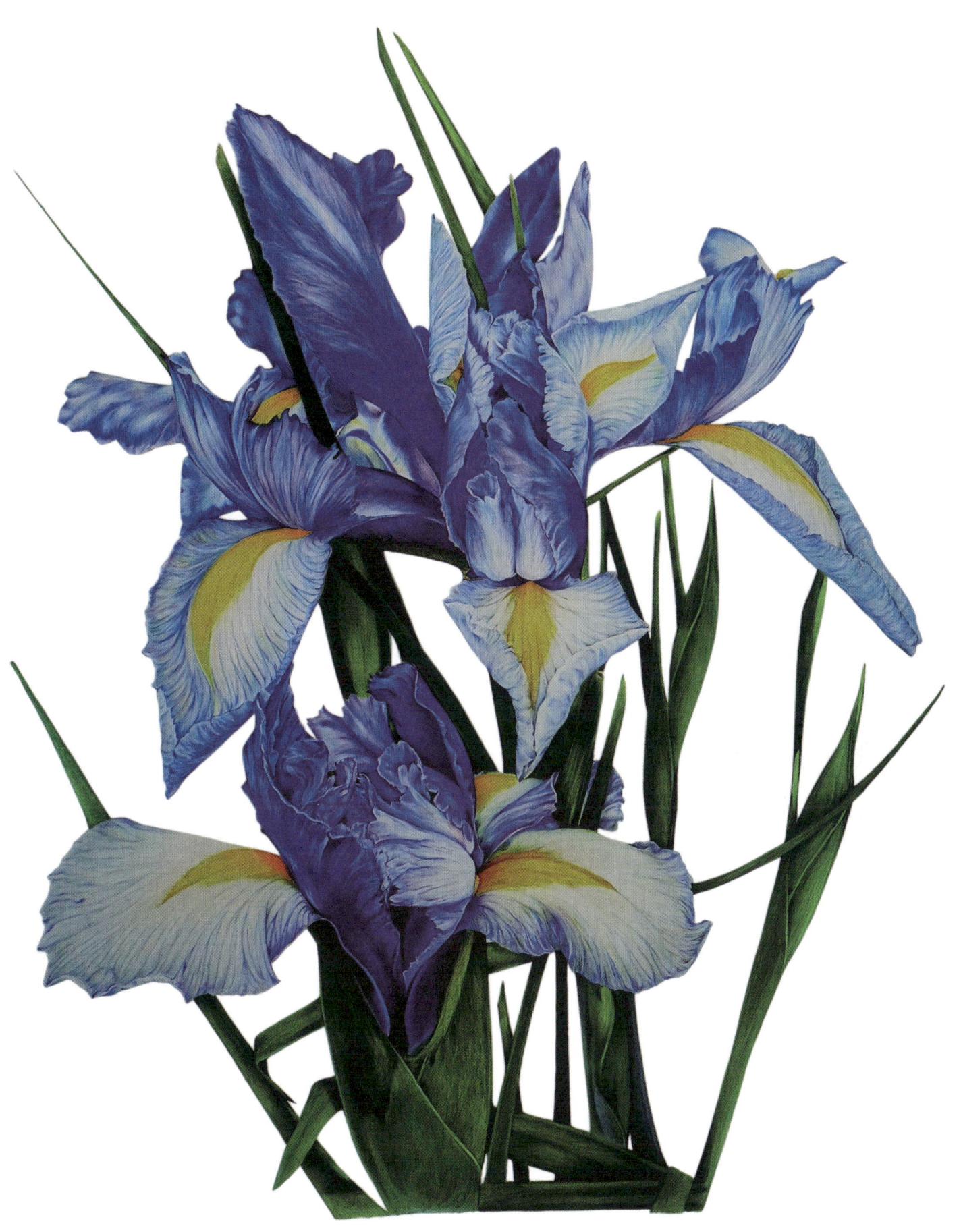

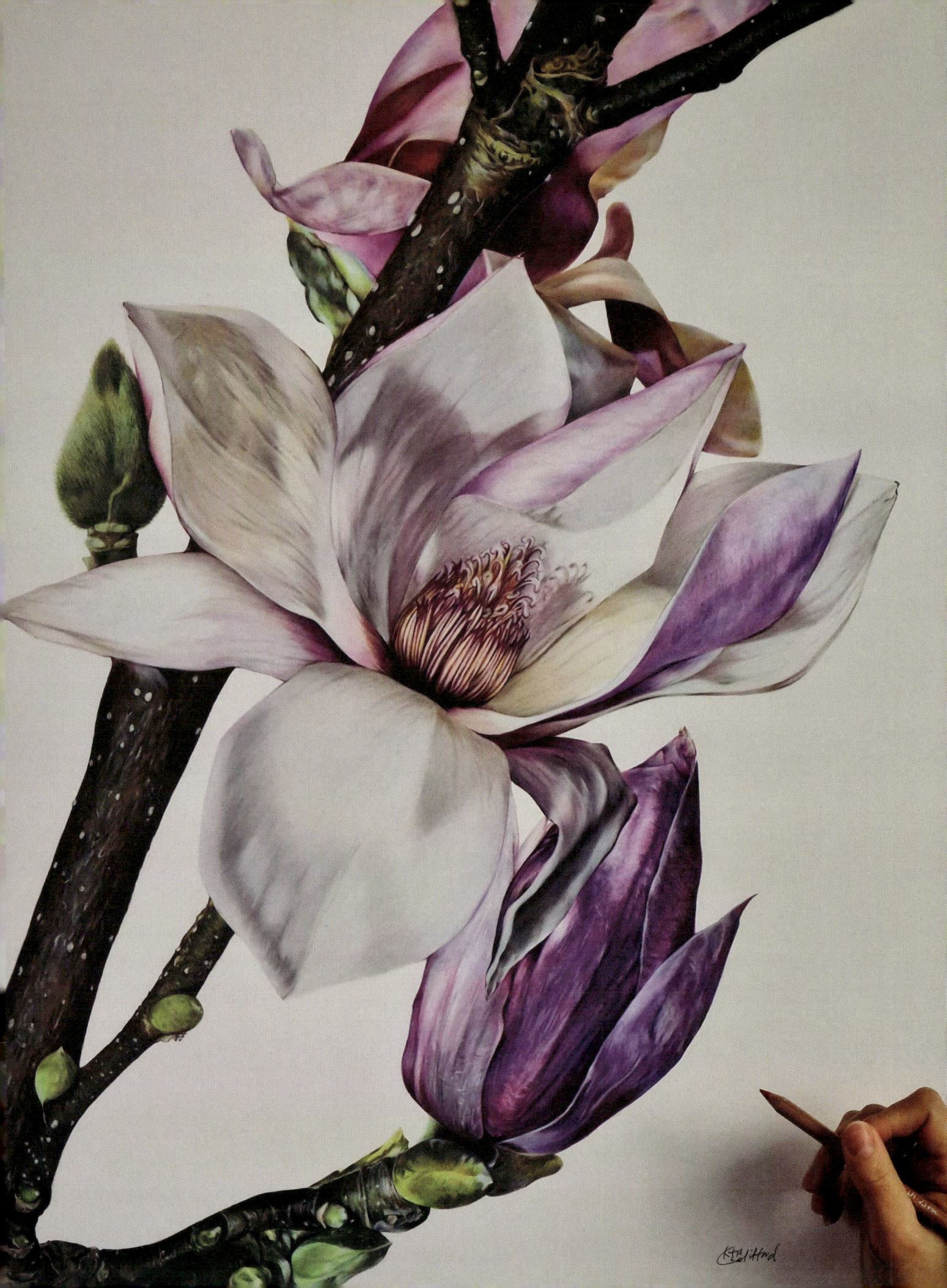

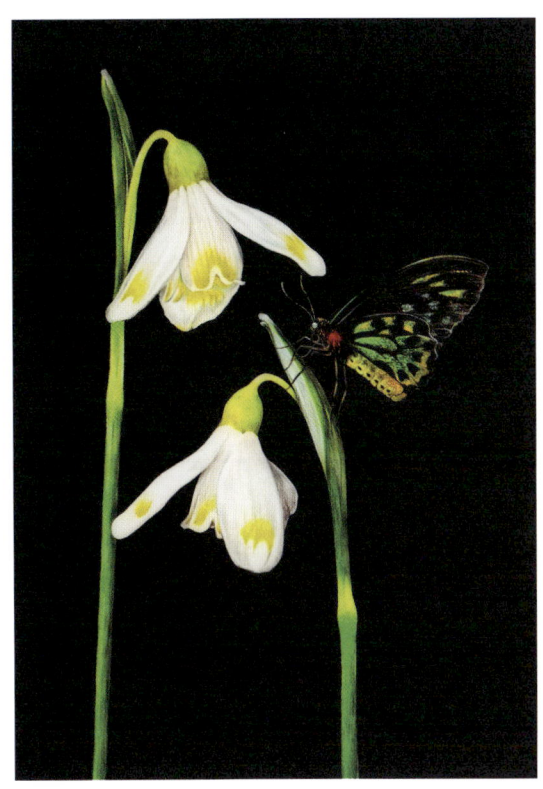

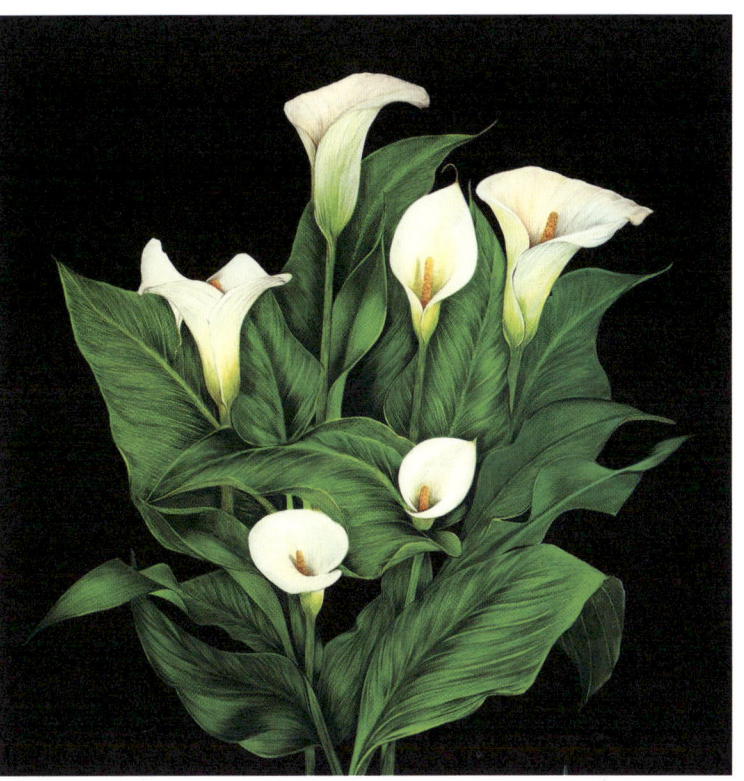

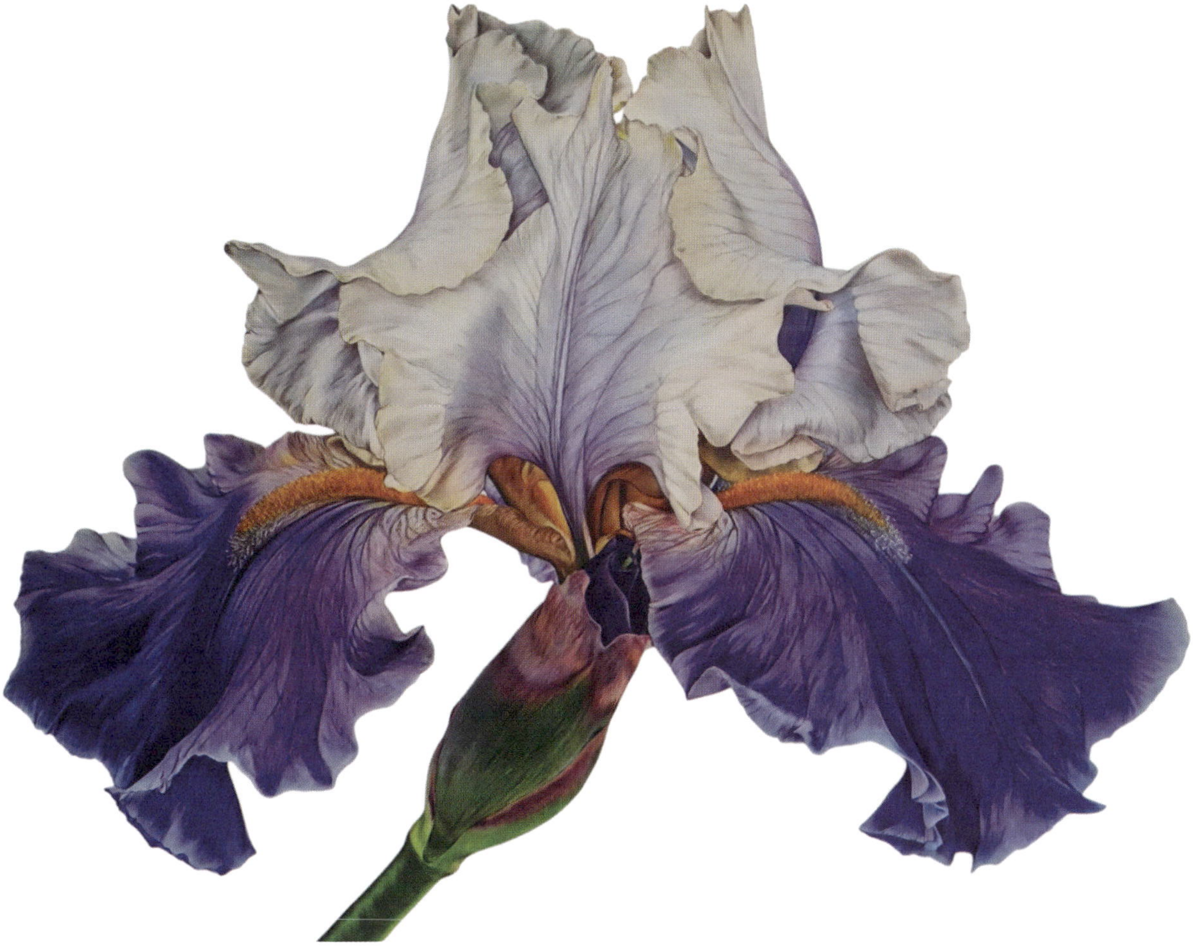

INDEX

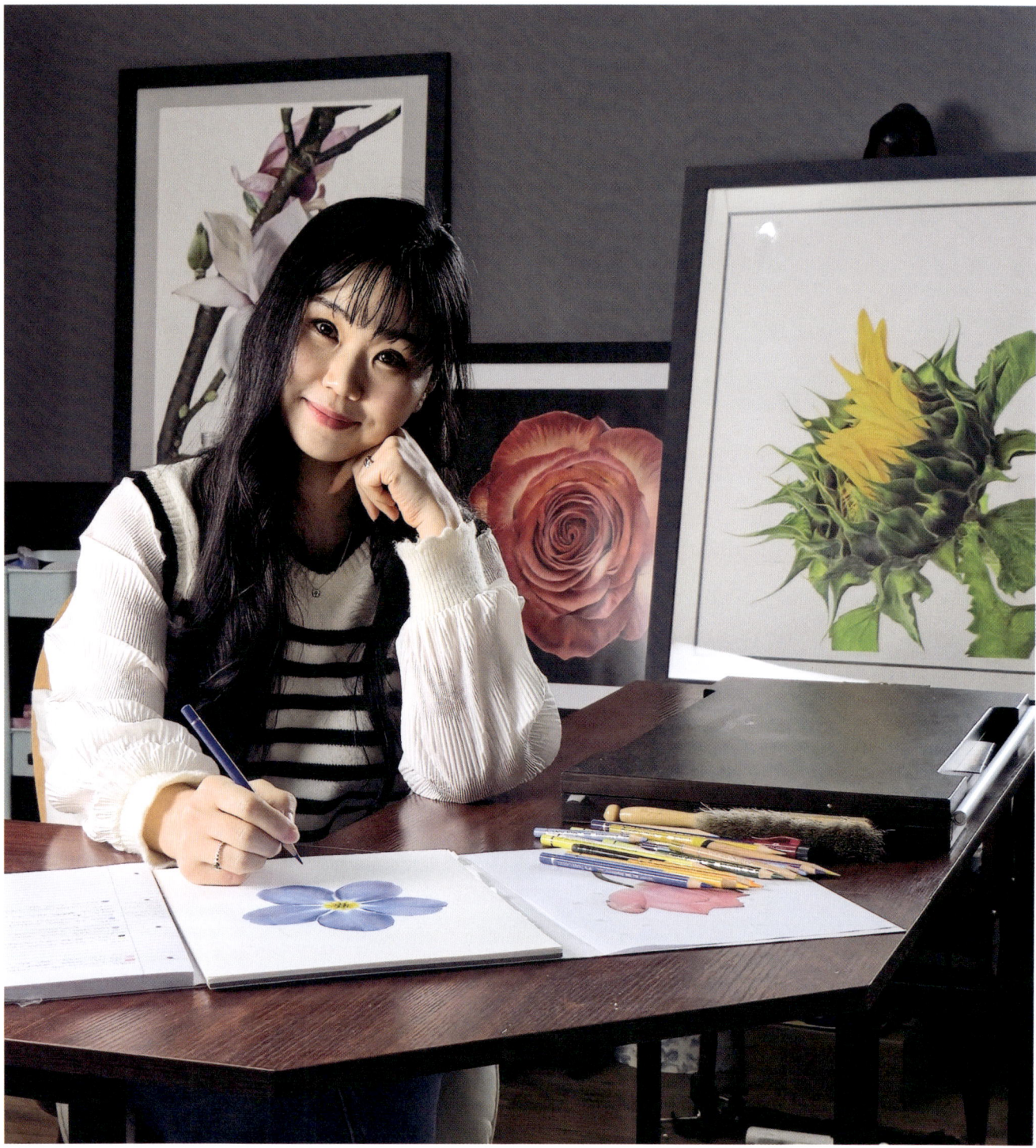

ABOUT THE AUTHOR

ORIGINALLY FROM SOUTH KOREA, Sun-Kyong Clifford is a self-taught colored pencil artist based in South Wales. She always had a passion for art, but it really grew when she picked up colored pencils again as a hobby in her thirties.

Sun started her professional art journey as a pet portrait artist taking commissions. She loved creating commissions but always looked to create her own original drawings. That is when her first colored pencil series, "Something Big Something Beautiful" was born. Sun loves to find the beauty in nature and capture this on paper, allowing these small, delicate flowers to bloom dramatically in her large-scale drawings.